A Shadow Falls

Andrew Beatty grew up in Warwickshire. After studying English at York University he travelled in Asia for two years and discovered an interest in anthropology which he later took up at Oxford. Among many odd jobs, he has worked in a banana plantation in north-west Australia, on a scallop trawler and in an Italian circus. He lived for five years in Indonesia, on the tribal island of Nias and in a peasant village in Java. Currently he teaches anthropology at Brunel University in London. He is married with two children.

by the same author

VARIETIES OF JAVANESE RELIGION
SOCIETY AND EXCHANGE IN NIAS

A Shadow Falls

In the Heart of Java

ANDREW BEATTY

First published in 2009
by Faber and Faber Ltd
Bloomsbury House
74–77 Great Russell Street
London WC1B 3DA

Typeset by Faber and Faber Limited
Printed in England by CPI Mackays, Chatham

A CIP record for this book
is available from the British Library

ISBN 978-0-571-23586-5

2 4 6 8 10 9 7 5 3 1

For Mercedes, Sofía, and Daniel

Contents

CONTENTS

Preface

We are all travellers now, all tellers of tales. In novelty there is a routine, and with today's frictionless travel, an easy familiarity with the exotic. Yet in the best travel writing the steady eye, the alert ear, catches more: a detail that suggests the whole, a turn of phrase that opens up hidden lives. To fix a moving world in words is a strange and remarkable art.

There is another way: to stay put, learn the language, live among the people as one of them; to make friends and enemies, be a good or bad neighbour; to be tested. For the anthropologist, engagement is the condition of knowledge. The tale told will be different from that of the traveller, the vision, though singular, more firmly rooted: as inside a view as an outsider can ever provide. Their story told through mine.

I came to Indonesia with my family in 1992 to work as an anthropologist. We lived for eighteen months in a village in East Java, then, three years later, returned for a further year. A rice-growing village on the slopes of a volcano, a people devoted to music and mysticism, a relaxed and easy way among men and women: it was not a hard place to like. This was an island where people of radically different ideology – orthodox Muslims, Hinduized mystics and animistic peasants – managed to live together in harmony. But the Java we first knew and the Java we left in 1997 were different places. The transformation – long prepared but still unexpected – was quite sudden and shocking. A puritan, ideologically driven Islam had made rapid progress, pushing aside older traditions, disturbing an ancient pact that allowed ancestral spirits and pre-Islamic deities a place among the prayer-houses. Like other villagers, we had to make our compromises and find a way to live with the new dogmatism. But the gentle world that we had known – of Muslims and mystics, of dancers and shadow plays – was in eclipse. And with the rise of an assertive piety, neighbourhoods and communities were splitting. Inside every family a struggle over the faith was taking place. And not only in Java. Repeated wherever Muslims live, this struggle will decide the future shape of the Islamic world.

Indonesia, the largest and most diverse Muslim nation – with Java at its heart – shows us better than anywhere how to live peacefully with cultural difference. That diversity and respect for pluralism are now under threat. Almost uniquely in the Muslim world, Java still has the cultural means to confront the challenge. It has lessons for us all. This is its story, told from the inside.

In telling the story I have drawn on my professional knowledge, but I have gone beyond what an anthropologist normally does. I am interested in how people get caught up in history, how ordinary men and women remake themselves in circumstances they can only partly understand. An anthropologist looks for broad cultural patterns. A novelist, by contrast, finds significance in the interwoven lives of her characters. In writing about Java in a time of crisis – and our effort to make sense of it – I have adopted a similar approach, with two important differences. First, unlike the novelist, I may not invent or imagine. I have changed names and a few circumstances to protect the privacy of my hosts. Otherwise I have stuck to what I experienced. Dialogues, though edited, were recorded or written down shortly after they occurred. Everything that happens happened. The second difference is more complicated. Unlike the novelist, I cannot assume background knowledge. Java is a complex and ancient civilization, strangely attractive yet profoundly unlike the West. As will be apparent from the beginning, almost everything people do, say and think is subtly, sometimes startlingly, different. Yet, as we shall see, by following a few characters through their lives, letting *them* show *us* what matters, it is possible to enter and understand this unfamiliar, entrancing world.

*

The debts of gratitude incurred in making this book are more than the usual. One by one, I should thank the Javanese people whose lives we shared and who showed us such great kindness; but there are too many to name, and I want to protect their privacy. So, having said farewell in the Javanese way – with feasting and apologies – and with a general vote of thanks, I preserve here their anonymity. My debts outside the village are fewer. My family shared intimately in the experience and made it not only possible but joyful. Mercedes, my wife, was as deeply immersed in Java as I was, perhaps more so. Our children's first words were Javanese. This book is filled with Mercedes' insights and I hardly know where my thoughts end and hers begin. She has also been my closest critic.

In England, I thank my editor at Faber and Faber, Neil Belton, for his faith in an unusual project and for his many incisive suggestions. My agent, Caroline Davidson, of the Caroline Davidson Literary Agency, has been a steadfast support and source of excellent advice. I am grateful to Cambridge University Press for permission to use passages from an earlier book, *Varieties of Javanese Religion: an Anthropological Account* (1999).

People

Names are followed by approximate age at the time of our first stay in Bayu. People are grouped by family.

Bu Mari, 53, our landlady (Bu = 'Mother', 'Mrs')
Arjo, deceased husband of Mari, a schoolteacher and organizer for the Nationalist Party
Wan, 37, adopted son of Mari and Arjo, a part-time mechanic
Sri, 19, foster daughter of Mari and Arjo; natural daughter of Sae and Sutri

Pak Lurah, 42, village head ('Pak Lurah' = 'Mr Headman')
Bu Lurah, 40, his wife ('Mrs Headman')
Dewi, 21, their married daughter, living next door
Jan, 22, Dewi's husband
Hari, son of Dewi and Jan, born during our first year
Witri, 61, Pak Lurah's mother, lives at the back
Winoto, 62, Pak Lurah's father

Drus, 35, landowner and dealer, lives next door to the headman's family
Siti, 35, his wife. They have a small son and an adult daughter

Misti, 35, our next-door neighbour
Jakis, 38, her husband
Ana, 13, their daughter
Urip, 17, their son
Tari, 60, mother of Misti, lives in fieldhut with her husband

Sae, 42, natural father of Sri
Sutri, 41, his wife, natural mother of Sri
Busono, 23, their son, a soldier
Benny, 27, husband of Sri

Untung, 38, neighbour
Nur, his wife
Katri, 13, their daughter

Noto, 50, carpenter, windmill maker and dance-master
Las, 45, his wife
Rita, 23, their daughter
Marko, 16, their son

Mystics and their families
Warno, 59, one of the leading mystics
Min, 50, his wife
Taji, 65, his brother
Arsad, 72, older brother, father of Untung
Purwadi, 60, regional organizer of the mystical association
Joko, 30, his son
Eti, 29, Joko's wife
Harsono, 74, former headman of Bayu, uncle of Mari and brother of Ran
Rupo, 72
Suyit, 70
Ma Suyit, 70, his wife
Suher, 65, brother of Suyit
Elan, 50, village irrigation official, former nationalist activist and follower of Arjo

Leading Muslims and relatives
Mustari, 58, leader of our neighbourhood prayer-house, a traditionalist
Andi, 8, his son

Aris, 33, factory worker and religious reformer
Tompo, 30, religious teacher in the primary school
Yusuf 28, paramedic from elsewhere in Java
Mosque official, 46, cousin of Noto
Jumhar, 35, head of a prayer-house, traditionally-minded
Matraji, 73, former mosque official
Sukib, 53, prayer-leader (imam) in various prayer-houses
Ali, 42, traditionalist orthodox Muslim

Other persons
Asih, 21, niece of Noto, a pious young woman
Bambang, 30, Bayu's 'head of youth', son of a mystic
Basuki, 57, keeper of the barong masks
Buyut Cili ('Great-grandfather Cili'), village guardian spirit, were-tiger
Hadi, 47, Jan's father; in-law to headman; arts impresario, owner of a rice mill
Hasan, 25, my assistant at the beginning of fieldwork; lives in town
Jona, 50, peanut dealer, lives at back of Mari's house
Panji, 36, our cook, a wandu
Mul, 37, performer in the barong
Pin, 52, caretaker of the village shrine, a spirit-medium
Poniman, 30, his assistant
Pujil, 37, official in the subdistrict office, friend of Wan
Pran, 42, headman of Mandaluko
Ran, 64, uncle of Mari, brother of Harsono; a curer-magician
Ramelan, 50, a ploughman
Jamsa, 50, Ramelan's wife
Rapi'i, 35, headmaster of a school in another village
Rasno, 62, performer in the barong
Sanuri, 65, Bu Lurah's father
Sarko, 60, head of security in Bayu, former nationalist activist, comrade of Arjo
Sugito, leader of the tambour percussion group

Glossary

Alas Purwo forest on eastern tip of Java
barong lion-dragon; drama of this name
Bu mother, Mrs (more formal than 'Ma')
buyut great-grandparent or great-grandchild; title for village guardian spirit
gandrung female singer-dancer hired for all-night performance
haj pilgrimage to Mecca
Haji title of person who has performed pilgrimage to Mecca
kyai traditional Muslim leader, usually head of a seminary
lair-batin 'inside and outside', 'with sincerity': salutation at Idul Fitri
Lebaran week-long celebrations at Idul Fitri, the end of the Fast
lurah village headman
Ma mother, Mrs
Man uncle (short for *paman*, the younger brother of a parent)
Muludan celebration of the Prophet's birthday
Pak father, Mr
Ramadan the fasting month
Sangkan Paran a mystical association
seblang a trance dance performed by a young woman
wandu 'man-woman', transvestite

PART ONE

1
The Prayer-meal

Joko pursed and plumped his lips, as he had often seen his wife do, adjusted his gauzy headscarf, and lowered himself, in tight sarong, to the ground, knees primly together, feet tucked to one side. Straining against his lacy jacket, he scraped at the bare, compacted earth with a fieldknife, then dug quickly until there appeared in front of him, just inside the threshold of the house, a molehill beside a neat, bowl-shaped cavity. Sweat beading his powdered cheeks, he took from his father a clay bowl, brimming with what looked like offal, and murmured a prayer.

'*Peace be upon you!* Mother Earth, Father Power, we commend to you our daughter's spirit sibling, born on the same day. May the baby be safe north, south, east and west. May she grow to be a real woman, a beauty like the goddess Sri!'

So saying, he dropped the bowl into the hollow with a gentle thud, withdrawing his left hand before his right so the baby would not be left-handed, then sprinkled flowers over the bloody swirl. From the corner of the room, half-daring to look, a little girl – his eldest daughter – watched shyly, giggling, a bit alarmed. The older man, slim and angular, stooped, straight-legged, to insert a cigarette paper among the purple folds of the placenta. He too murmured a prayer, this time without an Arabic salutation; something in Old Javanese. Perhaps this was what he had written on the cigarette paper.

With that, Joko smoothed the soil over and tamped it down, strewing more of the flowers (red, white, and yellow), while his father sprinkled cold water from a kettle over the fresh coppery earth. ('May you be cool like water, fragrant like flowers!') Then, ladylike, a little flustered, Joko rose and vanished behind a curtain.

Ten minutes later, having checked on wife and baby, and looking – but for a smear of lipstick – more like his old self, he resumed his position at a hatch, where a queue of villagers, unaware of what had passed, waited to buy lottery tickets.

'Any news?'

'There is.'

'Boy or girl?'

'Girl. Not half an hour ago. How many tickets do you want?'

'Three. Can I have them on credit?'

Java 1992, close to Islam's eastern frontier. A few islands along, the archipelago runs out and there is only ocean, and beyond that the West. Indonesia may have the world's largest Muslim population (over two hundred million), mosques dating from the fourteenth century, modern, Saudi-financed Islamic institutes, ancient Sufi lodges and innumerable madrasahs, yet six centuries after the first conversions, distance from the Holy Land still counts. Javanese soil retains its own sacred character, its rich, feminized fertility, its reigning goddess. The solemn burial of an afterbirth (a kindred spirit), the pantomime transvestism linking father and daughter, the mantras to earth spirits and Hindu deities, and the careful distinction of right and left would not belong in the orthodox Islamic heartland.

Nor, according to some villagers, did they belong in Java, which was why they were not on show. Nobody outside the family was invited: I was present by chance. But still, the ritual had happened. And it happened, by all accounts, even in devout Muslim households where 'Javanism', when it conflicted with the scriptures, was properly deplored.

Five years later, at the end of our second period in Java, babies were still born in the Javanese way; fathers still confirmed their daughters' femininity by imitation, though fewer would admit to it. But the mosque loudspeakers had grown shriller, the world had come closer. It took more than discretion now to resist the steady pressure of a globalized, resurgent Islam. In Java and all over the

Muslim world, local identity, of which local versions of Islam had always formed a part, was giving way to something more all-embracing and insistent. At the end of the century, to be a Muslim in Java meant, increasingly, to deny your Javanese self, and that meant renouncing everything you had grown up to be, all that connected you with others outside of your abstract faith. This was a deep and painful loss. And it could reopen old conflicts, raising the spectre of a violent and repressed past. Five years after witnessing Joko's domestic ritual, we left Java during an epidemic of lynchings, a witch-craze that brought the region of Banyuwangi, where we were living, to the world's front pages.

There is an expression, *He didn't know his Javaneseness*, which means 'he lost his bearings', 'didn't know what he was doing'. It denotes a kind of dizziness, even madness. To be Javanese is to be civilized and 'aware' – conscious, poised, 'knowing right from left', rooted in the soil; for Java is not simply a place, but a state of mind, an ideal, a way of being.

These things we dimly felt, without understanding, in our early months in Bayu, the village where I had come to work as an anthropologist. We knew them by their effects: a certain sympathy and concern that we should feel at home; a stoical good cheer that flattered the listener; a puzzling lack of resentment over the violent past. Javanese made good neighbours: they had learned how to get on with each other despite different, even opposed, philosophies. But it was village life, not 'national character', that made this possible. Empathy and a mild-mannered engagement were part of the compact, part of the compromise that was Javanese civilization.

The newcomer arrives on the scene as to a game in progress, armed only with a little background. To the players, who briefly glance up, what matters is how the pieces are laid out, who controls the knights and castles; for them, background is background; but their positions depend on a history of moves whose rules are determined elsewhere. Our experience of history is always local, but the local responds to broader historical changes.

Java has a surfeit of history: a pagan backdrop of ancestor worship and spirit beliefs; a millennium of Indianized caste-societies ruled by god-kings (Bali, next door, still has its Brahmans and princely castes); Islam from the fifteenth century; Dutch colonization from the sixteenth; the brief, brutal Japanese occupation from 1942 to 1945; the war of resistance after the Dutch returned; then Independence in 1949 and the creation of a unified, sovereign Indonesia with Java its political centre.

Political epochs have dates, but cultural change is less tidy. Animist, Buddhist and Hindu elements persisted into Muslim times, not merely as leftovers but as ways of thinking, handy symbolic forms. Each civilization was built over the last, layer upon layer, but the old ways remained too useful to be discarded – like the Hindu-style split-gates of the first mosques; so the past, even the forgotten past, continued to nourish the present. Village feasts still use a colour symbolism in their offerings that mimics the iconography of fifteenth-century Hindu Java (though the villagers do not know it); mystical practices blend Sufism with tantric yoga; the ancestors whisper through modern Muslim rites.

Cultural labels mask as much as they reveal. Yet dates too can mislead. Most Javanese will tell you that Java has been Muslim since the last Hindu empire fell to armies from the north of the island in 1527. But lesser domains converted peacefully, and the kingdom in the far east of Java, where this story is set, held out for a further 250 years, remaining Hindu until the end of the eighteenth century. And because Java is large – six hundred miles wide – and Islam took hold at different moments, it evolved quite different forms. The version of Islam established in the ancient inland kingdoms – elaborately ritualist, Sufi-tinged, a harmony of the old and new – was unlike the austere, orthodox faith of the northern coast. There, a simpler portable creed, based around the scriptures, enabled merchants and seafarers to deal with Arab traders, Malay pirates and halal shipments from across the Indian Ocean. Inland, among the volcanoes, the Central Javanese sultan, like his Hindu ancestors, was the 'axis of the world', joined in mystical union with the spirit serpent-queen of the Southern Ocean. In him, the local, the Hindu-Javanese and the Islamic converged.

Java's chequered history makes generalization dangerous. But over time, two rival positions crystallized. One looked to the rites and doctrines of Islam for knowledge and truth; the other turned inwards in contemplation. In this rival orientation, Java was the microcosm and 'Javanism' a kind of practical mysticism, equally suited to the royal court and the rural village. Javanism was not a sect or variety of Islam, but the result of what cultural historians call syncretism, in which the Indic past and the Muslim present were blended with local tradition. Sometimes the separate elements remained distinct, like the coloured threads in a yarn; sometimes the colours mixed so you could no longer tell what was Islamic, Hindu or native Javanese. Both rival positions – the pious and the Javanist – were avowedly Muslim, but while one cleaved doggedly to the Book, the other trimmed Islam to traditional Javanese concerns, or made of it a universal humanism unconfined by Koranic revelation.

Pious, orthodox-leaning Muslims still prevail in the urban markets and northern ports; their nominal co-religionists in the old court centres and rural hinterland. But every village has both types, and a fair range in the middle. Since the rural pious still share many customs with their Javanist neighbours, the distinction is partly one of emphasis – of which aspect of your cultural identity matters most. One man will say 'I am a Muslim,' the other, 'I am Javanese.' But there are also real differences in practice and outlook. In recent times, influences from the Middle East have somewhat blurred the distinction, painting even the conservative pious as slaves of custom unfitted to the modern world. And – as everywhere now – radical Islam, rejecting compromise, hostile to context, has sown seeds, torn up roots. In the villages recruits are still few, individuals countable. But that too is changing.

There are parallels in the Islamic heartlands, the orthodoxy of Middle Eastern clerics contrasting with popular 'idolatrous' saint cults. But the parallels are not exact because in Java orthodoxy was rarely the dominant form. The first Muslim missionaries came not from Arabia but from the more syncretic, Sufi-influenced Indian subcontinent, and newly converted rulers were happy to embrace a religion that left their sanctity and most of their customs unchallenged. The absorption of the old ways, the going beyond orthodoxy or its outright rejection, was not a matter of popular deviation from the shariah: the practice of the masses was also, in more refined form, the policy of the ruling class. This is why, in Java, as nowhere else in the Islamic world apart from Mughal India, a broader, tolerant, humanist culture gained a legitimacy and intellectual power that made it a match for more dogmatic forms of Islam. Only in the last decades has it lost ground.

Why? The worldwide resurgence of puritan Islam – begun long before the extremism of recent times – has many explanations: decolonization, the rejection of despotic Westernized rulers, petrodollars, Palestine, mass education and literacy, the Iranian revolution. But the progress of orthodoxy in Indonesia has had two local impulses, one violent and abrupt, the other gradual, half-intended. On 30 September 1965, a group of junior officers kidnapped and killed the army's top generals. Within a few days they were captured and the blame conveniently pinned on a communist conspiracy. At the time, Indonesia had the world's third biggest Communist Party, after China and the Soviet Union: three million members; twenty-seven million workers and peasants allied to left-wing organizations. Factories had become unionized, co-operatives were set up. Here and there across Java, peasants had seized land they farmed as sharecroppers. But there was no prospect of revolution. The nationalist president, Sukarno – a brilliant, erratic demagogue, more Nasser than Nehru – had included the Communist Party in his cabinet as a foil to the army and the Muslim parties. When the storm broke and the communists were caught out – wrong-footed rather than complicit – the rival forces came together. Sukarno, raddled and decaying, stood aside as the decapitated army, now led by Suharto, an undistinguished major-general, went about its business of arrest, torture and execution. Civilian killings were spearheaded by Muslim groups – lynch mobs crying jihad, village sheiks and their followers, but also student leaders, the next generation of clean-cut party spokesmen. In obscure villages, former Sukarno loyalists, stirred by the propaganda, put on black and formed death squads. Across Indonesia, between half a million and a million people died; a hundred thousand disappeared into the gulag. Until Pol Pot's revolution in Cambodia, it was the world's largest peacetime slaughter.

Java had been a workshop of social and cultural ideas, alive with experiment, out of control. To the hungering, marching masses Sukarno had promised a Year of Living Dangerously. But by 1967 Java was an ideological wasteland. With tanks ringing the presidential palace, the usurper Suharto formally assumed power. Backed by the army and with grudging Muslim support, he ruled unchallenged until 1998. Sukarno's old Nationalist Party, the home of pluralists, secularists, Christians and a vast following of syncretist Muslims, was disbanded. Henceforth, Javanism would have no political protector. The new man was a Machiavellian, not an ideologue, even less a friend of Islam. The goals of power and plunder always determined his policy. Yet despite his Javanist leanings – among his advisers, diviners rubbed shoulders with Harvard-trained technocrats – he cultivated orthodox Islam, promoting it as a bulwark against communism. And the Muslim parties, shut out of power, were bought off with institutional patronage. In the later years of the dictatorship, a surge of educational funding and mosque-building – some of it financed by Saudi Arabia – created a more Islamic society, or rather a society closer to the orthodox model, observant of the 'pillars of the faith' – prayer, fasting, pilgrimage – disdainful of tradition, fearful of ideas. Many, perhaps a majority in Java, did not conform (Sumatra and the Outer Islands were different: they lacked Java's cultural resources, its deep civilization). But Islam had come a long way. This was the quiet revolution that the killings of 1965 had begun. Thirty years on, we would see its partial unravelling, as revival met resistance and East Java descended once more into violence.

*

History could take you so far. It showed you the lie of the land, the paths and dead ends, the point where you came in. But that was all. As newcomers, we knew nothing of how the long cultural struggles had shaped village life. Our concerns were immediate. How to get on. How to win acceptance.

I had come to Java with my wife, Mercedes, after a long stay on the island of Nias in the west of Indonesia. We did not arrive in Java as innocents, but we were badly prepared. After two and a half years among a tribe of former headhunters, we were battle-proofed, ready for anything except gentleness and grace. Anthropologists adapt; their adaptation is the way they learn about another culture. The field remakes them as people. Set on our mettle by Nias, we were disarmed by Java, frustrated by mildness; for Java was culture shock in reverse: a featherbed so soft one was hardly aware of its sustaining presence.

This time around, what made a difference – apart from all that separated peasant Java from tribal Nias – was that now we were a family, a mother and father and child. In Nias, our childlessness had sharpened our strangeness. In Java, among villagers devoted to the simple but hallowed things of life, we were recognizably human.

To prepare the ground, however, I arrived alone, equipped with the gifts I would have dispensed in Nias, ready to negotiate our presence as among Javanese headhunters. I wasn't new to Java, only to its villages, but a week in the port town of Banyuwangi, shuttling between police and immigration, had done nothing to dispel my trained cynicism. My research application had already made a year-long odyssey through the state security archipelago, drifting, barnacled with stamps, between offices, marooned for months in the headquarters of the secret police. Now I was almost free of bureaucracy, but I was not yet ready to encounter Java on even terms. A youngish man in need of company and information, proficient in Indonesian and lacking the tourist motley quickly attracts the curiosity of people with designs: touts, guides, pimps, local experts, and language teachers. The local experts – all of mixed ethnic descent, locals by preference – had strong, violently-opposed theories about the origins of certain Banyuwangi dances. They tried hard to enlist me, a Gulliver among the Big Enders and Little Enders. Was the trance-dance more archaic than the flirtatious wedding dance? Were they both originally performed by transvestites? Were the songs anti-colonial messages in disguise? Over long noisy dinners in Chinese restaurants, they quarrelled endlessly about these matters.

The language teachers – young men in polo shirts and sunglasses – formed a fractious yuppie fraternity, cruising Banyuwangi on mopeds, poaching one another's pupils and girlfriends. Every week, in rented classrooms, one of them would open a new, ambitious-sounding private school: *The Academy of World English*, or *English for the Future*. Each of them wanted a 'native speaker' to give his school a head start.

Then one of my guides took me by motorbike around the uplands. Away from the flat, dry plains that slide gently into the ocean – dust, silt, sea: you could hardly see the joins – the land lifts suddenly towards Mount Ijen, last in the chain of thirty-eight volcanoes that is Java's backbone. Ijen is 2,400 metres high, its crater an acidic well of sulphur. To local people, the bubbling white liquid and reddish sulphur coughed from the well are human symbols – sperm and blood, male and female – and the poor men who descend into the hissing fog to gather rocks are sacrilegious figures, reprobates who have somehow betrayed their origin. But the lower slopes, with their steady rainfall and rich alluvial sediments, make good farmland. Java's great agrarian civilizations were built on volcanic soil. And it is rice that has formed the landscape: broad, stepped fields with narrow mud walls and trickling irrigation streams; on the steeper slopes, smaller plots in scalloped terraces, some planted with fresh green shoots, some dry stubble, some flooded, reflecting stands of coconut trees that fringe their edges. In the fields, at intervals, little huts with red roofs, byres for the buffaloes, and windmills, like giant toys, whirring on the tops of the highest trees.

With each rise of a hundred metres the temperature drops a

degree, the air thins, the mind clears. Above the rice belt fruit trees start to appear, orchards of citrus and rambutan, and then, higher still, flecked with cloud, the big Chinese-owned clove and coffee plantations – enclosed worlds of colonial-style industry, of workers' barracks, overseers in grimy uniforms and lines of slanted pickers in conical hats. Beyond the dark-green plantations, forest, then mist and the bare top of the mountain.

One day we stopped at a village called Bayu on the lower slopes. I drank coffee with the headman, took a walk around, and asked to stay. It was as simple as that. Unimaginable in Nias: I thought, *This isn't going to be too difficult*. Over the next weeks, as I relaxed into Bayu's measured rhythm, the same thought recurred. And the contrast between the poverty and drama of the tribal world – the world I had left behind – and the easy harmony of the Javanese village haunted me as I found my way in the new setting. At night, I dreamed obsessively of my old friends and enemies in Nias.

Why Bayu? It could have been any of the Osing villages on the Eastern Cape: a crowded settlement of neat, red-tiled houses, some of cross-hatched bamboo or teak, some whitewashed stucco, amid rice terraces and coconut groves. The layout was unlike other parts of rural Java, where houses are often scattered or separated by compounds; untypical too in its intimacy, its positive, inward-looking sociability – but then that was what had brought me here. The Osing are that Javanese stock descended from the Hindu kingdom of Blambangan, the last realm to be colonized by the Dutch, the last to accept Islam. These two events coincided, as nowhere else in the Indies, when, in the late eighteenth century, the colonists imposed conversion to the alien faith, believing that it would protect Blambangan – or what remained of it after their scorched-earth conquest – from the meddling of Hindu Bali, an unconquered and troublesome neighbour just three miles away across a narrow strait. In this they were right. But the belated conquest, the half-hearted conversion, and Bali's enduring cultural influence made Blambangan – now renamed Banyuwangi, after its port town – a distinctive and interesting proposition. So much had already been written about

Java, but here, at the eastern tip, was something different.

At that first encounter, as our glasses of coffee cooled on the table, the headman – a man of about forty, with square shoulders and deep-set ironic eyes – had put it neatly. 'The thing about the Osing', he said, 'is that they are stubborn. They don't like people telling them what to do, especially outsiders. Blambangan defied Mataram [the Muslim sultanate] and refused to pay tribute. It held up the Dutch for two hundred years. Wouldn't pronounce the *Bismillah*! We said "No!" [*Osing!*]'

Needlessly – for I had heard it several times – his deputy, also in khaki uniform but less relaxed, added: 'That's why outsiders called us the Osing, or Jawa Osing: Javanese – but not.'

'We like to have things both ways,' the chief laughed through his smoker's cough; then, in English: 'Yes-no!'

It was as good a theory as any. Java but not Java; not Bali either, though the Osing dialect of Javanese had borrowed many Balinese words, including the trademark *osing*. I too liked things both ways. Contradiction makes good anthropology, good drama.

It's a truism that who you are affects what happens to you when you enter another culture: that age, nationality and gender shape the experience. I arrived in Bayu alone, which meant, in local estimation, single, since in Java a man away from his wife is as good as single. The life the village presented to me was quite different from the life that we lived as a family, so different that I am hardly able to believe my diary of those early days. Yet without this solo entry I would never have grasped an important undercurrent of village morality; the glimpses I was granted as a regular householder might have passed me by.

Without fuss, I had settled into the house of a middle-aged widow. She lived near the headman on the opposite side of a narrow tarmac road that cut through the village and led uphill towards the mountain. The houses that lined the road, shaded by trees, were of a similar kind: single-storey, as simple as a child's drawing, with a roof like a broad-brimmed hat and projecting eaves that rested on poles creating a sort of verandah at the front. Javanese houses were narrow but deep. Behind the front parlour was a windowless room for sleeping and storing rice seed. It was here in this dusty bedroom-granary that the rice goddess – a sprig of rice tied with a scrap of cloth – was kept, pinned on the wall. Further back a big airy kitchen was the real living space.

A few dwellings were built of whitewashed concrete or brick with shutters and cold smooth floors; some were of wood – painted green or blue or left untreated, the dark wood fading and spotting in the heat. Most were of bamboo, their wall panels formed from woven strips. Bamboo was light and cheap. A bamboo house, resting lightly on the bare earth (all the weight was in the roof), could be dismantled and moved to a new plot, or rearranged as the family grew. Houses, like families, came and went.

Surrounded by a picket fence and loosely shaded by a mango tree, the house where we were to live was in the exact centre of the village. Sitting on the bench under the tree, you could watch people setting off unhurriedly to their fields in the morning or returning at dusk, the women with headloads of vegetables, the men quickstepping under a yoke of coconuts or ambling behind a cow. Along this same road, at staged intervals, filed blue-uniformed children on their way to the kindergarten, older schoolchildren in ochre shirts, and the pious in sparkling prayer-garb bound for the mosque some three hundred yards uphill at the western end of the village.

The east–west road is a straight line connecting town and countryside, village and government. But to either side a different geometry prevails, as paths and alleys lead off into a maze of low, red-roofed houses crowded haphazardly together, some with clean-swept yards, others squeezed into rows. Under the eaves hang bell-shaped birdcages and strings of laundry above off-duty bicycles and neat stacks of rust-coloured coconut husks. The ground is bare, but wherever the sun can penetrate, trees sprout – bananas, papaya, starfruit. The paths and yards are loud with children and squawking chickens. The village is as crowded as a town. Apart from the two cemeteries, one open to the sky, one half jungle – smaller overgrown villages of the dead – there are no green spaces. But the fields press close, encroaching on the settlement, bringing mice, the nocturnal glugging of frogs, and stray snakes that wander into kitchens and chicken coops. On dry days, the breeze from the fields carries a faint tang of the sea.

The widow – our landlady – lived with her ancient father and unmarried adopted son. In the polite but familiar way of the village, where names are coupled with kinship terms, I called them Mother Mari, Grandpa and Elder Brother Wan. It was an odd household, composed around a missing centre, the patriarchal figure of Pak Arjo, recently deceased.* Pak Arjo had been headmaster of the school he himself founded in 1956, when he arrived in the small and backward village from Malang, a city to the west. In those days, Bayu was still surrounded by forest and was accessible only on foot or by horse, though it was less than five miles from Banyuwangi. The village did not even possess a mosque. Bayu's pious – the score of men who had attended rural Islamic boarding schools – would file through the ricefields to a nearby village for Friday worship or gather in one of the leaf-thatched prayer-houses beside the river. Built soon after his arrival, Bayu's mosque was not Arjo's innovation: he was a Christian, a Protestant of the East Javanese denomination. But he had helped to raise funds for its foundation and in all things was regarded as a pioneer, a bringer of civilization: at least that was how – in the minor cult that had grown up around him since his death – family and followers described him. On the wall in the parlour hung a framed black-and-white photograph, enlarged past the point of clarity, of Arjo in middle age. It was only a half-body portrait but somehow you knew he was short: a stern man in a suit, hair combed back, his gaze fixed beyond the viewer.

Before Arjo's advent, dwellings were the windowless wood-

* Javanese mostly use only one name. 'Pak' means Father or Mr, and is respectful but less impersonal than our 'Mr Jones'. To most villagers, I was 'Pak Andrew'. Likewise, 'Bu', Mother, can mean 'mother' or 'Mrs'. To simplify, in this book I have mostly dropped the kinship epithets.

panelled houses or bamboo huts prescribed by tradition; yards were dirty and unornamented; water was hauled from the stream. Arjo planted flowers and dug wells. 'Your homes are like tombs,' he told people. He cut windows in the façade of his house and neighbours followed suit. 'People here are slow to change, but when they see a good thing they imitate it,' said the current headman, a boyhood admirer.

The early 1960s was a time of slogans, agitprop, heroic, chain-breaking statuary in the cities, land-grabs in the countryside, workers' rallies, Muslim counter-rallies and great poverty. In the feverish politics of post-colonial Indonesia, there were three power blocs: the nationalists, the communists, and political Islam. Arjo was a local organizer in the Nationalist Party, loyal to President Sukarno. The Muslim parties, strong in nearby villages, had no adherents in Bayu – even the pious were Nationalists – but most of the eastern part of the village was solidly communist, or at least affiliated to peasant organizations under the communist umbrella. Sukarno's trick – almost a miracle – was to hold these three forces in balance, much as, it was often said, the Javanese shadow-puppeteer holds in equilibrium the dozens of heroes and villains of the Indian epics: a feat of impersonation, manipulation and sheer willpower. No real synthesis could result since the rivals were too different: instead, an ever-renewed contest of left and right, darkness and light, that lasted until the catastrophe of 1965. In the countryside, many communities were polarized or dominated by a single party. But in Bayu, and many Osing villages like it, the solution was different. In the village there was no Sukarno-puppeteer above the fray: what kept things from falling apart was not a charismatic centre but a shared tradition, a common culture, and the fine mesh of kinship and intermarriage which meant that anyone, however ideologically driven, had ties to people all over the village. Puritans shared prayer-meals, wedding celebrations, even genes with proletarians. This arrangement, too, would be tested by Sukarno's downfall, just as it would be tested three decades later by the fall of his successor and the breakout of religious reformers.

It was this wary tolerance of diversity that permitted Arjo a painless acceptance and even an influence. As with the windows and the wells, he had a knack of making his desires the wishes of others. When he announced, unsurprisingly, that he was looking for a wife, Mari, then a girl of seventeen, warned other girls not to speak to him, a Christian and pork-eater. But within a month she had agreed to marry him. 'I have always done things my own way,' she told me. 'People say I'm obstinate.' It was also, of course, Arjo's way.

I soon saw that Bu Mari was unlike the other village women, who seemed to regard her with a mixture of amusement and apprehension. Beside their mild expressions and ready smiles, she was a little sour and disappointed, with a sharp tongue and a face clouded by worry. She showed me photographs of when she was young: a slim, tall, defiant girl in a batik sarong and jacket of the kind she still wore. 'See, I was once considered beautiful.' This was said boastfully, but as of somebody else. 'Now I'm an old crone.' Perhaps her thin, ascetic figure and the grey smudges under her eyes were the effect of long years serving the local hero. She was also – and this too was obvious – a clever woman. 'I was illiterate when Pak Arjo arrived, but he taught me to read and I was the only woman in the village who read the newspaper and knew anything about the world.' He had never let her work in the fields.

With me she struck a tone that was both teasing and scolding. If I got up late, or spoke Javanese incorrectly, she would prod me in the ribs and emit a coarse laugh. When a pretty visitor arrived to get her coconuts milled (Mari had a small diesel-powered mill in the back yard), she would goad me, often in front of the woman. Seeing my discomfort, Wan said: 'Don't mind Mother, it's just her way. Everybody accepts she's like that.' Knowing that I was wifeless for a month, she teased me tirelessly about young widows in the village who would be happy to receive me. 'Widows' came in two varieties. 'Cool' widows had lost their husbands and were in mourning; 'hot' widows had been divorced or had left their husbands and were eager for company. She herself – she explained – had long since lost interest in men; indeed, she had 'freed' her husband to go wherever he wanted years before he died. But younger women, and some not so young, normally took lovers between husbands. Wan explained, as though justifying a difficult government policy: 'You see, a widow over thirty can't quickly remarry, especially if she has children, but she can always get a man; and the man usually leaves a gift. The young men of the village need some outlet, so it suits everyone. Older widows say the man's essence keeps them young, gives them a lustre.'

'What happens if people hear about the affair?'

'As long as it's discreet no one minds. If the woman is still married, that's a different matter.'

'What if the man's married?'

'As long as his wife doesn't hear. Even then, some turn a blind eye. Some people –'

But a glance from his mother cut him off.

Pursuing this line of research, I was curious about a local refreshment, found only in certain parts of Banyuwangi, called 'coffee with a pinch'. Young women seeking a husband, or perhaps merely short of cash, would set up a coffee stall and would entertain there youths who, for a modest tip, could buy a 'pinch'. It sounded fairly innocent: behind a curtain, she might sit on the customer's lap and – a step further – allow herself to be kissed in the Javanese way – an upwards browsing sniff along the cheek. Nothing more was permitted. Several village women had met their husbands in this way. One morning, Bu Mari embarrassed a matron queuing at the coconut mill by telling me loudly (shouting across the noise of the machine): 'She used to sell coffee with a pinch. Ask her.'

'I did not!' protested the woman.

'She did! Ask her husband there how they met.'

Behind the matron, a meagre man holding a bundle of coconuts looked sheepishly away and Bu Mari nodded significantly at me, as if to say: 'There! You didn't believe me, did you?'

It was part of her humour that whenever I went to town alone she told callers it was 'to look for coffee with a pinch', and this was her euphemism whenever Mercedes and I retired to our half of the house and closed the curtain.

One of the oddities of the family was its lack of blood ties. Another, evidently related, was a tendency to conversion, although 'conversion' seems too definite a word for something so unsteady. Born to a Muslim family, Arjo had been adopted by a Dutch schoolteacher and became a Christian. He married Mari, born a Muslim, and converted her. When they discovered that they could not have children they adopted a cousin's son who also converted. Wan was the first boy in the village to be circumcised by a doctor – another of Arjo's innovations. Circumcision, though a Muslim rite, was also Javanese and therefore, conceivably, Christian. You could join in Muslim rites – funerals, weddings, domestic feasts – forswear pork, even, for a few days, do the annual fast, but still be a Christian. Nothing was absolutely fixed. Wan had more or less cut ties with his real mother, now very old, who lived in the big coastal city of Surabaya where his brother worked as a prison guard. (He once explained to me, again justifying: 'They don't torture all the prisoners, only the recidivists and the politicals. For the others, it's not as bad as you'd think. They eat rice twice a day. Even get conjugal visits.') They paid one formal visit during our first year in the village to mark the anniversary of Arjo's death. The visit seemed to cause Wan no confusion, no awkwardness about how to behave or what to feel.

Not long before I was installed in this rumpled, irregular household (which was less an exception, it turned out, than an exaggeration of the norm) another member had returned to the fold. She had dropped out of university in Malang due to lack of funds and was now back in Bayu. Aged nineteen, Sri was the daughter of Mari's brother, but she had grown up between the two households and therefore had two mothers. To make the distinction, she called Mari 'Bu' and her birth mother 'Ma', the second term being a little more intimate, like the difference between 'Mum' and 'Mother'. 'Bu' was standard Javanese; in the Osing dialect it belonged to the polite register. 'Ma' was demotic, your first word and probably your last.*

Although brought up a Christian, Sri had lately switched to Islam 'to be like my friends' and had attended the Muhammadiyah University – home of a reformed, modernist Islam quite different from the old-fashioned spells-and-amulets religion of Bayu's pious. But Sri was unconcerned with doctrinal matters. Miffed at having to give up city life, she spent her days in front of the television clutching a neighbour's child or a cuddly toy, or lazing about with her childhood friends, their limbs entangled, giggling and snorting. She never joined them in the fields. Neighbours and age-mates helped out with planting and harvesting, but Sri was a step further from the land than her adoptive mother. She was happiest when riding off to town on the back of a motorbike. With her loose mane of black hair, which she proudly tossed over her shoulder, her tight jeans, her giggly manner, her dazzling white teeth, and her perfect Indonesian, she was like a girl from the pop magazines she brought back from town. I liked her, though I could not talk to her. She was young enough to regard me – at thirty-five – as very old, and this made things straightforward.

Wan was my early escort around the village. Never married (or never quite: the weddings always fell through), he was one of Bayu's few bachelors. I did not press for reasons – things would come out in time – but he did not seem to me homosexual. Java offered several accepted forms of homosexuality and he could have chosen one of them, had he wanted. Soft-bodied and sleek, with a greasy quiff – an Elvis in his rhinestone period – at thirty-seven he was less an old maid than a superannuated teenager. He called our social visits *adaptasi*, using the English loan-word, and told me that, as an incomer, he too had done a lot of adaptation. He still felt a bit of an outsider. Being Christian – at least nominally (he never went to

* Javanese is a richer, much older language than the national language, Indonesian. It has several levels or registers. To speak to a superior or in refined company you use High Javanese; to speak down or among peers, Low Javanese (the basic language). The Osing dialect is a variant of standard Low Javanese. Among Osing speakers, High Javanese is not much used outside ceremonial occasions and with strangers.

church) – made things slightly harder, although there was practically nothing he didn't do: attend ritual meals and weddings, go to the mosque on the Prophet's birthday, serve at funerals. He was on the prayer-house committee and organized visiting preachers. He even knew Arabic prayers – more than some of the neighbours. For two years he had worked as a mechanic in the merchant navy and had 'seen the world – or at least Taiwan'. But now he had no job, other than ferrying villagers about on his motorbike or doing odd repairs. Perhaps I could help him find his way. 'Sometimes I sit up all night meditating,' he said earnestly one day. He cupped his palms on his knees and shut his eyes in supplication, showing me what he meant. 'I try to imagine a better life and what I would have to do to obtain it. I screw up my concentration to a pitch and let the world float away.'

'What do you see?'

'Nothing!' He switched tone suddenly and guffawed: 'I fall asleep.'

His laughter that day was interrupted by the growl of a motorbike and the arrival of a short, sturdy man in khaki uniform who appeared at the door. Wan got up and they spoke hurriedly, the man glancing at me occasionally, a little warily, and then advancing on me with a full, confident smile. It was a smile I recognized from my visits to government offices, suggesting access to patronage and a comfortable venality – winningly human for all that. He was only an officer in the subdistrict headquarters, but any position outside the village counted trumps; hence the swagger.

Wan said: 'Pujil's going to bless his motorbike – sort of a baptism. I fixed his carburettor and we're invited.'

Later that evening, we went a quarter of a mile up the road to the top of the village. Pujil, smiling, slightly abashed, welcomed us at the door. He had changed out of his uniform and was now clad in a dark sarong and shirt, with the regulation black rimless cap worn by all Javanese men since Independence. The fez-like velvet hat was Sukarno's nationalist trademark but it was also Muslim, so you couldn't go wrong with it (unless you were tall and white, when you looked like Tommy Cooper). Inside the small, brick house, dimly lit by a dangling bulb, nine or ten men dressed like Pujil were seated on the floor around a long rectangular mat. Along the mat, like a path with an ornamental rockery, were arrayed rice mounds of varying colour and height, dishes of leafy vegetables, saté sticks, bowls of stewed buffalo meat and chicken in rich, oily gravies, and a big conical mound covered with leaves. At the far end, atop a pink pillow, was something for the ancestors: a packet of face powder, clove cigarettes ('ideally, 76 brand'), and to either side, brass bowls of water and ingredients for a betel chew, including a mortar and pestle 'in case the spirits lack teeth'. This was a prayer-meal.

The Javanese way to deal with the untoward in life – bad feelings, uneasy dreams, ghosts, rice pests, structural weaknesses in bridges – is to hold such a banquet. But I had heard that practically anything could be the object of a prayer-meal: a harvest, a newborn child, a married couple, a cow, even a motorbike.

We took our places beside the mat. 'A thousand apologies,' began a dignified elder, as he crumbled benzoin onto a tiny clay brazier and waited for the white smoke to rise. 'I call on you to witness the wish of Pujil and Jal: their desire to send prayers and give food to their ancestors who have returned to the realm of eternity; may none be passed over.'

The rest of his address – of which I understood little – appeared to be a dedication of individual dishes – I counted fifteen in all – to the hosts' parents, the Prophet, sundry spirits, Adam and Eve, and 'the four siblings born on the same day'. After each phrase of dedication, the guests, in unison, pronounced the High Javanese word for 'Yes'. As the speech drew to a close, Pujil, who was standing in the background – a grateful bystander to the ceremony conducted on his behalf – leaned forward and whispered something in the elder's ear. The man coughed and made a wry face.

'Finally, may Pujil's motorbike be safe and sound, and may he go north, south, east and west on it, without hindrance.' ('*Yes!*')

After which he broke into an Arabic prayer, spoken very rapidly, each phrase answered with a collective '*Amin*' from the witness-guests. At the end, each man rubbed his hands over his face, as if emerging from a dream.

'Gentlemen! Help yourselves, don't be shy,' said Pujil, gesturing towards the food. And calmly they did so, taking a morsel of meat here, a scoop of sauce there, unhurried, and without a show of appetite. Though the mat was laden with choice items, nobody reached beyond his nearest neighbour for a favourite delicacy or took more than a modest amount. The talk was quiet and friendly, Pujil patrolling on the sidelines urging people to eat their fill, his wife, Jal, standing at the rear with clasped hands, looking pleased and relieved. Murmuring a prayer, the elder who had recited the litany pocketed a coin from the pillow as his token reward. Then, after each guest had smoked an ancestral cigarette, they got up to leave, touching the hands of Pujil and Jal and saying, 'Your wish is granted!'

The men had left more than half the dishes untouched, and now their wives, who had spent two days preparing it all, set to, and with less decorum and a good deal more noise devoured what remained. Jal took over Pujil's role, superfluous this time, of coaxing them to enjoy their meal.

We stood outside in the night air, smoking our handrolled '76' cheroots (*The brand the ancestors prefer* – it would make a novel marketing line), each drag emitting an audible crackle along with a blast to the lungs of harsh, grandfatherly tobacco. It was like smoking Woodbines dipped in candy or being pickled from within. A neighbour, who had been called away and missed the meal strolled over.

Pujil said: 'Let's go to town. You ride pillion on my motorbike; Wan can take Rapi'i on his.' Rapi'i, who was married to another woman whom Bu Mari had informally adopted, was an occasional caller at our house. About my age, dark and fastidious, he was headmaster of a school in another village and had ambitions to become a schools inspector. He had published articles in regional newspapers on local issues and customs. He was interested in the dissolute morals of the West.

From their glances, I had the feeling this was not something they would normally do, at least not straight after a prayer-meal. It was like going on a binge after church. But a trip to Nighttown was either what they wanted me to think they did, as salaried officials, men of the world, or what they thought I expected. At any rate, as we chugged downhill through the village, lights off to avoid attracting attention, Pujil said to me over his shoulder: 'What shall we do in town, eh?'

'You're my guide.'

'That Rapi'i knows the places, we'll ask him. Another time I'll show you where I go.' Then, with a sharp laugh and a decisive rev, 'We'll start with coffee with a pinch!'

We breezed down the wooded slope, engines off to save petrol. A brilliant moon flashed through the tops of the trees that lined the narrow, bumpy road, and as we left the village behind and the trees thinned out, the grey spaces of ricefields filled out on either side. Even at night, it was a landscape in which you could feel safe from the world; or, when trouble came, very cut off. Pujil told me that the midpoint between Bayu and the next village had been a favourite place of ambush in 1965, after the military coup, when communists all over Indonesia were hunted down. All it took was a pole across the road. He nodded to the spot where villagers had been waylaid and butchered, their heads left in the road 'as an example'.

We entered the lit up, broad avenues of Banyuwangi, a town of government bungalows, flagpoles, pedal-rickshaws and dusty football fields, with two streets of Chinese shops (shops were always Chinese – the exception being stalls selling Muslim books and paraphernalia), a covered market, a beautiful big-domed mosque, and warrens of whitewashed back streets, each with its own colony of Bugis seamen, Arab cloth merchants, Malay fishers, Madurese hawkers, Balinese, Chinese, and Mandars. Each such quarter was a tiny, invisibly bounded village with its own residents' association, its leaders and enforcers, its mosque or prayer-house, coffee stalls, and roaming workforce of rickshawmen, herbal medicine peddlers, prostitutes, artisans, saté vendors, street singers and scavengers.

These townspeople were really villagers separated from their roots: home was always, nostalgically, somewhere else. And during Lebaran, the holiday at the end of the fasting month, half of them would 'go back to the village', wherever it was in that vast and ethnically mixed corner of Indonesia, while the other half welcomed Lebaran visitors from the big cities of East Java, migrants doubly cut off, for whom Banyuwangi – small and intimate, a sentimental terminus – was still home.

Passing through the town's split-arch gateway, like horseback riders on the rim of an unexplored valley, we hove to by the side of the road and took stock. The salty heat of the sea-level town surged over us; motorbikes and rickshaws buzzed past. 'Let's get something to drink,' said Pujil, wiping his forehead. 'I thought we'd take our English friend to "dine on cheek" over in Pakis. Are you ready?' Wan began to laugh and I thought anxiously of the ribbing I would get from Bu Mari. My reputation would be sealed within a month of arrival.

Rapi'i, dark-faced, correct, said, 'We'd be very noticeable. I'm dressed for work.'

'Half the customers are in uniform,' said Pujil. 'Without people like us they'd go out of business. Bankrupt.'

'I'm not sure,' said Rapi'i with an awkward laugh. 'I might meet a pupil.' He eyed me thoughtfully and I sensed he was weighing up how I would judge him.

'You can say we're helping Andrew with his research,' said Pujil. 'And you could write another article for the *Java Post*. Promotion points.'

'Perhaps this isn't the best time,' said the headmaster. 'Why don't we see what's happening down in the Malay quarter?'

Remounting, we rode through back alleys to an area near the harbour and tethered our steeds in front of a dingy cinema where a hoarding promised guns, hirsute villains and full-breasted women, their livid faces running with purple tears. But the film had started and the crowds were thick, so we drifted into a nearby billiard hall.

Inside it was oddly quiet, but for the clicking of balls and the dull throb of traffic through the door. At half a dozen tables, each spotlit by a hanging lamp, tough-looking youths chalked cues, swigged beer, or leaned over and shot balls with swift, unconsidered strokes. Each table was served by a girl who set up the balls and brought drinks. When a partner was lacking the girls too would play.

'Who goes first? You with our guest,' proposed the headmaster.

'No, you go first,' said Pujil. 'It's been a long time – I've forgotten how to play.' But Rapi'i said he felt hot and would take a breather outside. I played a game with Wan, but it was plain he had never handled a cue, and when a stranger – evidently a regular – came over and watched us, Wan meekly stood aside.

I was prepared to be thrashed, but my opponent kindly did not keep score. The others watched in respectful silence as he sunk the balls, and when he flipped a cigarette into his mouth, his chin poised over the cue, Pujil sprang forward with a match, holding the flame there until the man had completed his shot. After my presumed defeat, Wan and Pujil, now eager for a turn, played a round. I went outside and found the headmaster talking to three young women. I caught only the end of their banter, but he seemed to be teasing them, calling them 'you fine ladies', and telling them he'd be along another day if they could keep a time for him. Warmed by this exchange and no longer worried about my opinion, Rapi'i turned to me, his eyes shining, and began to question me carefully over the cost of the game – only six hundred rupiah, less than a dollar – and I wondered whether this concern explained his hanging back. When, at last, Wan and Pujil came out, smiling bashfully, chests puffed, not for the first time I had the impression that they were taking me on a tour of the sin spots of Banyuwangi but were hardly less new to them than I was.

We huddled under the awning of an outdoor stall and drank a sweet coffee (no pinch), chatting with the plump, gold-toothed woman who ran it, and across our steaming glasses with a man whom Wan recognized as an off-duty security agent. (Wan whispered to me, '*Intel.*') In Java one was never far from the secret state.

The security man said, 'How do you like Banyuwangi?'

'I like it.'

'He feels at home,' said Pujil.

'Then you must have the spirit of a soldier,' said the security man.

'Why?'

'Because they feel at home anywhere.'

But no, it wasn't that. On the way back, Pujil told me that outsiders always felt at home in Bayu. Pak Arjo, the paramedic, the agricultural extension worker: they were all welcomed and never wanted to leave. That was the virtue of the neighbourhood feasts: nobody was left out.

I doubted whether the security agent had ever attended a prayer-meal.

We got home before midnight, Wan tapping on the front door to be let in. His voice had the quiet, pleading note of someone wishing to awaken without startling. 'Ma!' *Tap, tap, tap.* 'Ma!'

'Where have you taken Andrew? Or where has he taken you?' said Bu Mari from within. 'What will I tell Bu Mercedes when she comes?'

Pujil had parked his motorbike outside the house under the mango tree and now, with a casual goodbye wave, he swung astride it. But the bike wouldn't start. With fixed grin and an unlit cigarette in the corner of his mouth, he stamped on the starter, each bounce and engine shudder producing a guffaw from Wan. *Stamp-stutter-laugh. Stamp-stutter-laugh.* It was a comic routine that could not tire.

'That's *your* carburettor again,' retorted Pujil still grinning.

'And he's just held a prayer-meal for it!' said Wan, slapping his knee in delight. 'All those bananas: "north, south, east and west"!'

'Did we or did we not get back safely?'

Stamp-stutter-laugh.

And there! It started.

2
The Headman and the Pilgrim

An anthropologist's tale should have a headman, preferably a flamboyant one, a man who would be king. In the autocratic Indonesian system where officials owe everything to their immediate superiors, the village head is still a man of the people, a figure who can look on the president's ubiquitous portrait without fear or gratitude. Unlike district officers and provincial governors, or the thousands of functionaries beneath them, village heads are chosen by the people. They control village funds, collect taxes, maintain order, and can bring down the law; these are their official functions. But their personal authority and the ethos over which they prevail largely rest on character.

The headman of Bayu, who was always known simply and respectfully as Pak Lurah (Mr Headman), had no ambitions to kingship. That comic possibility is entirely denied to me. His solid, phlegmatic presence, his deep-set, observant eyes, and his air of expectant mockery – as if waiting patiently for a practical joke to spring – all suggested someone who preferred to respond to events rather than shape them in his image. Pak Lurah was into his second year of a six-year stint and, so far as I could tell (people are never entirely happy with their headman), was making a fair go of it. Unlike some of the other heads I had met, he did not take the job – or anything else – too seriously. His was a light touch. It wasn't his style to steamroller his opponents or impose his will on the village. Indeed, it would be fair to say that he didn't really have a will. When things were going against him, he would sigh: 'Ah, let them get on with it, we'll have a good laugh at the mess!' or 'So be it!' He ruled by shrugs. Perhaps this was the key to running a village like Bayu where – as everybody kept telling me – you could find all sorts. A headman too partial to the modernizers or the conservatives, the puritans or ritualists, would provoke a split. True to the Osing spirit of Yes-No, of having it both ways, he sat on the fence. In fact, he lived on it. This was frustrating for the hotheads and 'fanatics' who were always spoiling for a fight. He would wear them out with indifference or deflate them with a smile.

How Pak Lurah came to his position was not entirely clear to me. What passes before you arrive in the field comes to you as legend. Though it happened only a month beforehand, it already has the fingered, bowdlerized feel of ancient history. I hated leaving the village for more than a day or two because anything that occurred while I was away was virtually lost. Either I would never hear about what had happened (people sparing me the bad news), or the event would be turned into anecdote or personal propaganda. 'We cried for a month after you left,' they said, on our return to Bayu in 1996. Of course, the interesting thing about such a statement was not whether it was true – which of course it wasn't – but that people wanted to tell it to us. It was a claim on our sympathies, an endearing lie. But in other matters it would have been nice to know the facts. All I know of the headman's election was that, as is usual, there was a certain amount of influence-peddling, a sweetening of enemy supporters, a nobbling of the diehards – and a sign from heaven. On the eve of the election, a smallish star was observed to hover directly over his house. Several people claimed to have seen the light; others had meditated all night to that end. It was the emblem of victory, a sign that the gods were with him.

The headman lived diagonally across the road from Bu Mari. He and his wife, Bu Lurah (Mrs Headman: in local terms, the First Lady), had only one child, who lived next door in a house they had built for her. This white, spacious bungalow, with its concrete floor polished to a sheen and its town-style, imitation-leather sofas, was much better than their own. It was an Osing custom for the older to retreat before the progress of the young. This was why the headman's own parents were content to live at the back in a bamboo structure not much better than a hut. He had built them a brick dwelling but they preferred the homely, permeable, split-bamboo shelter which was never hot or cold, which let out the smoke and let in the light, and through which talk and laughter could pass freely. Barefoot, they liked the body temperature of an earth floor.

Resting against his parents' limewashed hut was a narrow bench on which Pak Lurah would take a nap or sit and watch the women coming and going with headloads of washing. After a marital tiff he would sit there eating meatball soup his mother had prepared for him. He conveyed a sense of leisure. And until I realized that a headman's principal function was simply to exist – to be around, as a focal presence in village life – I had an impression of indolence, of time hanging heavy. In fact, Pak Lurah's unhurried manner was not the result of laziness but economy of effort, a recognition – very Javanese, it now occurs to me – that exertion and efficacy are inversely related. In Java it was a well-established principle, from the president down, that the man who shouts loudest is least heard. Pak Lurah had extended this principle to every aspect of life. There was a way of doing things that involved minimal fuss – less grunt. In the empty house he had built for his parents, the pale-green walls had been painted *around* the furniture, leaving white silhouettes when the armchairs were moved. But why waste paint if the chairs were fine where they were?

Every morning, in khaki uniform, he strode the hundred yards up to the village office where his team of development, irrigation, and finance officers – all ordinary villagers – totted up statistics, drew pie charts and fulfilled targets. Beneath government mottoes exhorting discipline, cleanliness and service, he would hear petitions, dictate letters, sign permissions, reprimand delinquents, and advise on divorce. (Following government policy, the advice was always *against*.) The master of thirty-seven different books (down from forty-three during a recent reform), including birth-control registers and land records naming the size and ownership history of every rice terrace in Bayu's 175-hectare territory, nothing could happen without his say-so. Yet the work was not particularly onerous and much of the time was spent in smoking and drinking tea. On the few occasions I turned up, my interruptions were welcomed and nothing happened until I left.

The rest of the day he would stay at home receiving visitors, or go off on his motorbike to check his fields. He owned several hectares of prime land – all worked by sharecroppers – but his main income was from the four hectares granted him as headman. Before his election he had been a harvest broker: someone who buys the standing crop from the farmer, organizes the harvesters, and sells the paddy on to a rice factory. Before that he had done a little dealing, and had even been known to plough a field. But I could hardly imagine him capable of such energy. By contrast, his father – an emaciated veteran in the battered hat and black smock of a peasant – was active from before dawn, chopping wood and forking hay for the cattle, while his mother rallied the chickens, cooing and chivvying them as she scattered coconut shavings.

Like many others in the village, Pak Lurah lived surrounded by family. Three generations – presently four – lived within earshot of one another. This might have made for a certain continuity, even uniformity, but the generations belonged to distinct eras, overlapping rather than successive. And to walk the few yards from one dwelling to another was to be reminded how rapidly Java had changed since Indonesian independence in 1949, how so much history had been crammed into so little time and space. It was as if the world had changed too fast to allow the full, ripened shape of the past to emerge, and each truncated era, each human type, persisted alongside its successors. The headman's parents, in their peasant attire, could speak only the Osing dialect of Javanese; neither had gone to school or had ever been outside Banyuwangi. As a cattle dealer, the old man could handle figures, but neither he nor his wife could read or write. Their granddaughter, Dewi, fluent in Indonesian, a graduate of high school, was trained for a different life – she had never planted, weeded, or even cooked – but she had no clear conception of what that life might be. (What was a modern villager to *do*?) Yet she could read aloud from the Arabic (without understanding) and had completed a recitation of the entire Koran as part of her wedding celebrations. With her big, mild face and sturdy, pale calves, her shortish hair – the fashion for her age – and high voice, she seemed an overgrown child. Her husband, Jan – dark, smirking, strongly built – was the son of a rice-mill proprietor, one of the bigger landowners in the village. He, too, had been handed prosperity on a plate, and thanked not his parents but divine grace. Since moving in with his wife, he had begun to pepper his conversation with *insha'allahs* and *bismillahs*. When he spoke these Arabic words – self-consciously making a claim, but unsure of the effect – his expression changed, becoming defensive, alert to anyone who would question his right.

Jan was a new Muslim. In ways I did not yet understand, the growth of orthodoxy – the scriptural, literal-minded side of Islam – had become entwined with modernization. All that the headman's generation had rejected as backward, wasteful, divisive, even foreign (*Arabism*, they quietly called it) had returned, rebranded as modernity. Where the old man knew nothing of Islam, and the headman was, as he put it, *nasional* – by which he meant, Sukarno-like, that he did a bit of everything – the son-in-law had aspirations to go on the pilgrimage to Mecca. Dewi would have to follow his lead. If Jan made this commitment, which meant a lifetime of mosque attendance, annual fasting, and conspicuous almsgiving, she could not persist in her parents' indifference. She would have to pray and put on the headscarf, like a proper pilgrim's wife.

The three interconnected houses showed different faces of Java, different visions of what Java could be. There were other, more compelling visions I had yet to encounter, but, with variations, these three household types – oriented to the village, the nation, and the community of the faithful – could be found all over the village.

The headman, suitably enough, was poised in the middle of things. I took to him immediately. And when I think of Bayu, and dream of going back, it is often Pak Lurah I remember, capering with children in the yard, sitting gloomily on his mother's bench, or cackling hoarsely at some joke. He had the gift of friendship. In

Bayu, friendship was unusual – probably because friendliness was everywhere – but I was made to feel a friend. Like three or four others he had kept up with since his schooldays – men he took fishing in a leaky, rented boat, or accompanied to all-night puppet shows – I felt included in his trusted circle. Friends received confidences, were taken to view mistresses (then quickly hustled away), and knew one another's business. Perhaps this was why his wife, Bu Lurah, through her cheerfulness, always regarded me with a hint of suspicion.

You had only to glance at the headman to know that he lacked the ascetic strain, the puritan streak which is a persistent element in the Javanese mix. His largish, slow body – heavily built for a Javanese – and his groomed finish, with small, trim moustache and back-combed bonnet of black hair, suggested a discreet vanity, the dapperness of a lady-killer. He had the same mildly cynical view of human nature as Pujil (it was a common disposition among officials), and this made him reluctant to moralize, a useful virtue in the headman of a 'mixed' village. He expected people to be no better than himself. A few days after our trip to the fleshpots of Banyuwangi, Rapi'i, the headmaster, called in and contrived to leave on the table, so I would find it, a newspaper open at a page-long article on Western mores. The headman would never have done such a thing – though, reading its prurient condemnation, he might have asked me about a ticket to Europe.

The West – fabulously rich, dissolute, bellicose – was part of our baggage, what we had to live down. Visiting preachers paraded the horrors of life in the West – the drunkenness and nudity, the 'free love' (this phrase always in English, love having a price in Java), the enslavement to money, the incontinent 'anger' that led to war. Television made it all real. I struggled to persuade people that *Baywatch* was no more a reflection of my world than *The Flintstones*. It must be like that, they said: we could never make such a film here.

News broadcasts showed the outside world to be in a constant state of war. After the obligatory pictures of the president opening cement factories and visiting prawn farms, the foreign reports consisted mainly of explosions and tank convoys. The purpose – certainly the effect – was twofold. As we gathered in the evening before a blue-screened television, Wan would comment gratefully: 'Indonesia is such a peaceful place.' And Jona, a woman who lived at the back, would say, in disbelief rather than reproach: 'Ah, you people are always at war!' In a few houses they were saying: 'Always murdering Muslims,' but neither Jona nor Wan thought in such terms. Killing was killing.

The villagers' other source of information on the West was to the east. A tour of the tourist hotspots in Bali – Kuta Beach, the Monkey Forest, the romantic coastal temples – was now part of the annual post-Fast holiday. Villagers returned from exhausting, titillating daytrips convinced that these exotic sights – fat girls in bikinis, bronzed surfers, lager louts throwing their women into the sea or puking in the street – were part of our 'culture'. We belonged to that world of wealthy savages.

On my early 'adaptation' visits around the neighbourhood with Wan, he helpfully explained that the tourists were Australians or criminals who had been sent into exile by their countries. England was a cold country and the English did not go naked in public. But not all villagers understood these distinctions.

'Why are they always reading?' asked Ramelan, a ploughman who had done the beach tour. 'I've seen them, lying on the sand, drying. They have books thicker than the Koran. The women have underpants like this.' And he made a V with his hands at his crotch.

'Oh, shut up!' scolded his wife. 'You couldn't tear yourself away.'

'Do they have widows in your village?' he asked me.

'There, Andrew. He's already planning his trip. Shameless man!'

I would have saved a lot of time had I worn a placard disclaiming responsibility for white mischief. But my handling of these questions, in repetitive conversations, was good language practice. What I could never reply – in the early days at least – was that, while my wars raged in the Middle East, the Indonesian army, cheerfully impartial, was busily killing Muslims in Aceh, Christians in East Timor, and pagans in West Papua. Nor, when they tackled me on Western promiscuity, could I remind people of what they seemed so eager to show me closer to home – the philanderers and randy widows, the village notables with secret 'second wives', the brothel visits after Friday prayers: for them, these things had no equivalence.

An early caller – I think it was my second day in Bayu – was Pak Drus. He lived directly opposite – next door to the headman, who was his father's cousin. Drus's Indonesian was weak, and my Javanese basic, so it was difficult to talk. But he wanted to tell me one thing: that he intended – indeed longed – to go to Mecca. Why? 'Because performing the haj is an obligation on those who can afford it.' This seemed to me fair as justification but weak as motivation. There must be more to it. But when I pressed him on his reasons he simply repeated his answer, as if I had not understood. 'I am a Muslim. It's my duty since I can afford it.' He stared at me intensely and I felt prompted to respond with some word of praise, but nothing came to me. Perhaps feeling obliged to expand – Javanese are invariably polite – he explained that he had built up a sum of money from his trading. He dealt in motorbikes and was in partnership with a Chinese man who lived in town. The Chinaman provided the capital; Drus knew the market. His 'interest in religion', as he put it, made him well known to hajis and the like, 'people with money'. Business followed religion; religion followed business. 'One day I will be a haji too,' he said. 'Hajis are the most respected people. They have sacrificed their wealth for religion.'

It seemed a rather self-rewarding form of sacrifice but I did not say as much.

A few weeks later, I was buying something at the little store his wife kept, when he called me in. Ducking under the lamp glasses and balls of plastic string, he led me past stacked bags of fertilizer into a big overfurnished room. He had bought two three-piece suites hoping to sell one of them, but nobody was interested and now he was stuck with them. 'So you can sit wherever you like,' he joked, waving a hand. With a speed that suggested they had planned my visit, Siti, his tired-looking wife, set out glasses of tea and smiled at me in a welcoming, if slightly reproachful, way. 'Why haven't you been to see us yet? You're always with Pak Lurah or Wan or off somewhere. Where do you go? When is Bu Mercedes arriving?'

'In two weeks. With Sofía.'

'My son's friend,' she said. The boy, age five, was their only child, though each had children by previous marriages. There was a girl of seventeen or eighteen, Siti's daughter, who (Wan told me) had gone mad after being jilted by her fiancé. She lived with an uncle in another part of the village. Now she was 'settling down', but before I arrived she would walk stark naked around the yard. Nobody had done anything about this for fear of giving her a further shock. It was 'shock' that had caused her madness.

Thinking of this terrible story, and confronted by their expectant faces, I was stuck for something to say. On the wall was a photograph of the smiling couple in full pilgrim garb, he with the white cap of a haji, she with a white headscarf. 'That was the carnival,' he said, following my gaze. 'Last year, on Independence Day. Call it a practice run!' There were other tokens of piety – Koranic mottoes painted on little wooden shields, a big calendar showing crowds swirling around the Kaaba in the Grand Mosque in Mecca. On the sideboard was a framed picture of Drus standing beside a gowned cleric. 'That's my kyai,' he said. 'I go to him for advice. I do whatever he tells me. His word is sacred.' Kyais are the heads of rural Islamic seminaries, the face of traditionalist Javanese Islam. Beside this portly, self-satisfied figure, Drus looked small and insignificant, his thin moustache outdone by the kyai's full beard. He leaned forward and fixed me with a black stare. 'The kyai gave me this ring. It protects against sorcery.' He held out a dark, gnarled hand – the hand of a farmer, not a trader – and showed off a big silver ring whose centre was an arabesque, presumably a *Bismillah*. Around his wrist was one of those black snaky bracelets that grow on sweat. His fingernails were bitten down to the quick.

'I would follow him to the death,' he continued, as if I would stop him.

I said, changing the subject: 'I hope your daughter is a little better.'

'No, she's the same. Still like a zombie.'

Zombies in Java? He had probably got the word from a horror film. Cannibals, zombies, Dracula: Western imports to the Javanese pantheon. *Our culture*. But the ideas of soul loss and spirit kidnap were standard in Javanese magic.

'She's had injections, but the doctors can't do anything for her. It's sorcery. She's been like it before, got better, and then relapsed. There's a lot of sorcery in this area. You'd better be careful.' Then, indicating our tea, 'Drink up!'

I felt I was getting out of my depth. These were matters best left for a day when I had a fuller command of the language and knew who I was talking to. But Drus persisted, determined to impress.

'My four brothers were killed by sorcery. In the space of a few months. They were already grown men, but none could resist. We knew who had done it and denounced him. They took him to the mosque, wrapped him in a shroud like a dead man and made him swear an oath that if he was guilty he would die by his own hand.'

Drus fell silent to let the words sink in, and Siti added: 'A few months later he was found dead in his fields.'

'Not a mark on him,' said Drus. And with this triumphant phrase, no doubt often repeated, his leer returned. 'He was lucky not to have been murdered by our father.'

'Why did he want to kill your brothers?'

'Human nature.'

'I don't understand.'

'Isn't it human nature to afflict one another? That's why the magicians are always busy. Banyuwangi is the warehouse of black magic in Java. You tell anyone in Jakarta, "I come from Banyuwangi," and they'll run a mile.'

I had thought this reputation – like the regional epithet *Osing* – was an outsiders' construction, a slur. Drus seemed proud of it.

Crouching forward in his seat, he began to describe to me the effects of sorcery – the sudden haemorrhages, the waking nightmares, the incurable diarrhoea – and I had the sense that he was trying to scare me. When he boasted, 'I know all the magicians in this area; or at least I have experience of them,' I countered: 'Doesn't that conflict with religion?'

'Not if it's in self-defence.'

'Isn't it interfering with God's will: like trying to change one's fate?'

'No. Because you are using the Holy Book.'

'But is that using, or misusing, the Holy Book?'

He looked at his wife in exasperation and I regretted my question.

Siti said: 'You don't have to worry about these things, Pak Andrew. There aren't as many magicians as there used to be, at least not of the bad kind. Many were killed as communists.'

'Many killed themselves in terror,' said Drus, his grin returning. 'Some were victims of the Mysterious Killings.'

This was a wave of extra-judicial executions allegedly ordered by the president across the country during the 1980s. They were known as Petrus, an acronym derived from the Indonesian for 'mysterious murders'. The victims mostly belonged to criminal gangs – the tattooed thugs, pimps, and racketeers who ruled the slums of Surabaya and Jakarta. But in the countryside, reputed sorcerers met a similar fate. As in the anti-communist pogroms of the 1960s, local leaders had supplied army commanders with names; masked killers took away the victims at night. It was a demonstration of state power, but more terrifying than an open crackdown. In Banyuwangi, Petrus stalked the hinterland until a death squad hacked to pieces the regional military commander's son. After this 'accident' someone ordered the killings to stop.

It was bad to conclude on this note, but I was called away – a visitor from town wanting English lessons (refused) – and I left them with an uneasy feeling, disturbed by Drus's manner and annoyed with myself for having said too much.

3
East–West

My solo days in Bayu were drawing to a close. In over two years of fieldwork I would never establish sensible hours – the raucous night life of the village made that impossible – but my trips to coffee plantations in the hills, pool halls and roadside stalls, locally famous dancers and puppeteers had come to an end. So too, my evenings on airless town verandahs among Banyuwangi's scattered, rivalrous intelligentsia. I had to settle down and learn what it is to live in a Javanese village. But before anything I needed to find somewhere to live – something suitable for a family of three, with a well and a bathroom of sorts. This would not be easy. The village had a neat, scoured, spruce appearance – none of the patchy squalor of town – but it lacked piped water and sanitation. Most people bathed on their way to and from the fields in one of the streams that ran down the mountain. In the evening, they squatted in the shallows, half-clothed, unembarrassed, sometimes hailing passers-by or shouting conversation up the bank. The biggest stream, the Sobo – a silver trickle in the dry season, a brown torrent in the wet – was a place of communal washing. Knee-deep among smooth black rocks, the women – some stripped to the waist and gleaming – would pound and thrash their laundry, swinging wet sheets above their heads like sails, working soap suds into airy meringues. It was a happy sight. On my way to Sumbersari, a hamlet to the south, I would brave their ribald humour.

'Come down and join us!'

'When does Mercedes arrive? Can you hang on that long?'

'You won't come out of that room for a week!'

'Who will hold the baby?'

I had grown used to this banter. But sometimes I was taken aback by its bluntness. One morning a crowd had gathered at Mari's coconut mill, and a woman who had been pointed out to me as a 'widow' – in this case, a divorcee – said aloud: 'Aren't you lonely at night? You can sleep with me. I'm still young.'

Mari's was one of the few houses with a bath, or rather a concrete tub, fed by the well, from which you scooped water in a gasp-inducing shower. Behind the tub was a French-style latrine connected to an irrigation channel. This, too, was a rarity in the village. The well had been dug by Arjo. He had 'taught' the villagers to boil water, and this was something that Mari did every day. But her unsophisticated neighbours drank it fresh. Well water was good enough to drink; spring water, even better, was 'medicine'.

In Nias, we had lived next to a big, fast-flowing river. We had swum in its pools and carried slopping buckets back up the hill to our house. Only when we switched from boiling to filtering did we get sick (and then I had nearly died of dysentery). But Javanese streams were more like sheep-dip. They drained pesticide and fertilizer from the rice terraces, turning red shirts pink. Nothing less than a tub and a well would do.

Pak Lurah, the headman, had offered me his parents' vacant house, a white concrete building complete with traditional panel-walled kitchen. A Javanese kitchen was like a bamboo cave, warm and windowless but pricked with light, cosy yet dimly vast. It could amount to half the house. More intimate than the front parlour, it was a gathering place where you could relax with neighbours in workclothes or sit barechested after the shower. In the kitchen you could spit tobacco juice on the dirt floor, conspire with friends, or sleep off the heat of the afternoon. It always had a bed-platform, one or two earth ovens, a resident cockerel (or songbird in a cage that hung from the rafters), benches strewn with drying spices, sacks of rice grain, piles of odorous chopped wood, half-finished pandanus mats, rolled and frayed, and sometimes a well, but no taps, sinks, or 'kitchen appliances'. Pans and ladles hung from the walls; knives were thrust in the bamboo wattle. The kitchen was backstage, and things could be said there that could never pass in the front parlour.

This particular house was to be our home in the second period of fieldwork three years later, but for the moment I wanted something more independent, less compromising. I began to make a map of the village. It was never more than a sketch – how could you fit such human variety into centimetre squares? But it gave me an excuse to circulate, to be seen around, and to spy out a suitable house – perhaps even persuade a 'widow' that a monthly rent would make it worth her while to move back with her family. (A bad idea: young, popular widows did not want to be encumbered with parents; old widows generally lived in hovels.)

I quickly discovered that the village, though small in compass, was unexpectedly large inside – like a fabulous chest whose chambers open into other chambers, or a system of subterranean caves. (How else could a population of two thousand be fitted into so small a space?) And it came in parts. West and east were the points of reference, geographically and socially, but between them, and to either side, the cramped space was subdivided into quarters or wards. Each ward had its own cluster of blood relations – often the descendents of a single ancestor three or four generations back – its own character and even speech style. People remarked on the fact that folk at one end of the village – the west end, furthest from town – spoke slowly and clearly, with a more archaic Osing vocabulary. They said *gurau* for *guru*, and *Byalai* for Bali. These drawlers were what linguists call Norms – Non-mobile Older Rural Males, sticklers for tradition. But family idiolects, just like Habsburg chins and strong right hooks, were also passed down the generations. So within a ward you could hear differences of intonation and style, accumulations of family speech habits.

Norms – and Normas – were peasant farmers, smallholders, whereas the rougher, slangier tongue of east Bayu was spoken by day labourers and artisans, people exposed to the street argot and generalized Indonesian culture of town. The poorer eastern section was more proletarian, more mobile, less Osing than the west.

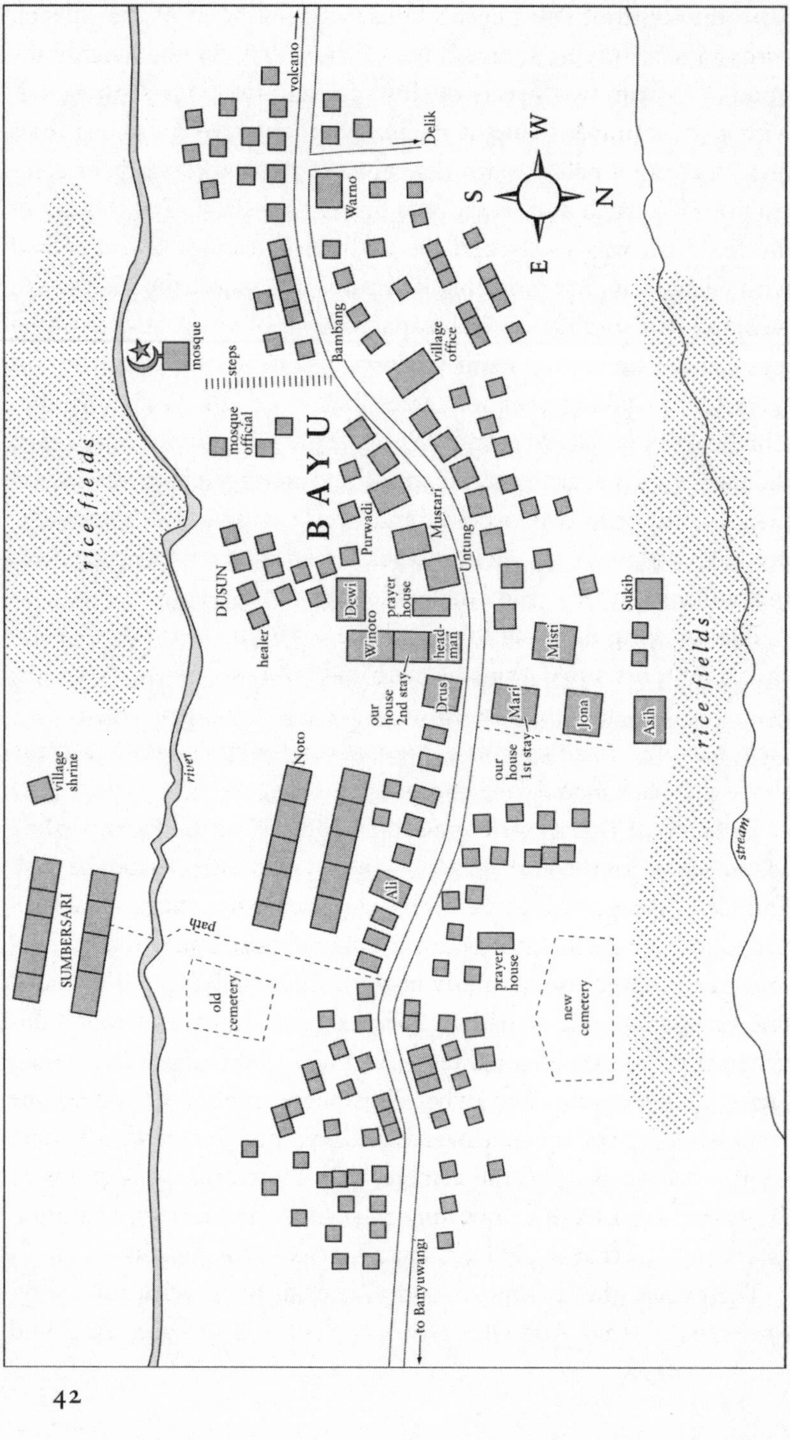
volcano
Delik
W
S
N
E
Warno
Bambang
village office
mosque
steps
mosque official
BAYU
rice fields
Purwadi
Mustari
Untung
DUSUN
healer
Dewi
Winoto
prayer house
headman
our house 2nd stay
Drus
Sukib
Misti
Mari
our house 1st stay
Jona
Asih
rice fields
village shrine
river
Noto
stream
Ali
SUMBERSARI
path
old cemetery
prayer house
new cemetery
to Banyuwangi

To the south of Pak Lurah's house (the midpoint of the village), across a leafy ravine spanned by a footbridge, lay the neighbourhood of Dusun, two streets of close-packed dwellings forming a T, with a small prayer-house at the junction. Between the facing rows of houses ran a pebbly path that divided the fenced yards of compact reddish earth and served as a gutter in the rain. But the day of my first visit was sunny and the washing lines puffed and bellied with village laundry: faded batik sarongs, big purple brassieres with webbing like surgical corsets, capacious bloomers with elasticated legs, school uniforms, scout uniforms, babies' swaddling. An old woman was raking peanuts spread out to dry on empty sacking. Chickens – black-feathered, long-legged, half crow – scratched in the path; goats tugged at gateposts. In blinding sun, a fat woman heaved a mattress over a bench and beat it with a curly rattan carpet beater: thwack, thwack, thwack. *Humph! There!* she grunted, the punishment over, and laughed loudly at my grin.

The working day was long and there was no hurry. Under the eaves, mothers stood chatting with babies in slings on their hips; grannies sat with children between their knees, crooning as they picked the lice from their hair; an old man, shirtless, reclined in the shade, his back against the bamboo wall.

The men of Dusun were graduates of the rural Islamic boarding schools that dot the East Javanese countryside and provide the rank and file of Indonesia's conservative religious association. They happened to live together not because a shared faith had brought them together, but because of family history: their ancestor had attended one such school and so had his sons and grandsons, and even – this generation – his granddaughters. (And what a difference that would make.) Twenty years ago, when Dusun became too crowded, one section simply shifted southwards and founded Sumbersari, a quiet hilltop hamlet beyond the cemetery. Sumbersari was as pious as Dusun; it even had its own tiny prayer-house, a creaky bamboo affair on stilts that could hold seven or eight worshippers.

These were the two most solidly Muslim wards. But not everyone was the same. And wherever you went in Bayu, you could find people who did not conform to neighbourhood type. Consider Pak Ran. His was the poorest house in Dusun, a weathered bamboo and plywood shack among gabled wooden houses and brick bungalows. On my first reconnaissance he called me in, sketch map in hand. As we sat uncomfortably on his plastic string chairs and smoked the clove cigarettes I had brought, it seemed to me incredible that a man of sixty could have acquired so little in life. The dirt floor, the newspapered walls, the damp-stained sagging ceiling with solitary lightbulb: it was like a Surabaya slum. Ran was an uncle of Bu Mari (my claim on his hospitality), but he was poorer than any of the family. 'I've been married many times,' he told me with a rueful smile and a flash of gold teeth. Perhaps this was his vice, the cause of his poverty. His wife, preparing coffee for us on a smoky fire, had a long-suffering look. She was his first wife and he had come back to her, the mother of his only child. It was a common pattern – the roving husband, the woman awaiting his return like a sailor's wife. Ran's big, brawny body suggested a life of toil – he could still handle a plough – but the smooth, muscled arms and long, beringed fingers spoke of vanity, sensuality. What made him different from his neighbours, however, was his calling: he was a healer, a diviner, a magician.

We heard the afternoon call to prayer, a taped broadcast from the mosque. It was a good two hundred yards away but loud enough to make conversation briefly impossible. Ran looked coolly away and waited until it died. As he gave me to understand, he was not a pious man. He had served as the mosque caretaker, and he knew more Arabic prayers than most people in the village. Indeed, he routinely led the prayers at weddings and funeral commemorations. (I must have heard him twenty or thirty times in the course of my stay.) But he did not perform the five-times-daily prostrations, the prescribed ritual of Islamic worship. Nor had he ever learned to 'recite' – to read aloud from the Koran. 'What is the use if you don't understand?'

'You mean, understand the Arabic?' I said.

'Understand the body, the self. There's a saying: Don't learn to recite without learning how to recite your body.'

One's body, oneself: in Javanese this was a single expression. But the meaning of the saying was lost on me.

'In my day,' he went on, 'only the older youths learned to recite. Girls never. Now everybody does it, boys and girls of eight. And there's lots more tunes, more swagger. Loudspeakers! We all have to hear it. But look at the Balinese: they don't know how to recite their scriptures, but they're honest, afraid of their gods.'

Their gods. It was a phrase his neighbours might have wondered at. Wasn't Allah singular?

I asked him whether he fasted in Ramadan. No. Nor did he bother to hide the fact, as he would have had to do in certain other villages. If neighbours saw him eating his midday meal as they passed by, let them! If people wanted to fast, that was their own affair. 'Each person carries the burden of his own sins. If I pray, it's for my benefit, if I don't it's my loss.'

'What about the hereafter?'

'There is no hereafter. There's only *here*.'

'And no heaven or hell?'

Ran sighed and explained slowly, as to a child.

'Everything is in the visible world. In the town square, look west and you see the mosque. North is the palace of the lord [the regional officer's mansion]. South is the market and pleasure – heaven, if you like. East is hell, the police station.'

I had visited Banyuwangi police station – though not its innermost cells – and could not agree. The warders of hell could not be so polite. (Though an Indonesian hell surely contains uniforms.) My question was too simple, his answer a little too pat. A toytown cosmology: even as an analogy it was trite. But I was soon to realize that he would not debate a point; he was not a thinker, rather a collector of arcana. And his esoteric lore, picked up here and there, was something he jealously guarded – as a fortress against the pious. In his divinations and prayer-meal addresses he displayed it to good effect; for he was always the man called upon to preside at neighbourhood feasts. His long, incense-laden dedications of the 'five-coloured porridge' and the 'rice-mound of misfortune' always had a few extra ornaments, symbolic curlicues that sounded vaguely powerful but only made sense at the moment of hearing, like a Dylan Thomas poem. An archaism here, an earth spirit there, a mantic reference to the 'three-in-one': nobody questioned him on these embellishments for fear of seeming ignorant, or out of habitual courtesy. What did they mean? That the spirits of the above and below were at his command; that with Ran you were in safe hands.

Here, then, was a paradox: a doubter among the pious, entrusted with their welfare, leading prayers at their most sacred domestic rites.

I had met several non-practitioners who allowed the pious a certain superiority, as if religion, like athletic prowess, was a talent and a privilege. But the magician was not particularly respectful of his neighbours' piety. As he put it on that first visit, waving airily in their direction: 'Behind good, there's bad; behind bad, good. Who knows what is in men's hearts!' To him, their diligence in prayer, so public and noisy, was just 'showing off'. But nor did he express any interest in Bayu's most effective reply to orthodoxy: the mysticism of the Sangkan Paran sect. Adherents of a pantheist doctrine, the mystics were concentrated in the west of the village, among the rice farmers. He spoke of them dismissively: 'They say, "I am Allah." Well, we know that, don't we?' (*Do we?* I wanted to ask him. *Your neighbours would not accept it.*) 'But what of it? Does that make them any better than me? They're all talk! Words, words, words! The meaning of this and the meaning of that, the "three-in-one", the "five-in-four", the essence-and-origin-and-destination and whatnot. But when it comes to playing with one another's wives . . .'

The slur was already familiar. I could not credit it and wondered at his bitterness. But what surprised me more was his ignorance. Had he spent more time with the mystical Norms and monist Normas he would have had some ballast for his scepticism; something solid to cling to in the sea of faith. (For a lonely doubter, it is faith which is disturbing.) Yet knowing nothing of mysticism beyond a few heretical and pretentious-sounding formulas, he saw it merely as another form of arcane knowledge, a species of obscurantism like his own. Had he dropped his guard and dared listen to its practitioners, he would surely have been astonished by its earthiness, its unexpected rationality. But perhaps such qualities were not valuable to a diviner.

These cross-currents were, as yet, barely perceptible to me. I knew something of the variety of belief in Bayu but assumed a simple antagonism. I assumed that you were one thing or another: a mystic or a pious Muslim or an animist – or perhaps a rank materialist, if such could exist in Java. (Ran's 'all's in the visible world' was at odds with his spirit-mongering.) But even at this stage, as I went on my rounds, it was obvious that the *shape* of the village affected who knew what – that the map of knowledge I was discovering, house by house, ward by ward, was criss-crossed by invisible barriers: what you were permitted to know was limited by who you happened to live among, who you met on a regular basis. And to learn about mysticism, you had not only to make contact – that was unavoidable – but to be alert to the coded meanings slipped into prayer-meals and casual conversations, to be curious and persistent, to *want* to understand.

A guru does not seek pupils, said Sahari, one of the mystics. *The pupil seeks the guru. It's not for me to encourage others; even less my children. It has to come from them.*

Ran's brother, the former headman Harsono, had been an active mystic for fifty years. Yet none of his children or neighbours had followed him; and they had only the vaguest idea of what he believed. His daughters were ordinary lukewarm Muslims; his son – a neighbour of Ran – a stern pietist. In this human hive where people mingled so easily, buzzed so sociably, it was as if certain words and ideas didn't carry: either that or people tuned out. The really important things passed unnoticed, or did not pass at all. Pantheists, idealists and god-fearing theists might live side by side but, mentally, inhabit different worlds. As a system of knowledge, only Islam moved freely.

More typical of Dusun was the headman's father-in-law. Sanuri, unlike the diviner, had spent time in a seminary and could 'recite', though again without understanding the Arabic. He performed the prescribed prayers, the annual Fast, and the Thursday night chanting in the prayer-house, when the faithful gathered to sing the names of Allah. He also did all the other things that Bayu people did: hosted feasts, sent blessings to the ancestors, left parcels of chickens' feet in the fields for spirits, and visited the shrine of the village founder, a were-tiger who was the guardian spirit of Bayu. When he held a prayer-meal, it was Ran whom he called to burn the incense.

For men like Sanuri, orthodoxy was not a matter of avoiding what is unorthodox (who could say what that was!), still less of shunning the lax, but rather the faithful performance of one's obligations, one's traditions. And where, after all, did obligations end and traditions begin? It wasn't for him to decide whether a prayer-meal, with its invocations and spirit-offerings, was Islamic or not. 'All I know is that it was good enough for my grandfather,' he said. 'And good enough for my teacher.'

We sat in his big wooden house, on his firm, upright chairs at a marble-topped coffee table. It was a standard Osing house, with a swept earth floor, a glass-fronted cupboard stocked with crockery and, to the side, a platform which served as a bed at night (it could sleep a whole family) and a bench or table in the day. An ornamental wrought-iron lamp hung above us from the rafters. On the biscuit-coloured teak walls were nailed Koranic mottoes of the kind I had seen in Drus's house. But here was no ostentation, none of the younger man's desire to impress or cut a figure. Instead, the owner, like the house, wore a solid, settled, defensive air. When I asked him about the purpose of the Thursday chanting, what the Arabic phrases meant – from hearing them repeated hundreds of times, I already knew them myself – he stiffened. 'They mean something to God,' he replied, a touch irritably, as if to ask about meaning was to put Islam itself in question. (But it was a good answer, worth remembering.) What, then, was the chanting for?

'To build up merit, to help the ancestors achieve tranquillity, to be safe-and-well [*slamet*].'

I supposed he meant by this salvation. But he corrected me:

'*Slamet* is when you go to bed at night, get up in the morning and you are still there; nothing has happened. *Slamet* is not being bothered by demons.'

It was the same, he explained, with the daily prayers: they bring you peace and *slamet*. But this only lasts a short while, so you have to be regular and diligent. 'It's like filling your belly with a bowl of rice: it satisfies for a while, and then you are empty again.'

Was there no more to worship than the quest for *slamet*? Sanuri took off his black hat and wiped his broad, balding head, as if unaccustomed to the effort of explaining. God made humans and spirits for no other purpose than worship, he said. Performance of prayer is the only repayment he expects. In worship we give thanks that we have arms and legs, that we can feed ourselves, that we exist.

What about the uncommitted, the non-fasters, the people in Bayu who did not attend the mosque?

'That's their business,' he replied gruffly, and quoted: '*In religion, there is no compulsion*. But obligations are obligations. Those who deny Allah are killed by him.' And with this he made a throat-slitting gesture.

His son came in and sat quietly on the bench, observing from a distance. And Sanuri, perhaps regretting his gesture, said: 'Of course, that doesn't mean people of other religions. You Christian folk follow the prophet Noah, don't you?'

Talk turned to the West, and he drew a contrast. 'Your people are pugnacious. That's why they're always at war. Whereas we Muslims turn the other cheek.'

I denied this. But he insisted, saying he had seen it on TV. 'Iran–Iraq. Iraq–Iran. On and on until there's nobody left.' And then the inevitable conclusion: 'Indonesia is a peaceful country.'

When I pointed out that Iran and Iraq were Muslim countries, not Christian, and certainly not Western, he stared at me in disbelief as though I had lied to him. (What matter that 'we' were aiders and abettors?) Then he looked to his son for confirmation.

But the son shook his head.

The old man raised his eyebrows and harrumphed. 'Ah well! In that case, I suppose we're all the same after all. Come, Andrew. Drink up!'

So we concluded with this (as I now see it) typically Javanese admission – tolerant, accepting, frankly humanist. I liked him for it. But it showed up a contradiction, a division. It was as if there were two contending voices, almost two people. The dogmatist had excluded me; the tolerant Javanese Muslim had embraced me.

Dusun would have been a good base from which to observe the progress of Islam; and unlike its inhabitants I was free to roam and sample other ways of thinking. If I wanted to ask what 'the three-in-one' meant and nobody felt inclined or able to answer I had only to walk west. But in Dusun there was no room for another family. I would have to look elsewhere.

As word got around that I was househunting, I received much advice, most of it opposing any shift eastwards. The headman came over specially to warn me. He sat down solemnly and cleared his throat, looking round in vain for somewhere to spit. 'I would be careful about where you're going. Not everyone is like Bu Mari here, or Wan. They understand what you want. Bu Mari can cook, Wan can help you. *I* can help you. When Bu Mercedes arrives she'll have a civilized house to come to. They can make room for her. Sri can take care of Sofía. Down there [nodding east], things are different. Simple folk. They don't understand about boiling water or hygiene and all that.'

He leaned forward and whispered: '*Communist!*'

'Not now, surely!'

'No, of course not now. But old ways of thinking . . . Some of them still have to report to the police station.'

I said: 'Pak Saki has offered me his empty house.'

I had met this bluff, untalkative farmer the day before and he had made me the offer. He was moving out to join his new wife. His old wife had gone back to her parents.

'Saki's a good man. No problem there.' He leaned forward again, tight and paunchy in his uniform. 'The father was executed. Don't ask him about it. He was *implicated*.'

Implicated (it was always said in italics) meant involved in the alleged communist plot to take over the country – the plot which General Suharto had crushed in 1965 on his way to becoming president. Saki's father had been one of the half-million killed, one of Suharto's necessary rebels. Fishing for background, I mentioned two or three other people I had met in east Bayu and again Pak Lurah seemed caught between warning me about them and admitting that they personally bore no blame. The 'ringleaders' were killed, he explained – executed by local death squads or arrested by the army. Those who remained were the small fry – sympathizers and camp-followers. But they were not full citizens. Some were denied the vote.

'How many were killed?'

'Ah, nine or ten. Far more in other villages. In Ulih-ulihan thirty-odd. In the southern villages, hundreds. Banyuwangi: thousands. Here it was under control. Pak Arjo saw to that.'

'Who did it? Arjo's men?'

'Well, not exactly. Each village handled the cases sent to it. Our people were taken away and died elsewhere.' He held his thumbs together like a prisoner. 'You didn't see them again. That way there were no grudges.' He lowered his voice. 'A few died here, messily –'

It was not easy for Pak Lurah to talk of this, the great political taboo of his lifetime (and doubly taboo to a foreigner). But his reluctance wasn't just prudence. He was personally uncomfortable. It was as if a collective taint had fallen upon the east, like the aftermath of some terrible plague. Involvement in '1965' was a heritable stigma – in Suharto's Indonesia, the original sin. But the terror of those times had given way to shame. And this was how the headman put it: the victims and their families felt shame – at the past, at their blighted lives. So you couldn't talk of these things – these people whom you had known all your life – without feeling some of that shame, without feeling in some way, well, *implicated*.

Others were less awkward, less compassionate. I met a man in

Banyuwangi who had ferried prisoners to their deaths from Kalibaru, a plantation used as a holding camp. Some were allocated for civilian execution – the village quotas – others were trucked up the mountain towards Jember. Half way there, they were thrown alive over a cliff. 'We used to dump twenty loads a day,' said the man with a pained grin. 'Sometimes they'd douse them with petrol and drop a torch over the cliff. You could see them twitching in the ravine below.'

When he heard that I was prospecting for a house in east Bayu, Pujil, with a callous laugh, said, 'You would have found a lot of empty houses in 1965. Could have taken your pick!' We were sitting in Bu Mari's kitchen – the usual mixture of neighbours and callers, men whom Wan called Pak Arjo's 'followers'. One of them, a quiet, mournful man of about fifty, was a member of the village staff, an irrigation official. Pujil pointed to him and said, half in jest: 'He killed quite a few himself! Ask him about it. How were they killed?'

The man looked embarrassed and mildly shook his head.

'Chopped up like fish,' Pujil continued. 'It was Wan's father who gave the orders.'

'Pak Arjo saved the village,' put in Bu Mari, justifying. 'It wasn't murder, it was civil war.'

'Did they kill anybody in return?' I asked. Which was my understanding of civil war.

'Not here,' said Wan. 'But they did in some areas. South, there were whole villages that went over to the communists. It was us or them.'

Bu Mari's old father nodded grimly and repeated, 'Us or them.'

'How did they defend themselves?'

'They couldn't,' said Wan. 'Once they were named, they were done for. The problem was to find out whether you were on the list. Women used to come at night and offer themselves to Pak Arjo.' He made a wheedling voice: '*Scratch out my husband's name. He never did nobody wrong*. But he didn't waver! It would have been a sin.'

'It was the time,' said Elan, the quiet man. 'You can't blame the individuals on either side. It was the time. A time of madness.'

The east is red. The headman's warning called to mind the old Maoist slogan. But what could it mean, thirty years after the massacres? Even in Suharto's Indonesia, built on the ruins of communism, the cold-war rhetoric had begun to look threadbare. Strikes and riots were still blamed on 'certain organizations', meaning the banned – annihilated – Communist Party. But nobody believed this any more. Aside from Islam, in its various forms (and these were mostly non-political), there was no ideology of opposition in Indonesia. In this area, at least, there were no rebels left. All that east Bayu could show, if you cared to look, was an old scar. Otherwise it was not very different from the rest of the village: poorer, more haphazard in layout, with scruffier yards and more children. (As I wandered about, map in hand, two old women asked me for money.) But some people had made good. There were motorbikes among the bamboo houses, and the odd substantial dwelling. People told me proudly, 'We are more sociable than the west end, not so selfish or concerned with our own prosperity.' At the same time, there was a slightly muted air. The big things could not be said – least of all to me, but perhaps not even to each other.

I called on a man who was a clown in the village theatre troupe. He was dressed in ragged pyjamas, a rim of white greasepaint outlining his face. We sat outside on a bench before a crowd of children, and he asked me – probably for their benefit – about snow. Could you put it in a glass with syrup and drink it, like an ice juice? (Yes, I said, by the bucketful.) Then, sculpting a feminine form in the air, he asked about the naked tourists in Bali. (Australians, I said.) Finally, were there 'widows' in my village? (Yours for the asking.) These matters settled, he began to demonstrate a set of puppets he had bought in town – figures from the Indian epics, Bhima and Arjuna, and the bumbling guardian spirit of Java, Semar. To the children's laughter, he made the voices and twirled the flat, angular figures. They were mere cardboard cut-outs, not the real buffalo-hide puppets of the shadow theatre. But he had bought them to teach his son. He was an artist, a man of the theatre. 'If you want to meet the folk of east Bayu,' he said, turning to me amid the laughter, 'it's no good coming in the day. Come at night and see the show. We're all in it.'

The show? In Bayu, there was only one show that mattered: Barong.

4
Barong

Children in Bayu can do the barong before they can walk. They waggle their hands beside their ears, imitating the lion-dragon's wings, and rock their heads and shoulders from side to side. They make the noise of the percussion orchestra that accompanies the dragon's show. And like marionettes, they awaken to its prompt. Just go *ding-dang ding-dang, gong-ding-dang* and automatically, helplessly, they begin to dance. Within a week of her arrival, Sofía was pronounced expert. So coached and practised in the movements was she, so tormented with *ding-dangs*, that she would rock, hands fluttering, in her sleep. The barong is benevolent but scary; and appropriately, one of her first words in Javanese – at some kindly adult prompting – was 'Scared!' For the people of Bayu, it is hard to imagine growing up without the barong.

An articulated four-legged, two-man beast, a locomotive off the rails, a jabberwock. Think of a Chinese dragon joined to the rear end of a pantomime pony, bristling and boisterous, fearsome but lovable. But be careful! *The jaws that bite, the claws that catch!* A youth in Kinjo who dared to kick it had two fingers bitten off at the knuckle and was flat on his back for a week in a catatonic trance. (Possession, they said.) Only a family apology and a visit to the village shrine saved him. Another mocker was struck dumb. As the keeper of the dragon – a man not noted for long speeches – said at the time: *He had disbelieved.*

Nobody from Bayu makes this mistake. They know that the village mascot is more than entertainment, and the guardian spirit to whom he belongs does not take insults lightly. Buyut ('Great-grandfather') can afflict as well as cure. For villagers, however, the dragon's principal role is protective. A rattling, jangling procession begins the annual village cleansing, as bad spirits are led up the road and pushed back into the forest. Like the expansion of the first settlement, the direction is always uphill, east to west. And when the road was paved ten years ago and the contractors took the practical downhill route – against local advice – their steamroller predictably stalled. I could not exactly discover the logic of the offence. Perhaps the road crew, with their monstrous machines and bubbling tar, were a kind of hellish parody of the ritual procession. Perhaps they had simply forgotten to notify the guardian spirit. At any rate, no amount of kicking and cursing would shift the steamroller; no merely mechanical tinkering could fix it. How they must have snorted when the little dragon keeper came out with his incense and began to flick water over the engine! How they laughed at him perched in the high seat, uttering mantras! But they had to pay up. Only a full east–west procession – not cheap on the day – would get the steamroller moving again. As the keeper said to me: *They had disbelieved.*

A performance of the full drama (called simply Barong, like the dragon itself) is auspicious for weddings and circumcisions. It is part of the spirit cult. And for ordinary ungodly folk, the guardian spirit is the real thing: not an idea or dogma or an obligation to be shirked. The spirit world epitomized in Buyut is as tangible as a breeze on wet skin, as close and elusive as your shadow. And the drama is a brush with that otherworld, the spirit's frightening, alluring domain. 'Sacred' (*sakral*) was the foreign-sounding word used by one of the better-educated young men in the village to describe Buyut's shrine. For the mosque official, who sometimes officiated there, it was 'holy'. And for an elderly mystic, a woman who had never in her life prayed, the guardian spirit was *sakti*, magically powerful.

Sacred, *holy*, *powerful*: in Javanese, the words belonged to distinct vocabularies with different histories – European, Arabic, Indian – rival takes on the numinous. But they converged in the guardian spirit. And here was another of Bayu's paradoxes. On theological matters, the modern, the orthodox and the mystic disagreed; but on this they were one. There was simply nothing to dispute: you might as well argue about the blueness of the sky.

No doubt about it, the dragon show was serious fun. But to see at what point the fun spilled over into the sacred you had to see the entire performance: you had to stay until dawn. Then it was hard to disbelieve.

Tresno's circumcision was in the morning. At dawn, his mother woke him and he squatted in a nearby stream until he was numb. Then, seated on his father's lap, he submitted to the knife. The circumciser distracted him by pointing to an aeroplane in the sky. By the time Tresno had realized there was no plane, the job was done. Now he sat in state on an ornate sofa specially hired for the occasion, propped up by cushions and fanned by proud relatives. Beside him lay plates of sweets – fried bananas, sugary coconut balls and other concoctions in suggestive shapes. He wore a black cap, and his face was made up like a prince, with frowning eyebrows, powdered yellow cheeks and a curly charcoal moustache. Across his lap lay a white cloth, lifted clear of the wound by a pole between his legs. With this princely erection, Tresno had arrived at man's estate. He was eight.

The entertainment would be a dragon show. Tresno could have chosen a gandrung – a female singer-dancer – but the last three circumcisions had all featured dragons, and he wanted the same. Besides, he loved the clowns. His hamlet, Sumbersari, had been transformed for the event. Traditional houses have movable walls: the panels of wood or bamboo weave can be lifted clear of the frame. Home can expand or shrink with the changing shape of the family. In this case, the two rows of houses – five or six either side of a bare yard – had been opened out, the facades tilted up or lifted out and the party walls removed, revealing the front room of each dwelling like a cut-away doll's house. It was like walking through the furniture section of a department store, domestic life displayed in its material form. There were small variations, but each parlour had its round coffee table, platform-bed, crockery cabinet, calendar (usually old) and faded photos pinned to the wall. But for the oddity of banana trees in the middle of the yard, a hamlet of a dozen households had become one very big house.

Sumbersari had been electrified the year before, and the quietest place in the village (the furthest from the mosque) could now celebrate in the proper way. A ten-foot tower of loudspeakers, fit for a heavy-metal rock concert, stood at the entrance to the arena, anchored to a coco palm. The speakers pointed outwards across the paddyfields, like a missile system, and would broadcast intermittently for the next three days and nights. We could hear the noise – amplified to distortion – from a quarter of a mile away. It was Indonesian pop, mostly the same song (that year it was 'Drunk Again') or the high-pitched wailing of gandrung cassettes. When I asked one of the hosts why it was so loud, he said, or rather shouted: 'I don't hear it.' And he was not being ironic. After a time, you adjusted and stopped noticing. Noise became the element you swam in, like a fish in water.

The effect of pure noise could be enhanced by staging a competing event elsewhere in the village. Not to be outdone, the rival wedding party would aim its speakers back at Sumbersari. And if you were caught in the crossfire, you might hear 'Drunk Again' coming at you from both sides but out of step, like a baroque canon. Fortunately, neighbours, who collaborate in organizing events, never overlap in their major celebrations. Fortunately, also, breaks are imposed for the broadcast of the call to prayer and for the ceremonial greeting of guests, who are piped aboard, as it were, by a resident gong orchestra. Naturally, the main event – the dragon show or gandrung – commands the airwaves for its nightlong performance.

We never learned not to hear, and sometimes we suffered. But the sound of a wedding or a circumcision – the sound of happiness – felt different from the mosque's summons. It had no designs on you; it was not a reproach or a demand. And it did not fracture the silence and drag you from sleep. Unresisting, overpowered, you sighed and slept. Nobody had ever stoned a wedding, but the prayer-houses and the mosque all had broken tiles. The insomniac's revenge.

By the evening of the morning – Tresno still sitting in state, by now a little wilted – about a third of the village have called. They come in groups, by neighbourhood, filing through knee-high green fields, women to the fore, each in a lacy jacket of maroon, dark blue or yellow, with a batik sarong, a sash or cummerbund, and hair drawn back into a bun, emphasizing their delicate cheekbones and mild, serene expressions. (For such occasions, Bu Mari keeps a row of hair switches, like trophy scalps, in her kitchen.) Feminine, graceful, Javanese: a style becoming to young women and matrons alike. Each woman bears on her head a brass bowl containing two kilos of rice, sometimes with an egg on top. These they surrender to a quartermaster, who tips the rice into a sack and notes down their contribution in a book. In their wake come the men, soberly clad in black caps and ironed shirts. Relieved of their burdens, the women sit behind trestle tables laden with biscuits and sweets. The men are ushered to tables, a group at a time, and are served, in quick succession, a clove cigarette, a cup of thick black coffee and a doughnut; and then – dessert over – a dish of rice and goat's meat.

I arrive with Wan and Pak Lurah, both men smart in dark-brown batik. There is a pride in appearance, a desire to present oneself well and show respect to the hosts. A pleasant appearance is part of good manners. We sit at a table with six others, smoke our clove cigarettes and view the scene, attempting a comment or joke above the noise. Then we eat, holding plates close to chests, careful to time our meal so all plates touch down at the same time and no one is left eating alone. The usher returns with a pen and paper and Wan lists our names and contributions: Rp1,500 from each man, rich and poor alike. Feasts, like prayer-meals, equalize: all villagers are the same, and no one would have things any different. The poorest are admitted with as much respect as the richest, for which dignity their donation (half a day's pay for a labourer) is a small price to pay. To be gonged in, ushered and fed, and then entertained for a whole night amongst friends. What could be finer?

Wan flattens the wrinkled notes, counts them out, and returns them to the usher who passes them to one of the host's party seated behind a ledger and a jar full of money. By the end of the event, he will have recorded contributions amounting to two tonnes of rice, one million rupiah in cash (about $1000), 450 coconuts, eighty kilos of sugar, 350 eggs and two thousand cigarettes. In monetary terms, the host's family might break even (they sell the rice and boil the coconuts to make oil), but they are indebted to every single guest. Their festive debts will take years to repay as they donate rice and money to their guests' future weddings and circumcisions. In this way, the entire village is knitted together with festive obligations.

Everything is efficient, free of fuss, polite, cheerful, and obliging. No one is shown any special favour or greeted with more than the usual alacrity. The smile and the handshake are intentionally the same for all: the headman, the mosque official, the haji, the anthropologist, the peasant and the gravedigger. It is an atmosphere of absolute equality, oddly relaxed and achieved without strain. Only the mosque, with its forward-facing rows, can achieve this kind of uniformity – the obedient faithful before God – but strict equality, fellowship, dissolves the moment worshippers step outside.

Once we have eaten and made our contribution we can leave or hang around to watch the play. I go to the rear of the arena, behind the dolls' houses, and confront a scene from Fellini: women stoking enormous fires and working bellows, laughing raucously in the smoke. Some are chopping slabs of meat with machetes; others wield yard-long spoons in vats of bubbling lava. The walls separating the five kitchens on one side of the hamlet have been removed, creating a single vast cooking area open to the fields. From the darkness, a youth arrives with an armful of firewood. Two girls are wiping and cutting banana leaves, a third and fourth are wrapping sweets. Half a dozen more women ladle meat stew and dole out rice. And beside a tiny stream, at the edge of the yard, is a line of dish-washers, shrieking and splashing, their bare feet churning muddy puddles. All the women of Sumbersari are here; but so too are their female relatives and in-laws: far more help than is needed. Even Bu Mari, having sat sedately in the front, has come behind to take a turn at stirring. They are having much more fun than the men.

At nine o'clock, attention shifts to the end of the festive arena where the men of east Bayu have set up their theatre. It consists of a proscenium arch, a backdrop of painted forest (not unlike the woods that lie just beyond the hamlet), and a ragged half-moon of baked earth bordered by spectators – the stage. The orchestra – ten men seated on the ground behind xylophones, gongs and drums – strikes up a prelude and then changes pace with a new theme, a hectic rattling of drums, cymbals and gongs that is the dragon's leitmotif.

Ding-dang ding-dang, gong-ding-dang
Ding-dang ding-dang, gong-ding-dang

Enter the dragon – head rocking, body shivering – with a quickstepping, swaying motion like a rumba on hot sand. Its four legs jangle with bells as it bustles about, ducking and pirouetting, bulky and powerful but light on its feet. Three times round the stage and it comes to an abrupt halt, its wings, tassels and fringes still quivering. The percussion slows to a steady purr, the deep gong marking time. *Chung, tuk-tuk-tuk . . . Chung, tuk-tuk-tuk.* Someone in the crowd whistles and the dragon swivels round. Brow lowered like a raging bull, it lunges forward in an explosion of drumming. Children scream and fall backwards. But just in time the monster pulls up, panting, one leg raised, and stares vacantly ahead, jaws clapping. The shouting children edge forward: it jerks its head towards them, snapping. They scramble over one another in terrified delight. The orchestra purrs, *Chung, tuk-tuk-tuk.* Like everyone else, I am alarmed and amused: afraid it will interpret my laughter as an insult when I intend nothing but respect. But the fear seems mutual. What the glaring eyes, shuddering wings, and gaping jaws personify is startled arousal; and in Java, where loss of control is deplored, this is a very unpleasant emotion. It's as if something the villagers fear –

perhaps what they fear most – is represented by the beast and, at the same time, conquered by it. The dragon is haunted by invisible horrors.

But what does it see? What terrors lie in the darkness beyond the crowd? I think suddenly of 1965 and remember that Mul, the dragon's bearer, lost his father to the death squads. What is inside the head of the man inside the head?

A clash of cymbals, a flurry of wings, and the dragon dashes off-stage.

A woman enters to a gentle, lilting rhythm of rippling gongs. It is a gandrung, a singer-dancer, in bodice, skintight sarong, and tiara. More whistles. She wiggles voluptuously round the stage, with outstretched arms (a trifle muscular for my taste) and hands fluttering coquettishly. She flicks her pink scarf, preens and pouts. Her feet – somewhat on the big side – are clad in white socks.

Stage left, a clown enters. He rubs his eyes, unsure whether he is dreaming, and looks around. He waddles, bandy-legged, towards the audience and peers into the darkness. 'Eeee! What a strange place this is! Looks like the end of the world!'

Scratching his head, he waddles back, an upside-down smile on his white face. 'Eee! What kind of people can live in a dump like this?' He looks down at the nearest children. 'Smells funny too.'

The laughter is louder and coarser than Javanese character is supposed to permit. The women scream helplessly, beat their thighs and shout remarks at the players, like the umbrella-waving women at wrestling matches in Britain. The men, a bit more concerned for their dignity, shake their heads and echo the comic repartee. But I catch little of it: my tape recordings are like the improbable laughter track of a TV sitcom.

Another clown enters stage right. I barely recognize him as the man with the toy puppets from east Bayu. He too is white-faced, with a pink skullcap and multicoloured shin-length dungarees, tall where the other is short.

'Eh! A native!' exclaims the short clown, approaching and sniffing him. 'What are you, man or beast?'

'Man.'

'What's your name?'

'I've lost it.'

A third clown enters and they assess him warily.

'Is it a human?'

'No, a person.'

But it turns out they are brothers, with the unlikely names of Oarsman, Sailor, and Depth-tester. Mariners adrift in a forest.

They separate to explore their new world. Sailor finds a branch of bananas overhanging the stage. He takes one, gobbles it, and tosses the peel into the audience. Depth-tester comes across a leaf parcel. He unwraps it and finds another parcel inside, then another, and so on until he comes to the last wrapper. Inside there is nothing.

Oarsman is standing dumbstruck before the preening gandrung.

'Eh! Eh! Eh! What on earth is *that*?'

He circles her, gawping in astonishment. 'Eeee, I begin to like this place!'

He leans forward and hazards a pinch. But she squeals and slaps him with her fan.

'What are you? Male or female?' he asks.

'Female,' comes the squeaky reply.

'Virgin or widow?'

'Virgin.'

She flicks her scarf at him flirtatiously and does a turn; infatuated, he staggers after her. Then they dance. She confides that she has lost her 'charge', the dragon, and will marry him if he brings it back to her. But when he returns with the beast snapping at his rear, she breaks her promise and they fight. The gandrung soon has him pinned to the ground, gasping for breath under her sturdy thighs. She is about to feed him to the dragon ('That's no way for a woman to behave!' he screams) when his brothers return and carry him off, half dead. Gandrung and dragon dance triumphant across the empty stage.

In the next scene (apparently unconnected to the last), the brothers obtain permission from a forest spirit to clear trees for cultivation. But the creatures of the forest – fanged, ape-like monsters – rebel and make war on the humans. Only the intervention of an aristocratic warrior saves them.

The backdrop changes, trees and waterfalls giving way to concrete houses and telegraph poles festooned with wires. Briefly, the orchestra improvises 'Drunk Again'. We are in town. This time it is heavenly spirits who threaten the world of humans. Again the princely warrior drives them off, but Oarsman detains one of the nymphs for his bride (another falsetto, but not half as butch as the gandrung). A Muslim official conducts the wedding ceremony, asking the couple embarrassing questions and encouraging them to take up birth control. 'Can I have some pills for my mistress, too?' asks the bridegroom. The scene ends with the gandrung whining popular songs to the happy couple.

By midnight many of the children have fallen asleep in the laps of mothers and uncles or lie sprawled on the ground among the gongs. There is a brief interval – a lull in the laughter – and I can hear the distant blare of another event, far away across the fields.

I go backstage behind the curtains where the players sit among costumes and stage props. Some are eating cooked sweets or scooping rice from banana leaves. No one is talking. In their greasepaint, half-undressed, they look tired and – I realize for the first time – professional. They are men doing a job. Bareheaded but still with striped gorilla-muzzle, Rasno, one of the ape-monsters, is smoking a huge hand-rolled cigarette whose tip glows like a bonfire in the gloom. The gandrung is powdering her nose and squinting at a mirror. I tell her how beautiful she looks. She beams at me and exclaims in a high squeal, 'Ooh! Listen to Pak Andrew there, what a flatterer!' (But those arms, and that stubble!) The ape-man says, in tired jest: 'Be careful. Her boyfriends will be jealous.'

Beside the dragon's head, which is mounted on a trestle like a gigantic startled cat, sits a small dark man who is its keeper. Basuki tells me that the craftsman who made the monster used a cat as his model, stretching back the scalp to achieve the desired expression. 'Two cats died in this way.'

Why does it have wings, unlike the Balinese dragon? 'It's the lord of the forest. It has a bit of everything: the wings of the hawk, the fangs of the ape-monsters, the jaws of the lion.'

I try to figure out the connections between the scenes, why the characters metamorphose, switch roles, or appear out of context in different stories. But he seems puzzled by my question. 'That's how it is. Buyut, the guardian spirit, won't allow it to be any different.'

The show means nothing, said one of the mystics. *It's like the joke with the banana-leaf parcel, layers and layers but nothing inside. You waste your time if you go looking for a meaning. It's not like the shadow play. There's no philosophy in it, no symbols. It's just entertainment.*

During the 'troubles' of 1965, Basuki tells me, east Bayu lost control of the show. 'We were *implicated* and had to change or be closed down.' One of the nationalists, Elan, was put in charge. He introduced a new story about a girl who became a queen. He called the heroine after his adopted daughter. But Buyut disapproved because 'there's only one crown in the play and that is worn by the dragon himself'. The new man fell ill and the queen story was dropped. (I later remembered that Elan was the mournful visitor to Bu Mari's who had been pointed out to me as one of Arjo's death squad.)

No script, no direction, only a vague sense of plot. Instead, what people register are particular episodes: the abduction of a nymph, the taming of the monster, the empty parcel, the thing that happens at dawn. And strictly there is no acting, no attempt to put across feeling or character. The players run through their lines in flat, expressionless voices. The gandrung and the nymph are men pretending to be women, just as they do in real life. Of the clowns, only Oarsman has the gift of comedy. Before each show he visits the grave of a famous predecessor and 'asks for his humour'. In performance, he feels himself possessed by this genial spirit. He *becomes* a clown.

Under a canopy, a little to the side and not really a part of things, I notice Ran, the diviner, bare-chested, his strong hands hanging loosely over white-scarred knees. 'They don't need me until the end,' he tells me coolly. 'But I can't leave the arena.' He waves a hand around, meaning, *All this*. As one of the caretakers of the shrine he has overall charge of the show in its mystical aspect. Yet while the players and musicians receive a portion of the hire fee (150,000 rupiah between twenty-six of them), he receives nothing. His priestly service to the village cannot be compensated with money.

Ran often gets bitten by the dragon, said an elder. *Ever wondered why? He's not fitting, not right for the job. It's sacred. You can't have someone who's after men's wives. Buyut doesn't like it.*

He's not from the dragon family, said Basuki. *Not from the east. But none of us was allowed to be leader after 1965. He was Pak Arjo's choice, but Buyut has never really accepted him. That's why he gets bitten.*

Ran looks at me with a cool eye, his mouth moving slightly as if about to say something. I had met him a few days before, seeing off a 'client' at the bus stop – a buxom young woman from the south who, he said, had 'stayed the night to study with me'. She was clad in spectacular green satin like a mermaid or a stage star. The villagers gawped at her as she undulated past, twirling her umbrella and smiling defiance. Ran helped her onto the bus with exaggerated gallantry and bit his lips as he walked away.

Beside Ran, impaled on a pole like the victim of an execution, stands another mask, a 'tiger'. Compared to the dragon it looks unimpressive, hardly bigger than a man's head and oddly inexpressive: plainly, its eyes see nothing. Nor does it resemble a real tiger: a green face, red jaws, a collar spotted like a leopard (*macan* means tiger or leopard), and a beard of black fur made from the tufted bark of a sago palm. Like Blake's Tyger, it has been forged in the imagination. But the forests of the night are real: the tiger is Buyut's avatar. The bearer – who in earlier scenes wears the dragon's head – now carries the tiger's mask between flat palms, holding it just above his head. In trance, his hands are 'fused' to the wood: they cannot be wrenched free. For villagers, this is a kind of proof. Possessed by a tiger, he possesses the strength of a tiger. Only two men in the village can perform this task: Basuki, the keeper, and

Mul, a man from east Bayu who lives somewhere out in the fields.

I have never met Mul, but his old mother, a small, anxious woman, with unkempt grey hair, came to the house one day to grind coconuts and told me her story – which is also his story. Bu Mari told me she was one of the poorest people in the village and hinted that I should give her some money, which I did. She kissed my hands and blessed me, apologizing for not speaking in High Javanese. Then, as if to justify my charity, she began to tell me about her life. She used to be well off, with a big house in east Bayu, but her family got mixed up in things – 'It was the time of the parties.' Her older children squandered the family money and got into fights. 'In those days, the smallest quarrel would blow up and everyone joined in. Everything was politics. Our boys in the east would go courting girls in the west end and would be pelted with stones. When they came after our girls we'd do the same – all chanting slogans.' Her husband, a gong player, devised a new dragon story about poor sharecroppers in which they took over the land and killed the landlords. Party members came from Banyuwangi and wanted to see it. The Muslims said it insulted Islam. Then *Gestapu* (the acronym for the coup of 1965) happened. When they came in the night for her husband, she ran to Arjo to beg for clemency. His house was full of crying women. He would have saved her husband, she was sure. Only the week before, he had stopped them from burning down a row of houses; he had turned back a squad of Muslim youths from Delik, all in black scarves chanting *Allahu Akbar! Death to communists!* But that night he was out – on some operation in another village. They pulled her husband into the road and butchered him in front of the family. (Who did it? 'I don't know who did it. It was the times.') Mul was a boy of ten. He became deranged for a month, wouldn't sleep in the house. He stopped talking to people and she feared for his life. Only when she took him to the shrine and begged the spirit's protection did he recover. 'That's why he is the tiger.'

The gong orchestra started again as I returned to my place. The audience was half asleep, alternately lulled and jolted by the choppy, wittering, slightly out-of-tune music. Was it the abrupt lurches or the slowing down and speeding up, like a clockwork toy winding down and then spinning out of kilter, that produced in me a queasy effect, a feeling that it would never end? I was tired of the bad acting and of not getting the jokes. (It is hard to watch people laughing for five hours.) I found myself wishing that Bayu had a shadow play, something with philosophy and meaning. If only there was more connection with what happened backstage – stories of wicked landlords and rebellious sharecroppers. Instead: plays about nothing; landlocked mariners and empty parcels; scene piled upon scene. Or was that the point?

The curtain swishes back on an old fashioned courtyard: open pavilions, women with fans, men in the neat brown turbans of the gentry, retainers bowing and scraping. An irrigation official takes leave of his wives (the gandrung and the nymph of previous scenes) and warns them not to be unfaithful. There is a brief, touching scene when the younger wife sings a lullaby which is also a love song.

Hush, hush! Sleep, my child.
If you don't sleep, I'll lay you down.
Come to me, come!
If you don't come, I'll put a spell on you.

Then we are back in the forest. But there is a change. Without the clowns, the lurid landscape of bluish trees and waterfalls looks different; the ghost-train spookiness and hilarity have gone. With no one to poke at the world, lift the lid on its oddity – no one whistling in the dark – a comic safety net has been removed. And sensing this, the audience has woken up, stiffening when a sinister figure in yellow and black stripes pads onto the stage. My neighbour elbows me and says, 'That's Lundoyo: from Alas Purwo.' Alas Purwo is the (literally named) Primeval Forest at Java's eastern tip – a place of ruined temples, crumbling cliffs, and bat-haunted caves; for the mystics, a place of origins; for the audience, home of the tiger Lundoyo. Restless in his forest domain, he wants to experience the world of the village, to know the life of men, to love a woman and marry. He consults a sage, a white-robed hermit who gives him the necessary spell. Then he slips into the village. Unconcerned by his tiger stripes, the retainers (our three clowns) offer him hospitality. But when he tells them he is looking for a mate, instead of directing him elsewhere they act as panders. As it happens, they have two rather nice ladies in their charge, if he would care to see. Does he prefer a modern sports model – a Honda GL Pro – noisy but fast, or a more old-fashioned CB100 with a well-padded seat and a smoother ride? Lundoyo doesn't care: he is irresistible to women and will let his charm work its magic.

As it turns out, it is the buxom senior wife – the CB100 – who is smitten. He warns her that he is a tiger, but she stares into his eyes and – nobody's perfect – they go offstage together.

*

The guest tables lie abandoned, the kitchens are silent. In their dolls'-house parlours the ushers doze, stretched out on benches or slumped like drunks over coffee tables. Little Tresno, under his tented sarong, is fast asleep. Wrapped against the night chill, only a score of spectators have stayed the course. But as dawn approaches the villagers return and soon they pack the arena.

For a Muslim, there's nothing wrong with the drama, said Jumhar, who runs a prayer-house. *After all, it's just entertainment. But you must leave before the end. I've never seen the end! Wouldn't want to.*

The irrigation official returns and interrogates his servants. ('It could have been worse,' they tell him. 'You're lucky he's not a polygamist like you.') He arrests Lundoyo and binds him from head to foot. Trussed and gagged, they kick him about the floor and bundle him into a cage under a table. Then the official challenges him: If you can free yourself, you can have my wife.

Shouts and whistles from the audience: they are impatient, but what do they want?

Within a minute, unseen, Lundoyo has cast off the ropes and can be heard beating a drum. The tattoo is hair-raising, the escape miraculous, and he steps forth to general astonishment. And then, as he goes off with his prize, something unexpected happens. The motley crowd suddenly pulls together and solidifies: huddled, erect, alert, a wall of aroused fright. It's the small, unconscious adjustments that disturb: a woman covers her mouth with her hand; a youth braces himself in the front row; children cling to their mothers. Around the floor, tough-looking stage hands move into position, screening off the orchestra.

Lundoyo is at last alone with his bride. Again he tells her: *I am a tiger; you will see the proof.* But first he must go to the river to drink. A bird enters, flapping alarm, but the woman is too madly in love to take fright. An urgent, tuneless rhythm strikes up – drums, cymbals, rattling metal plates – the dragon's theme with a vengeance. Through a gap in the curtain I can see Ran lighting incense: a man is put into trance. Then, as the bird makes its escape, the curtain flies open and the tiger is unleashed: not Lundoyo but the spotted mask, the spirit. For a second it confronts the circle of faces, its head rolling with a giddy, panting motion; then it bursts across the stage, breaching the wall of spectators who fly screaming in all directions. In the collective panic, one sees only the small grimacing head, upraised and shaking violently as it strains and plunges forward. Children scramble up trees; women hide behind tables or run for cover; men, oddly passive, step back, arms slack at their sides. The tiger's handlers hang onto it, dragged along, and attempt to steer it from danger. And then one sees the legs of Mul, the orphaned boy, driving the tiger forward. They give him his head and let him run from the settlement, plunging along the path, then draw him back towards the arena. One of the cast, a young man, is frothing at the mouth and begins prancing and rearing like a horse. Someone thoughtfully steps forward with a bowl of water and leaves which he begins to chomp and slurp. As it calms down, the tiger, too, claps its jaws and gobbles up a few leaves.

How can it eat, said Wan, *when Mul is holding the mask with his hands? It's impossible! But he vomits the leaves afterwards. That's the proof.*

Imposing and solemn in black pantaloons and turban, Ran takes control. He holds a lump of smoking incense under the tiger's jaws and nods to his helpers to lift off the mask. For a moment there is a scuffle as Mul knocks him to the ground and they grapple in the dust. Basuki bends to speak calming words into Mul's ear; then Ran holds Mul's shaggy head between his hands and blows on his crown. The man who was a tiger comes slowly round, a green drool flowing from his mouth.

There is no curtain call to round off the show. It is no longer a show, but something else: the drama has burst its confines. But the villagers – already on their way home – are satisfied. Day breaks on an empty stage.

5
Mother Seeks Child

If, as Javanese like to say, a child is the soul of a household, Bu Mari's house had been soulless for a generation. Her long marriage to Arjo had produced no offspring, though children had often been around: after a month in Bayu I was still discovering people whom she had fostered or 'acknowledged'. She blamed herself, not Arjo. 'There's something wrong with me,' she said one day, putting her hand on her stomach. Another despairing woman, in the far west of the village, had pulled down her bodice to reveal nippleless breasts. (How can you prepare for this kind of revelation?) But I knew other women married to men-about-town who had no children. I suspect they were damaged by diseases their errant husbands had brought home. Several women whom Bu Mari had pointed out as 'sellers of coffee and a pinch' were similarly childless, which supported my suspicion. One of the big differences with Nias – where women typically gave birth to a dozen children (half of whom died) – was the availability of extra-marital pleasures: the 'hot widows' and 'second wives', the 'market candy' accessible to any man with a free afternoon and use of a motorbike. Hardly ruffling the surface of village life, it was a discreet trade, with degrees of acceptability, from the respectable widow to the out-of-town brothel. Discreet, yet popular culture made an icon of semi-licit lust in the brilliant figure of the gandrung, the dancer whose stylized eroticism and allusive (never coarse) songs had good citizens politely infatuated. Perhaps this celebration of desire – transported to another level, but just as insistent, in Javanese mysticism – had its sad cost in Bayu's childless families.

But villagers had a different theory. Some women couldn't conceive because inside they were male: their urethras (in some cases, their eggs) were not properly female. Something had gone wrong in the womb or in their early childhood when sex was not yet fixed. Either the correct rituals had not been performed or someone had broken a pregnancy taboo and the girl had grown up a victim of her parents' negligence. Usually the husbands of such women divorced them and 'sought seed' elsewhere, marrying six or seven times before fathering a child. But it was never the man who was considered sterile.

Our women have few children because of abortion, said a man from Mandaluko. *They get the healer to invert the womb. Then, when they want a child, they can't have it. There's nowhere for it to grow.*

Between husbands number two and three, I stayed single, said a neighbour. *My lovers were old and rich. And how I ate them! But I took a lot of medicine in those days. That's why I can't have children.*

Ritual errors, straying husbands and quack remedies. Or was it the pesticide sprayed onto ricefields and carried home – a chemical souvenir – from sparkling toxic streams? For whatever reasons, in the era of green revolutions and birth control, there are fewer children to go round. This is unfortunate because the Javanese delight in children is truly wonderful. Half-human, half-sprite, in Javanese eyes a small child is 'not yet a person', 'not yet Javanese', but rather an exquisite pet, to be gazed at and admired, dandled, slung on the hip, jounced laughing along to the river, stuffed with sweets, teased, gently frightened and then comforted, crooned to sleep. Not to be denied these pleasures, the middle-aged and infertile work hard to win the affection of other people's offspring. Consequently, village children grow up believing that the whole world is there to love them, that they are the finest thing in creation, and that the smiling adults who surround them mean nothing but good. Java being what it is, this is not a cruel deception. I once asked an elderly man why he liked to carry his eleven-year-old grandson around on his back and he told me: 'So he'll grow up knowing he can always depend on me.'

The arrival of Sofía was an answered prayer. The household briefly went mad. Bu Mari was once again queen of the neighbourhood – a position she had lost since the death of Arjo. I had never seen her so happy (I had never seen her happy) and she flitted from room to room with Sofía in arms, singing and chattering. Deprived of college and career, Sri, the adopted daughter, found her purpose. Wan gave up what little work he ever had and spent his mornings imitating the dragon for Sofía's entertainment.

Mercedes was received with such warmth that she kept asking me (recalling hard times in Nias), *Is it really like this?* And yes, it was. On the first day, the headman's wife, Bu Lurah, dressed her in a sarong and jacket, did her hair, and made me photograph them together, posed formally on the grassy patch in front of the house. And seeing us, Siti came out and insisted on a similar photograph. (What has she done with that picture? Has Drus destroyed it?) Small and dark-haired, Mexican, Mercedes could almost pass for Javanese; but they knew she was different and accepted this. And unlike our Niasan hosts on that remote and sad island, they understood that she was far from home and unfamiliar with local ways, and they wanted nothing from her except friendship – and, of course, Sofía. Six months old and with the special geniality and sociability unique to that age, Sofía was our passport into a hundred houses. But more often the village came to us. I would return home from doing the rounds to find a circle gathered about her, watching her bounce up and down in her bungee seat (her seesaw, they called it), swaying sympathetically with each twist and turn.

Sofía's rapturous arrival showed us what children meant in village life. But it also revealed something of the struggle that takes place in any Javanese family. There is a saying in Mexico: *madre, solo hay una*; a child has only one mother. In Java a child has many mothers. Indeed, everything conspires to weaken exclusive ties, even to the point of denying the mother's 'natural' privilege. The ideology of shared motherhood is so strong that attempts to resist it meet with incredulity and a disapproval as strong as ours would be if we saw a mother reject her child: that would surely be something against nature. And so the new mother hands over her child, at first happily, but soon feeling guilty and even wretched.

When Sri was born, said Sutri, her mother, *we had promised her to Mari, my husband's sister. But I didn't feel good about it. She was my second child. Mari took her off me still red, and I'd fetch her to give her the breast. Soon they'd started giving her bottled milk. Pak Arjo said it was better than breast milk. We lived next door so it didn't matter that much. But Sri was like a shuttle going back and forth. When I weaned her I went away for a week and left her alone with Mari. I was so sad I had to get medicine from the healer. Sri was too. The healer blew spells onto her to stop her crying. Since then it's always been a battle with Mari. I don't know whose child she is. Both I suppose.*

In those early months, there was a popular Mexican soap called *Maria Mercedes* that drew women to the house of Bu Lurah. They would crowd round her television, commenting on the action: 'Ah, they're making up again.' 'Fighting – no, just cross.' 'Crying. Ooh! Really sobbing now.' They loved it for its exuberance and the un-Javanese way the characters shouted at one another. But the plot motive – *madre, solo hay una* – either perplexed them or passed them by. The running theme was that the heroine has committed the ultimate crime of giving out her child for adoption. All her tragedies stem from this act and from her bad conscience. But our neighbours could not see why she was considered guilty. For them, she was only a victim. There was no moral aspect to the drama: it was just a story of fortune, good and bad. Let the child go wherever fate took him, as long as he was happy.

Child-sharing was the way of things, almost the natural order. And yet, in so many cases, the heart said otherwise.

Our next-door neighbour was headman of Bayu for a couple of years after my father retired, said Jamila. *He and Father are great pals. When I became pregnant, he said: 'I dreamed that you kept a songbird but it wouldn't sing for you. You gave it to me and it sang.' Then he asked for the child and we couldn't say no. I handed the baby over still red, and his dad* [the ex-headman] *fed him from a bottle. When they moved to another village, I cried for a week. But they came to visit and we saw him growing. The boy is eight now and still doesn't know I'm his mother.* (*Or that I'm his father*, said her husband, smiling.) *Nobody ever told him. But sometimes we think he knows. We've done the prayer-meal and 'adopted' him, so he calls us Old Ma and Old Pa and comes here freely. Helps himself to food. His parents brought him last week and we gave him some money so he'll be fond of us. One day I'll tell him and he'll understand that it was all because of kindness.*

The habit of adoption had made Mari's household what it was: an adaptable, rather ramshackle contraption, a patched and doctored structure much like the house itself. But it wasn't unique. Most people had fictional kin ties to other families besides their own. What the passing visitor could not know, what no government census could capture, was the fact that children – fed here, washed there, passed from hand to hand – grew up between households. It was not unusual for a grandmother to take care of her grandchild and treat it as her own, so that the child's natural mother became more like a sister. Having a better hand, granny took charge; and the young mother (usually a first-time mother) let it happen, relieved but often regretful. In some families, the child grew up calling her mother 'elder sister' and her grandmother 'mother'. This was only one variation. Among neighbours, women took turns with each others' babies, and a favoured woman – either liked by the child or unusually persistent – would 'acknowledge' the child as hers. Like Jamila, she would hold a prayer-meal and ritually adopt the child, henceforth calling herself its Old Ma. (What made Jamila's case poignant was that she was actually the child's real mother.) In most cases this meant little more than occasionally looking after the child, feeding it, or having it round to sleep. But sometimes the arrangement became permanent, or the child went back and forth, as Sri did between Mari and her mother. I have used the word 'adoption', but Islamic law, which is the basis of family law in Indonesia, does not recognize formal adoption. And in almost every case, there is no legal entailment, no threat to the natural heirs. In

Bayu, borrowing, fostering, adoption, or whatever one wants to call it, is a sentimental arrangement, usually without economic value. And partly for this reason, if someone wants your child it is hard to refuse. A refusal breeds rancour and disturbs the highly-prized state of social harmony. Worse, it might lead to illness or death.

I dreamed that Busono's nose was dripping into my mouth, said Endro. *I told his parents – his father and I were old friends – but they didn't want to hear. They'd just given out Sri to Mari and her mother was still upset. But Busono kept getting sick. And then one night I dreamed that he was swept away in a flood and I was standing in the river and saved him. When I told them that, they agreed. Otherwise he might have died. I held a prayer-meal and became his Old Pa. He didn't move in with me, but I feel he's like my own son. I love him as much as I love my daughter. Now he's in the army but he always comes to see me and says: 'Pa, I'm home!'*

Sofía had many aunts. Aunt Jona took her to the river; Aunt Misti, next door, and her daughter, Ana, played with her on the verandah or took her to see the goats; Aunt Siti whisked her away in a sling to mind the store; and there was always Aunt Sri, waiting for her from the moment she awoke, arms outstretched, tireless in her enthusiasm. These requests Mercedes indulged, sometimes gratefully, sometimes regretfully. But they became too frequent, and the stand that a young Javanese mother could not make was less difficult for a Mexican. Sofía had only one mother. On this point of cultural difference Mercedes was unwilling to yield. And why should she?

Besides, Bu Mari was not playing entirely straight. By a curious feature of Javanese psychology, the rival claims of 'mothers' for their charge are at the child's whim. It is the infant who decides where he is 'at home', in whose arms he is happiest, or where he will sleep. If he falls asleep quickly in a neighbour's house, that neighbour asserts priority: *Better let him sleep here; it's where he's at home*. The mother withdraws. Between carers, the handover is always a delicate moment, a chance to assert claims. Held out unsupported, at arm's length, the baby cries. Then you can say, *He doesn't want to go with you. There, there! Come back with me!* Thus a child gradually learns that an 'aunt' is his favourite, or that grandmother is really 'mother'. Bu Mari was an expert at this game. She had outplayed Sri's mother and perhaps others too. We later saw it happen with neighbours. It would not happen with Sofía. But the general point – *madre, solo hay una* – so incomprehensible to our hosts, to us so natural – could not be easily made. It must be forced.

One day, Sri had worked Sofía into such a state of hysterical excitement that she could not stop laughing. Sri echoed her laughter; she mimed the dragon; she sang and clapped. And Sofía grew breathless and agitated. Disarmed by Bu Mari's crowing approval, we watched in dismay. And then, at the next gush of laughter, Mercedes marched over and seized the baby. 'Ah, but she's having fun!' Sri complained. Too late: a swish of curtains and they were gone. I remember a look of shock on Wan's face. It was the unaccountable rudeness of the West, something out of the foreign soaps. Or it was a mother recovering her daughter. For a few tense days, the family went into a sulk but saw they could not prevail, and after this things once again became easy.

Sri needed distracting: that was what her father kept telling me. 'Can't you teach her English or something? Sofía is good for her. Stops her thinking about college.'

'I've tried practising English with her, but she keeps laughing,' I told him. Sae grinned. 'That's Sri!' He gripped my arm in a sudden but friendly way. 'Listen, you're not still thinking of moving down there, are you? You're better off here, near us. We can see you're all right here. There were problems in the east. Can't talk about it. You know, don't you?'

Then back to his theme. 'I don't know what to do to make her happy again. She won't help in the house. I can't pay her college fees: they're more than I earn. But what can she do? Do you think she should marry? Some nice schoolteacher perhaps.'

I said I would introduce her to Hasan, a young man who had

been my guide in Banyuwangi. He had trained as a teacher but could not afford the bribe required to secure a job.

'Bring him along! Bring him along!'

6
The Fast

Ramadan, or Puwasa as the Javanese call it, had started. The Javanese year is based on the Islamic calendar, but the months are differently named and the holy days are Javanized, given a local significance. With its addiction to neighbourhood feasts, Bayu had a special way of ushering in the Fast.

Only Bayu could celebrate fasting by feasting! said the mosque official of Mandaluko. *You can't 'welcome the Fast'. What's that got to do with Islam? You can't find it in the Koran or Traditions of the Prophet. It corrupts a holy festival. And remember that most of Bayu won't be fasting anyway. So what are they playing at? We threw out such things a generation ago.*

But the point of 'welcoming the Fast' was to affirm its local meaning, its communal nature, and to fortify the faithful in their month of hardship.

The noise began long before dawn with a siren from the mosque: a mournful, curving sound that recalled the air-raid warnings of wartime Britain. A warning, but there was nowhere to dive for shelter, and moments later a fierce voice burst on the ear: *Sahur! Sahur!* This was the name of the daybreak meal, to be completed before another siren at 4 a.m. More than a wake-up call, the prayer-leader's screaming – so loud, it first struck me as a practical joke: his gaping mouth an inch above my sleeping ear – was a challenge. It was as if this otherwise quiet man, an unfriendly neighbour and shunner of feasts, could suddenly compel our submission, or at least our attention. And when he had finished, Sukib loaded a cassette into the PA and let it roar for an hour.

Even by the standards of Bayu, with its banked loudspeakers and competing weddings, Ramadan raised noise to a new level.

Overhead, high-voltage prayers crackled from electric loudhailers. The air jangled with feedback shrieks and trumpeted yells as rival prayer-leaders shouted their wares from Bayu's half-dozen places of worship. By 3.30 a.m. you could see people wandering about like stunned sheep in the unlit road, some merely lost, others ostentatiously greeting one another, showing that they had made the effort. *They* were up, at least: who knows what the neighbours were doing!

After the shock, a sense of excitement and purpose. The early meal, eaten half-asleep; the calming ablutions and dawn prayers; the collective step into sacred time; the individual bodily discipline; the sense of a big undertaking; the pride in doing it right. *I have proved my faith; I have tested myself. I am a good Muslim.*

The rules are strict: from dawn until dusk – more than twelve hours in equatorial Java – no refreshment, nothing to eat or drink. 'One may not even swallow one's saliva.' Some people, like the prayer-leader Sukib and the primary-school religious teacher, would have liked the rules to be even stricter. They would have liked them to be enforced by religious police, as in those shariah-governed states where it is an offence to be seen eating during the daylight hours. (Some devout villages further from town unofficially operated such a policy.) But they would have been wrong, even by their own lights, because in Java compulsion in religion leads to defection. Following the 1965 coup, a push for orthodoxy in the south of Banyuwangi caused mass conversions to Hinduism. The more people learned of their religion, the less they wanted of it. And now there were Bali-style Hindu temples scattered across the south – a legacy of the Islamic drive. (Javanese Hindus saw their conversion as a return to the pre-Islamic faith, the religion of Old Java.) Fortunately for everyone, under Indonesia's ecumenical constitution, Islamic obligations remain, so to speak, voluntary. And this voluntary aspect enhances the Fast's ethical aspect, making it attractive to Javanists – people who stress the Javanese part of their cultural inheritance and mostly have little time for formal Islam. In Javanist philosophy, following Hindu precedent, austerity is one of the paths to enlightenment. 'I fast, but silently,' said Rupo, combining a modest boast with a put-down. 'And I don't do it for anyone. I do it for myself.'

Thus, the fasting pious – a minority of about a quarter – are augmented by sceptics, principled slackers and quite ordinary folk who derive some consolation from the discipline. 'It helps me understand the hardships of the poor,' said a poor man in east Bayu when I asked him why he fasted. 'I feel I share in their suffering.' 'Fasting dampens the passions,' said his wife sadly. 'Teaches us to control our instincts. I don't do it because it's an obligation, but because it's good for me.'

This was not how the headman saw things. 'The thing about the Fast', said Pak Lurah settling back in his sofa, 'is that it forces you to think about food and drink all day. You are woken in the middle of the night to eat. You stuff yourself until the dawn siren. Then you spend the day dying for a drink. The dusk alarm gives you the all-clear; then you gorge yourself at night. I'll tell you my way to conquer the passions – no, don't laugh! – You indulge them, *then* leave them behind.'

Obliged to fast? said Warno, one of the mystics. *Nonsense! I see a ripe mango on my tree and I am* obliged *to eat it. The world is there for our appreciation. Our senses are divine and we must honour them, satisfy them. A woman is beautiful: I am* obliged *to make love to her. These figs: take, eat! Delicious, no?*

For a more orthodox explanation I turned to Matraji, the retired mosque official who lived in east Bayu. Elected by his peers, the mosque official is charged with heading Islamic affairs in the village. He looks after the deeds of prayer-houses and land donated by the pious, chairs committees responsible for the collection of alms, gives sermons in the mosque, and presides over Islamic rituals. Something between a functionary and a religious leader, he is influential, but not usually powerful. In Java it is the heads of Islamic seminaries who combine learning with political clout, patronage with prestige. Mosque officials, by contrast, are typically modest – men of the people. The character and opinions of a mosque official, nevertheless, tell much about the state of Islam in a village. In puritan Mandaluko, the incumbent had taken a lead in boycotting syncretic rituals: anything not in the Koran or Sayings of the Prophet he denounced as polytheist. Matraji was not of that party. He had retired some years ago, but he still led prayers in east Bayu and served at the shrine of Buyut, the guardian spirit.

We sat in his tiny dirt-floor house and his daughter served us tea, our ornamental glasses steaming on the low metal table. Children, barefoot, hung at the door and pressed against the window. At intervals Matraji shooed them away. The heat inside the house was intense.

Gnome-like, agile for his seventy years, Matraji spoke very fast, the words tumbling out of him, and it was only later, listening to the tape at half speed, that I was able to catch everything he had said. He was born in 1919, the year his father made the pilgrimage. In those days, the round trip to Mecca took six months: pilgrims were rare and distinguished persons, especially in Banyuwangi. When his father died – he was still a boy – he boarded at an Islamic seminary, working for his keep during the day, praying and memorizing the Koran in the evening. For twelve years he drifted between seminaries, roaming the Banyuwangi countryside. But he always came back to the village. The prayer-house of east Bayu had been one of his initiatives. There had always been a bamboo shelter, like the one in Sumbersari. But in 1966, after the political massacres, people were eager to prove their faith, and poor as they were, they paid for the concrete and tiles, providing the labour themselves. 'As far as the government was concerned, you were either a Muslim or a communist; and being a Muslim you had to pray, do the fast and suchlike. Few of our people had ever done that. They didn't even know how to do the prostrations. We had to teach them as if they were little children. Can you imagine: the dragon men all lined up to pray! But after Tapan and Sumi were killed, you couldn't keep them away. As things became peaceful again, of course, numbers fell away. But we still get a dozen every evening for prayers.'

'Are they the real believers, then?'

'Who knows what's in their hearts. Perhaps they're still afraid. The important thing is that they do it.' And he gestured to our tea glasses. 'Drink up, Andrew! I'm not fasting this year, too sick.'

The version of Islam that Matraji taught was straightforward and demanding but tolerant, forgiving of human weakness. When I asked him about non-fasters, he shrugged and said: 'That's their affair. Strictly, they miss out on the rewards, but who knows. Who can tell what God intends? In any case, people are different. You have to look at their bodies: are they strong enough? And hard physical work: can't do it on air alone, can you?'

Matraji took off his black cap and wiped his brow with the rag that hung round his neck. His hair, still black, was sparse underneath, his temples finely veined. He fanned his chin with the folded hat. I felt I would suffocate in the heat.

'What about the mystical sect, Sangkan Paran?' I asked.

'Some of them fast, but I don't know them well. They're mostly up at the west end. Good people, though. Solid.'

I asked him about the rewards of fasting. 'Removal of sin; tempering the passions. People will tell you that they do it to prosper in this world, but that's an error. The rewards are in the afterlife, not here. If you do the right things – stay up reading the Koran aloud, do the extra prayers – the whole month is meritorious. On the twenty-first of the month, the Night of Power, God lowered down profit and loss. If you do the supplementary prayers on those days you get compound merit, equal to that of a thousand ordinary days. It's simple: no prayers, no merit.'

We need these rules because times have changed, he explained. 'Nowadays people have too many wishes and a thousand ways to satisfy them; they are ruled by their passions. Islam saves you from yourself.' Thinking of this, he turned, quite suddenly, to reminiscing about the past – not the turbulent Sukarno period of early Independence, but a remoter past, the prelapsarian Java of his youth. When he was young, he said, people were more honest. They were as good as their word. If a man said to his wife, 'I'll sleep overnight in the fieldhut to guard the durian trees,' he wouldn't dare come home. If he told someone he was going to market, he'd have to go: couldn't change his mind. Why? Because to break your word was to betray yourself. That was why, in those days, words really counted: they were efficacious.

'We were different then,' he went on. 'Men and women bathed together in the river without shame, without lust. Women would only put on a bodice to go out of the village. Even then the navel showed.' Only pilgrim's wives (his mother!) wore headscarves.

Faithful words, simplicity, and a kind of purity or integrity: that was what he seemed to be evoking. 'Think of it: in those days, it was permitted for youths and girls to visit each other's houses and sometimes sleep over. But nothing ever really happened: you knew the limits.' He'd done it himself, home from boarding school. He laughed and shook his head remembering it all. 'We were different people. Only Bayu and the real Osing villages had these customs. Other places not. Here Islam had hardly got started.'

'When did all that end?'

He considered for a moment and then, focusing, made the effort to answer. 'I was a lad, about fifteen: say, 1930s.'

I was puzzled by him, astonished by his recollection. It sounded more like 1930s Bali – the stuff of Dutch colonial fantasy – than Depression-era Java. Yet he told me straight, and with a kind of wonder at a different world. Blue remembered hills? An old man's fancy? I could not quite believe his memory. But his picture of an untroubled, sunlit past, though dismissed by some (it seemed so incredible, I felt stupid asking), was confirmed by others: old people I learned to trust. I was reminded of what elders – old headhunters and revellers – in Nias used to tell me: 'Before Christianity came, we didn't have sin. *We didn't sin.*' Islamic orthodoxy, in this perspective, was what came after the Fall. Religion for a world out of joint.

After nearly two weeks, Sri was still fasting – she alone of our house. By day, she put aside her frivolity and lay dull-eyed before the television; even Sofía could not interest her. That she was fasting at all had surprised me. She had been brought up a nominal Christian by Arjo and Mari. And her natural parents – so far as they were an influence – were positively anti-religious. ('As long as you're good to the neighbours left and right, that's all that matters,' said Sae. 'Islam, Christian, Nationalist, who cares?') But at university Sri had started to call herself Muslim. She did not pray – this she had never learned. But some of her friends were fasting and she wanted to show solidarity. In the evening, restored to life, she joined the women chanting in the prayer-house: easy repetitive litanies that anyone could learn. Though not devout (she did not pray), Bu Lurah, the headman's wife, went along too, scarfed and gowned, with a tray of sweets. So did Siti, Drus's wife: her store unattended, merit balancing loss. Both of them were fasting. And there were daughters of other neighbours, men and women indifferent to Islam. Curiously, you couldn't predict from their parents which children would fast or pray. It was rarely the case that devout parents had indifferent children, but apathy and principled abstention were less infectious. Katri, the daughter of another staunchly non-religious couple, had fasted every year since the age of ten. Now aged fourteen, she looked up to Sri as to a big sister and sophisticate. But it was Sri who was following Katri's example.

I made quiet enquiries about who was fasting and who had given up. People sometimes lied about performing the daily prayers, but not about fasting. It was obvious. Fasters looked sallow and half-dead, with sunken eyes and grey lips. Their tempers were short. They were excitable. You could see in their effortful movements that it was a real trial. And they had a penetrating rotten breath, quite distinctive to fasters. In a close-packed minibus the smell was overpowering. As the month wore on, however, people began to fall away and there were pious mutterings about excuses. 'How can Muni have toothache when he hasn't got any teeth?' said Sanuri, pulling a wry face. But sickness, the strain of hard labour on an empty stomach and sheer exhaustion took their toll. Women were exempt during their periods. Nor could they pray in the mosque or join in the evening chanting, since menstruation (in Indonesian, 'dirtiness') defiled holy places. By the end of the month it was mainly men, either the old and inactive or the young and strong, who had held out. Whoever had lasted was happy and proud.

Ill with tiredness, we escaped to Hindu Bali to sleep off the last week of Ramadan. So, too, did Sri's father. Or rather, he went to work on building sites in Denpasar, the Balinese provincial capital, as did a number of other village men. When we got back and compared notes Sae was ecstatic. The last days of Ramadan had coincided with the Balinese New Year and the holy day of Nyepi when a sacred silence is enforced. 'They had to turn off the mosque loudspeakers in Denpasar for a whole day and night! They were forbidden to broadcast the call. No chanting, nothing. We all threw up our caps in the air. What a victory, eh!'

7
A Different Islam

'Seventy-five per cent of the villagers are identity-card Muslims,' complained Tompo, the primary-school religious teacher. 'They don't pray; they neglect their obligations. A lot of them belong to Sangkan Paran [the mystical sect]. They call Islam *the Arab religion*. Can you believe it! We need to bring them back to the straight path, make them understand, but that is a matter of psychology. Perhaps you can help . . .'

We were sitting under the eaves of Jumhar's prayer-house where Tompo, a tall, slender, city-bred man of thirty, still unmarried, had just given a class in Islamic law to a group of children. He did not know me, and I assume this was why he thought I could help. An unlikely ambassador for Islamic orthodoxy, I was, nevertheless, an educated person, like himself, interested in progress. And Islamization and progress were the same thing.

I wondered how much he knew about the sect. He intended to use 'psychology' to advance his cause. But his choice of words showed a confusion. For what he had actually said was not the loan-word *psikologi* but a Javanese phrase meaning 'the science of inwardness', and this was, coincidentally, a pretty good definition of mysticism. Indeed, the general term for mysticism is 'inwardness'. In the mystical view, it is Islamic orthodoxy which lags behind in the world of the senses, of prayer-mats and postures. Unlikely, then, that an application of 'inwardness' would lead the mystics back to the straight and narrow.

I said: 'Perhaps they have their reasons. Have you talked to them?'

'No, you can't talk to them. They are full of reasons – reasons I don't want to hear. Look, the rules are clear. If you call yourself a

Muslim you *must* behave like one.'

Tompo had begun to jab his finger at me and checked himself. But he couldn't restrain the hectoring tone. He gave his words a peculiar emphasis that was not usual in Javanese.

'Perhaps they think there's more than one way to be a Muslim,' I said.

'There's only one way. Only one *good* way. Of course there are many bad ways.'

I thought of something the old headman, Harsono, had said to me. '*Islam* means *slamet*, wellbeing and security, something all human beings crave. So we all follow Islam, even you.' He was doing what the mystics often did, using puns and etymologies to make links. The puns were fanciful, but they pointed to hidden affinities. Everything in the world was interconnected if you knew how to look: Islam was really a universal humanism. But this was not Tompo's view.

'Who is to decide which is the right way?' I said.

'Not *them*. Ordinary people can't decide these things for themselves. People are ignorant and need to be told. And if they don't comply, they should be punished. I've seen people in Bayu during the Fast eating in full view of the street, mocking the faithful. It's shameful. Those who don't fast should be punished, like in Arabia.'

Jumhar had fallen silent and looked embarrassed as if he did not want me to hear these things.

I said, 'You mean whippings and all that?'

'Yes, all that. That's why there's no crime in Arabia. People are scared.'

He drew a finger across his throat and laughed. But he was serious. He leaned towards me, sweating, his little moustache twitching, his voice louder than necessary.

'Listen. In less than a generation things will move our way. That's why I'm a teacher. I'm forming the young.'

As often when talking to idealistic young men in Java, I heard an echo of borrowed words. I could imagine a preacher at his graduation ceremony telling the class: 'In a generation things will go our way. That's why you're needed as teachers, to shape the young.' And the preacher would have heard the same from *his* teachers. There was a tradition of change, of wiping the slate and starting afresh.

But Tompo was practical as well as passionate. He said, 'I make them show me a record of mosque attendance and after-school classes: if they miss twice they get punished – extra Arabic instead of sports. That's how to do it. Not through their parents. You get nowhere with the old folks.'

This wasn't quite true; for Tompo had made a convert among the old, as he went on to boast. When he arrived in the village three years ago, his landlord, Rasno (an ape-man in the dragon play), was a mere 'identity-card Muslim', like most people in the eastern section. He even had a little shrine to 'some Hindu saint or other' where he used to meditate. Tompo ordered it closed and Rasno complied. As a former communist, if Tompo had reported him he could be in trouble. Now this sixty-year-old man was learning to recite; he had become a good Muslim.

I said, 'So you'd inform on the man who has taken you into his home?' I knew that Tompo didn't pay any rent but depended on Rasno's kindness.

'Yes,' he said hotly, 'if it meant upholding the truth.'

Jumhar sighed at this admission but still said nothing. At this point we should have sipped our tea and smoked a cigarette. We could then have talked of other things. But it was the Fast. We sat in silence for a tense minute; then Tompo nodded to me sternly and left. When he had gone, Jumhar said: 'That won't do in a village like Bayu. People won't be forced: they have their own habits and customs. You have to recognize that a tree has many branches. Tompo wants a trunk, straight up and down like a telegraph pole.'

'But he's in charge of the religious education of all the village children. He has a big influence.'

'Only in school; and he has to follow the syllabus. Outside school they are my responsibility, and the mosque's.'

Jumhar was a short, squat man with red-rimmed eyes, like someone who has been crying. He was mild-mannered, eager to please. Now in his early thirties, he had been a Koranic instructor for about twelve years. With help from the neighbourhood he had built his prayer-house, the Light of Paradise. A hundred and twenty-five people, from virtually every household within two hundred yards, had contributed. Although not many attended, the prayer-house belonged to all of them. Its management committee included non-active Muslims such as Noto, the carpenter, and even Wan, who was a Christian. Wan, with his motorbike, knew people all over the district. He was charged with recruiting visiting speakers on holy days. Noto was Head of Equipment: he had raised funds for, and installed, an electrified megaphone on the roof. This made redundant the traditional buffalo-hide drum, used for the call to prayer, that still hung from the eaves; but it meant that non-attenders could 'benefit from the chanting on Thursday evenings'. That was how Noto himself put it. In all other respects, the prayer-house remained traditional: a wooden structure on stilts with a mossy, tiled roof, walls of bamboo wattle and a creaking wooden floor polished by worshippers' knees. Jumhar's prayer-house looked a century old yet gave no impression of solidity or permanence. A firm shove from a well-aimed reformist foot would send the whole thing sliding into the ravine below. Yet there was a certain low-key resilience in Jumhar's religion: it was tolerant, flexible, humane. It had kept the peace in Java for thirty years.

Had I been a Muslim, I would have found prayer-houses like Jumhar's very pleasant places to hang out in. Cool, shady, leisurely, mostly quiet, and somehow reassuring, they reminded me of country churches in my boyhood. They had that same sense of human use and repetition, the soft gleam of worn surfaces: a religion cut to human proportions. You had a sense that God, or something, was there simply because everybody around you thought and felt that way. And being there – instead of in the fields or on the building site – you did not need an excuse for idleness, a reason to stop and stare.

The fasting month, however, was not a time of idleness but of more or less continuous religious activity. I went along several afternoons to observe the routine classes – the Light of Paradise was a short walk from our house – and sometimes stayed on to see evening prayers and chanting. There was a schedule fixed to the wall: Monday '*learning the Arabic letters*', Tuesday *Koranic recitation*, Wednesday '*building of faith*', Thursday *the prostrations and liturgy of ritual prayer*, Friday *devotional chanting*, Saturday *lawbooks* (with Tompo), Sunday *the Traditions of the Prophet*. These sessions were for older children, those who could already read the Koran. On the chart, beside each Indonesianized Arabic word (*Alquran*, *Al-hadith*, *Fiqhi*), the name of a teacher had been crossed out. 'Now I do them all,' said Jumhar, 'except for Tompo's session – *he* insists – because the other teachers are too dogmatic. The kids don't mind but their parents object.' I pressed him for details, but he would only say that Yusuf, the new paramedic, was a *fanatik* who boycotted prayer-meals and told the children that their parents were idolaters. Noto, the equipment manager, had heard of this and had complained. '*Our* Islam is protected by the Constitution,' he had said. 'It's not for outsiders to tell us what to do.' So Jumhar told Yusuf, 'I'm letting you go.' Another acknowledged *fanatik* – the word was freely used, and not disowned – lived just west of our neighbourhood. His name had been scratched out beside *Traditions of the Prophet*. Aris was a lathe operator in a factory and was an enemy of the headman – 'a bit of an agitator,' said Jumhar. But again, he was reluctant to elaborate, perhaps not wishing to repeat criticisms of the headman. Wednesdays had been taught by a nephew of the mosque official, a graduate of the reformist university in Malang that Sri had attended. 'Too strict: he frightened them off,' said Jumhar.

All these people, except for Jumhar himself, had been educated out of the village or – like Aris – knew the life of the city. They were the reformers, the despisers of custom, men who wanted trees without branches. And as modern men impatient of custom and politeness, less tied to the village notion of harmony, they dealt with opponents brusquely. They called them 'infidels' – a dangerous word in Java. During the 1960s, communists were killed as infidels.

To accuse someone of unbelief was almost to deny their humanity, to tempt violence. When Aris, in a dawn sermon, had spoken of 'our infidel leaders', he was summoned to the village office and forced to retract. (Strangely, he did not speak of *apostates*, renouncers of the faith: it was as if his enemies had never believed.)

With me, an outsider and presumed Christian, the scratched teachers were unfriendly but cautious. Tompo, who didn't know me, was polite. But the others sometimes addressed me in the familiar form, as to a child. I could not deal with this, and it embarrassed people, so I tried to avoid them. Unlike the French *tu*, which could be egalitarian, the Osing familiar 'you', to an unrelated adult of a similar generation, was a calculated put-down. Behind it, I felt, lay more than sectarian antagonism. Aris and his friends were different from the other villagers not merely in their religious conviction but in what they claimed to know about the West – our immorality and individualism ('I am I and you are you'), our denial of God, our worship of money – and of course, the Gulf War and my part in it. Their contempt was racial in that it permitted no differences, no exceptions, just as their certainties permitted no debate. The humanism of their parents – pious men like Pak Lurah's father-in-law who had conceded that 'underneath we were all the same' – was mere weakness. That same weakness had allowed people of different religious orientation to live together peaceably; but peace was a lesser virtue.

Jumhar had let his teachers go – he would not confront them – but they taught in other prayer-houses and were on the mosque committee. His mentor, the mosque official – a devout, decent, tolerant man – was still the head of Muslim affairs in Bayu; but once he retired the new men would have the stage.

In the afternoons, Jumhar coached the beginners. One damp Tuesday I duly turned up and waited an hour in the prayer-house, watching the rain slip off the eaves in a thin curtain. Of the registered 106 pupils (belonging to both groups) only nine showed up – six girls and three boys. They were aged about five to ten, all in the uniform of piety: sarongs, starched shirts, and black caps for the boys (they looked like little old men at a funeral); full plain gowns and maidenly headscarves for the girls. The Islamic headscarf completely covers the hair and is pinned tight under the chin, accentuating the roundness of the face and giving girls and young women – naturally round-faced and big-eyed in Java – a curiously uniform appearance. In sing-song voices, they greeted me politely ('Good afternoon, Pak Andrew,') and went straight to a shelf piled with cheaply produced books and pamphlets. Then they arranged themselves on the smooth wooden floor – girls and boys on different sides – to practise reading. After a while Jumhar's wife came in to hear them read, one at a time, while the rest carried on in loud voices, all reading from different pages. It was another hour before Jumhar returned from the fields, his legs muddy, his face reddened with effort. He disappeared for a shower and then, in the same smart garb as the boys (a thatch of black hair sticking out from his cap), stood beside the readers in a bubble of silence and performed his mid-afternoon prayers. With only twenty minutes left of the session he took over from his wife.

The books were primers with graded passages of Arabic. Each pupil repeats a page until judged satisfactory and then goes onto the next page. When they have completed six primers in this way, pupils can 'graduate to the Koran'. 'Before then, I won't let them, as they'd be confused and would mumble,' said Jumhar. The children read using a pointer stick, moving it along the line and reading the words aloud. The cacophony of nine readers did not seem to put anyone off. Naturally, it helps that there is no attention to meaning. One learns to recite classical Arabic without understanding. Even the more accomplished reciters, men and women who have passed years in Islamic seminaries and who have memorized entire sections of the Koran as well as dozens of prayers and litanies, have only a vague sense of the text's meaning. All the effort is on the skilled crafting of externals – tone, rhythm, correct pronunciation. Since the Koran is the literal word of God, as revealed to the Prophet, it is imperative – and meritorious – to reproduce it correctly; but merit is won by performing the ritual action, not by attending to its message. At junior levels, this applies as much in the illustrious boarding schools of East Java as in the village prayer-house. A famous Indonesian educationist, brought up in such schools, once wrote of his early life, 'God never said anything I was able to understand.'

At the end, the children chanted a brief litany (memorized so perfectly that they sang without paying attention). Then the girls pulled off their gowns and filed forward, one by one, to kiss Jumhar's hand and say the Islamic *Peace be with you*.

At the later session there were eight girls, aged about ten to fifteen, though it was hard to judge ages in their outfits. Jumhar and his father spoke almost apologetically about the fact that no boys had come. 'It's the rain. Normally we get four or five.' The schedule on the wall indicated *Pronunciation of the Scripture*, but Jumhar strayed from this and lectured the pupils on good behaviour. Switching easily between Indonesian, the Osing dialect of Javanese, Arabic and High Javanese, he led them through exercises and drills, sprinkling his discourse with prompts along the lines of 'We must be *cl—*?' ('Clear!' they chanted back.) 'And always *pre—*' ('Precise!') Individually, the girls answered him in High Javanese, but only in simple phrases – *Yes, Pak*, and *I don't know, Pak* – that did not imply a mastery of its difficult, polysyllabic forms. After all, they had come here to learn Arabic. The high culture of the Javanese courts – the shadow plays, poems, chronicles, and mystical treatises dense with allusion and wordplay – was not something they would ever learn. Only Bayu's mystics took a serious interest in such things: they were not for youth.

While Jumhar heard each girl recite – nodding, not needing to look at the text – the others distractedly fussed with their books and their gowns. Some of them had long sleeves with cuffs hiding the hands, the cuffs held in loops over the fingers, making it difficult to turn the pages. Others fanned streaming faces ineffectually with hands. 'Ah! Hot! Clammy!' they sighed.

It seemed an uninspiring, pointless lesson. I could not understand what kept them there. Jumhar's father, again apologetic, said that the children were unreliable and hard to teach. There were too many distractions these days. They heard one thing at school, another at home. People like Tompo made life difficult and complicated; the children felt pulled in two directions. He himself had been a Koranic teacher in his time, and he had wanted to go on the pilgrimage like his father-in-law, but he wasn't rich enough. In those days it took seven months, including a month each way for the journey. He didn't know what a pilgrim did the rest of the time. But his father-in-law, a man from a barren island off the north coast of Java, had told him all about the camels – how they could go up and down slopes and still keep the rider level by shortening or extending their front legs. Their padded toes stopped them sinking into the sand.

On my way back home I took a deviation, following a track south, and picked my way over steaming puddles to Noto's block. This double row of wooden houses was another village within a village, like Sumbersari: dappled by mango trees, always full of children, its raucous yard roamed by chickens and strutting cocks. (My tapes are full of roosterish interruptions.) I found Noto planing the door of a cupboard outside, his broad, slightly flabby chest speckled with sawdust, curls of yellow shavings round his feet. Beside him, on a bench, the tools of his trade – wooden spokeshaves, bradawls, old-fashioned planes with brass knobs, a hand-drill. Were such things still manufactured in the West? They seemed oddly familiar: my grandfather had been a cabinet maker and his tools, passed on to my father (an engineer, who rarely used them), were the mystery objects of childhood. As soon as he saw me, Noto reached for a cigarette – '76', the ancestral choice – and threw me the packet. It was a house where I was always welcome.

Despite his easy, bland air, his fondness for joking, and his informality – he was usually shirtless and barefooted, a panama hat tipped back on his head – Noto was an important man in the village. He was unofficial 'head of arts' with his own gong orchestra and dance troupe; he was leader of one of Bayu's four administrative sections (more or less a matter of keeping a list); and he was one of those ubiquitous figures who make village life what it is. A big, easygoing man, at weddings or circumcisions he was always on hand to usher guests to tables (a skill, since it requires tact in placing people and a knowledge of 'who isn't talking'). And when the hired entertainment was a gandrung, a female singer-dancer, he was master of ceremonies, presenting the guests of honour with the dancing scarf, leading them to the arena. He himself was an accomplished dancer, the best of his generation: always masterful and dignified before the retreating, alluring gandrung. 'The young men get too close,' he told me. 'They are like besotted fools in the gandrung's power.' Beside the gandrung's undulations – her hips rocking, her bottom stuck out – he was firmness and male pride, angles to her curves. With a sharp stride and a flick of the scarf, he would cut off her retreat, hold her gaze (with the suggestion of a kiss), then arc away smiling, letting her pass.

Noto's abstention from Islamic ritual was different from the headman's slightly shamefaced indifference. And it was different again from the principled scepticism of the mystics. (Of their ideas, which surely would have suited him, he knew almost nothing.) His manifesto, which he told me more than once, was: 'God told the Prophet Muhammad that you should do the five prayers; and if you couldn't do that, at least turn up to Friday mosque; and if you couldn't manage *that*, well, be good to your neighbours right and left, acknowledge His name, and you'd be received.' Noto was a good-to-your-neighbours sort of Muslim. His way of acknowledging Allah was to stand guard of honour during the celebrations for the Prophet's birthday at the mosque, or to sit astride the prayer-house roof, cigarette in mouth, and fix the megaphone. But he would not pray, fast or read the Koran. And he had reasons.

I followed him into the house – a spacious high-roofed building filled with the sweet smell of cut wood. We smoked the clove cigarettes and he began to tell me about his father.

'Father was a Muslim specialist. In those days, that meant anyone with Islamic learning who could perform weddings, heal the sick, and so on. He did a bit of everything. But he was an expert in magic: he could make rain, cast charms, repel sorcerers, find lost objects. Anything you wanted.'

I said, 'You mean like Pak Ran?'

'No, something more. Ran hasn't studied in boarding schools; nor has he spent time with gurus. My father could quote the Koran. He knew hundreds of spells. He could look in your eyes and know your fate. That's why he was feared. There were all sorts of accusations – I was too young to understand. I was twelve when he was killed – by a mob in the fields north of the village. After his death, he returned to the house one night and spoke to my elder brother: *Don't come looking for me in Alas Purwo. I am a tiger. Should you come to the forest to find me you will never return.* Since that day, none of my family has been there. You ask my cousin [the mosque official] if he would dare. So that's why I didn't learn to recite or pray: I didn't want a suspicion hanging over me.'

'What suspicion?' I asked, guessing.

'Of following the family craft. I didn't want my father to haunt me.'

Banyuwangi was Java's 'warehouse of black magic'. And Alas Purwo, the Primeval Forest to the south, was the sorcerers' last refuge, a sanctuary beyond the grave. When the old kingdom of Blambangan, the last Hindu realm in Java, had converted to Islam in the eighteenth century, following a long colonial campaign by the Dutch, it was there – and to Bali – that the remnants had fled. Long abandoned, it was now the lair of were-tigers and solitary magicians.

Islamic ritual was not just uncongenial to Noto; it was dangerous. His past made it so. To know the prayers and spells, in his case, was to arouse suspicion, the inherited taint of sorcery. His abstention was therefore excusable, even respectable. Yet because he had not stood entirely aside, he retained a voice, as a faithful layman, in village Islam. He had won a long-running battle with Sukib, prayer-leader in the Light of Paradise. When Sukib overstepped the mark in his dawn broadcasts, Noto had intervened. Lax Muslims – people who ignored the call to prayer – did *not* 'become ghosts', as

Sukib had said (this was, understandably, a sensitive point); they merely went to hell. In front of Jumhar, he had forced Sukib – Fast or no Fast – to eat his words. And towards the end of the month, fatigued by the megaphone he himself had installed, Noto marched into the prayer-house at 2 a.m. and shouted, 'We're all deaf, you damned fool! Deaf! Deaf! Deaf!' sending Sukib scuttling to the headman. (Pak Lurah had choked with laughter telling me this.) The night-long amplified readings of the Koran – the whole book, three readers, a third each – had also begun to grate. Several prayer-houses now had broken tiles from anonymous missiles. Who had thrown them? 'Don't ask,' laughed Noto. 'There are quite a few who miss their sleep.' The silent, snoring majority.

Noto's laughter drew his wife, Las, from the back yard. She barrelled in, screaming at me. 'Ah! Andrew! How long have you been here?' A plug of tobacco as big as an egg distorted the side of her mouth. Her lips were red with the juice.

'Where's Sofía? Why don't you bring her here?'

'I did yesterday but you were out.'

'Ah, you keep her to yourselves. Lend her to me!'

It was a big, noisy household. They had a daughter named Rita, a buxom, eager woman, barely contained in her frock, whose husband was usually away working on construction sites in Bali. Rita's daughter, aged five, was already a dancer, with a grace and delicacy I had only seen in the Balinese dance. One day the little girl ran into the road and was knocked down by a truck. She was thrown into the ditch, unharmed except that her right foot pointed backwards. Rita carried her home weeping and Noto, with something of his father's craft – was it carpentry or magic? – popped the foot back into place. Miraculously, within a couple of weeks she was dancing again.

There was also a son, Marko, a quiet, handsome youth of sixteen, in the shadow of his jovial and omnipresent father. 'Marko is shy of girls,' said Las, 'not like his old man! He's not ready for a fiancée yet. He won't dance with a gandrung.' Neither did he smoke or drink like other youths. But he was not one of the pious: he had no interest in religion. Instead, he played in the gong orchestra and helped his father with carpentry. A generation ago most young people were like him: unhurriedly biding their time, confident in their elders' judgement, wanting to do what their parents had done. These were the people Aris and Tompo would have to work on.

8
Lebaran

Lebaran – the Javanese holiday marking Idul Fitri, the end of the Fast – fell on a Sunday. We made it back from Bali two days early. Our ferryboat, brimming with homecoming Javanese, nudged along at the speed of a swimmer: an hour for the three-mile crossing. At the wharf, buses bulging like burst cushions sped off with passengers hanging from doors and poking through roofs. In a vast internal migration, trains rattled back and forth across Java in a get-home-or-die spirit. It was the festival when half of Indonesia 'returns to the village'.

Bayu awaited few such prodigals. Pak Sae's son – Sri's brother – came home from his barracks. In his neat, tight uniform he had a confident, glamorous air which, as often with Indonesian officials off-duty, owed something to the power of a threat withheld. You felt grateful for his benevolence. He had served in East Timor where, over a period of two decades, the Indonesian occupation had caused the death of a third of the population. Perhaps he had served on the 'hearts-and-minds' front: the big massacres were over long ago. At any rate, during his year in the field – and this astonished me – he had converted to Christianity. To embrace the faith of the vanquished showed, I thought, something honourable even if, as he admitted to me, 'I was never much of a Muslim.' Yet of his role, and the army genocide, he did not express the smallest doubt. Nor, of course, could I ask him about it except in the vaguest terms. To his parents he was simply a hero. His mother had once shown me an embroidered Timorese cloth he had brought her. She held it out limply, with an uncomprehending smile as though it were a book written in a foreign language – which in a sense it was.

Another village warrior, from a house opposite Sae's, was in West

Papua putting down independence fighters: bombs against bows and arrows. A surly thug (I met him during my second stay), he was not allowed home for two years. I would like to report that his wife led the gay life of a 'hot widow', but this was not the case.

The village was almost restored to itself when, just before midday, Sae and a ragged crew of fellow construction workers arrived from Bali. They brought clothing for their families, wads of sweated money, and stories of naked tourists. They had noted the honesty of the Balinese ('not like us Javanese'), their passion for ceremony, and their outlandish customs ('the women pee standing up'). Dark and shrunken from their days in the sun, they looked like men who had undergone a month of rigorous austerities. Yet some had gone there to escape the Fast.

As part of the preparations for Lebaran, villagers visited family graves to seek the ancestors' blessings. (One feared only the nearest departed: those more than a couple of generations back were simply forgotten.) There were two cemeteries, on opposite sides of the village. The old cemetery, to the south, was overshadowed by huge trees and creepers, its perpetual musty gloom lit only by the phosphorescent flashes of wandering spirits.

I had to go up to Sumbersari one evening and passed through the graveyard, said Sanuri, Bu Lurah's father. *I was just past the big banyan tree when I sensed a grey bulk to the side of old Sumi's tomb. I froze and couldn't advance a step. By God, it's a tiger: Buyut* [guardian spirit]*! I thought. It turned and arched its back, then raised its huge head. In the dusk, its eyes shone like lamps. I bit my tongue and – tasting blood – I was suddenly able to move. I never ran so fast in my life.*

The cemetery on the north side was open to the fields, overlooking gently shelving rice terraces. I went there that sunny, windy day with our landlady, Bu Mari, and Wan. Among the white headstones and shrubs, little family groups busied themselves with weeding and sweeping; some squatted to say prayers, their clothes ruffled by a warm wind that blew across the fields. In the distance, tall shaggy palms glittered and swayed. Far away on an embankment a boy was flying a kite.

Arjo, Bayu's modernizer, its 'saviour' during the sixties, was buried right at the edge of the cemetery, outside the community of the dead. The mosque official had not allowed him to be 'mixed' with the Muslim majority, even though he had mixed with them in life. ('It would be wrong. Muslims go here, Christians there, in proper order.') Mother and son knelt quietly beside the small chalky headstone, fussed with the flowers – no prayers – then rose and walked away, wiping their eyes.

At dusk, we heard the siren for the last time. Dates were eaten, thirsts slaked, cigarettes lit: the Fast was finally broken – though for most it had never started. (In Java you could have your cake and eat it.) And the end of the hunger – or the mere thought of it – was celebrated as it had begun, with a brisk round of prayer-meals. In each cluster of households, one man would join his neighbours in a brief ceremony; then the whole group would move next door and repeat the operation, this time taking only a mouthful; and so on, until each householder had served as guest and host and the whole cluster had 'broken the Fast' and 'welcomed in' Lebaran. All round the village you could see little groups of men in black caps and sarongs filing from house to house, shaking hands, greeting and welcoming. And behind them, women carrying trays of food, laughing and calling.

I joined Wan (since we occupied the front of his house we were effectively two households) and we crossed the road at the bidding of Ramelan, the ploughman, and sat around his mat to eat. The festive address was given by a splendid old peasant with a vacant expression and a battered bell-shaped hat. He was home from his fieldhut for the week. 'May this food reach the ancestors of Ramelan and Jamsa and may we all make it to Lebaran next year.' We raised our palms for the Arabic blessing, but after a moment he ran out of prayer. 'I know it, but I've lost my place,' he said. To which all replied, 'Amen!' Ten minutes later we were seated around Drus's mat doing the same thing. Drus was the intending pilgrim who had visited me on my second day in the village; the man who had scared me with his talk of sorcery and revenge. I disliked him, but he was a good host and his feast lacked nothing. Unlike his neighbour, he decided to say the prayer himself and show us how it was done. He had come late to Islam, but he was catching up. Though he had never learned to recite, at the age of thirty-five he was bent on a position among the notables in the front row at Friday mosque. The Middle Eastern wall-hangings, the visits to prominent Islamic teachers, the *insha'allahs* that sprinkled his conversation: all were statements of pious intent. But the prayer wouldn't come. 'Eh! I've forgotten!' he said, as Wan broke into a snigger. Embarrassed smiles. 'I know a prayer for a cow,' volunteered Ramelan, 'but I suppose it wouldn't do.'

In the morning – the biggest day of the year – villagers were out on the paths greeting and visiting. There was a simple formula: 'I ask your forgiveness, within and without [*lair-batin*],' or simply '*Lair-batin*.' The words were derived from the Arabic. *Lair* is the surface of things, the worldly and exterior; *batin* the hidden interior. But what, in a deeper sense, did the formula mean? Like so much else in Bayu, there was agreement on the basics – on correct form and practice – but different interpretations of the significance, of the relation between inner and outer.

The purpose of Lebaran, said Pujil, *is to cancel all the bad things people have done to each other over the past year and even things out. In football terms nil–nil. Just like in a family, you have to forgive each other. If you bear grudges to others and keep your anger to yourself you can't prosper. If you're going on the pilgrimage and you've hindered people* [he is an official], *you might never come back.*

'Lebaran' rhymes with 'birth', said Sahari, a mystic; *so it's a kind of rebirth. It reminds us of our origins. That's why at Lebaran you don't eat ordinary rice; you eat kupat-lepet* [leaf parcels of compact sticky rice]. *Look at the shapes: the kupat is a split diamond; the lepet is a seed-filled solid tube. What does that remind you of?*

'Lebaran' comes from the word 'to cleanse', so it's about cleansing yourself of sin, said the mosque official. *We build up merit dur-*

ing the Fast and purge ourselves of the year's accumulated sins. That's why everyone is happy.

There was a strict order of precedence. The young visited the old: first parents – 'they are your princes' – then parents-in-law and fosterers, then older neighbours, finally relatives. 'Neighbours before kin, because it's to them you turn for your daily needs.' The more traditionally-minded kneel before their elders, palms placed together, head bowed, to beg their forgiveness. It still happened in Bayu, but I saw it done properly only on television: the President and First Lady receiving their children and a line of humbled politicians. Seeing it, you understood the expression 'filial piety'. Official position generally outranks age and kin status, so the headman remained at home for the first four days, callers arriving from all over the village. ('I hate Lebaran,' he told me.) Only on day five of the festive week could he venture out to visit the local bigwigs.

Drus spent much of the week touring the district on his motorbike, cultivating Islamic leaders. For these trips he sported the Arafat-style spotted scarf favoured by rural clerics (kyais) but regarded in the village as an affectation. *There goes Kyai Drus*, they said. Siti, behind him, rode side-saddle in the Indonesian fashion, her gauzy headdress billowing in the wind.

Like everyone else, we kept open house. A row of jars with biscuits and homemade sweets stood on the coffee table, cigarettes and jugs of coffee at the ready. With each visit there was a standard exchange of tokens: women handed over half a kilo of sugar or some eggs; on leaving they were given a bar of soap. Children received a banknote of five hundred rupiah. These small sums, multiplied by fifty or more, added up. In a week, Siti gave out fifty kilos of sugar and forty thousand rupiah. Another neighbour, Misti, put her food expenses at one hundred thousand rupiah. Add to that the cost of forgoing work for a week. Like Christmas in the West, it was a time of obligatory spending: the only opportunity in the year for showing off wealth. Misti wore a gold hairpiece ('including a Turkish dinar') and a necklace that cost one million rupiah (about $1,000). Siti bought her son a gold necklace and ring. If you couldn't afford jewellery, you bought a shirt or sarong and wore it with the price label showing. Among the poorest, there was a pre-Lebaran panic as people went into debt. And every year there were reports of suicides. Just after my call on Noto, the carpenter, a poor woman in his block was cut down, still alive, from the rafters.

We received a good many of our landlady's callers. She held court, at the back, to Arjo's followers – his former teachers and Nationalist Party recruits. One of them, the school caretaker, who had also been a member of Arjo's anti-communist death squad, had recently had a stroke. His wife, a retired dancer, had taken soil from Arjo's grave and rubbed it on his chest and arms. Now he was 'better' and they came to thank Bu Mari. As with Elan, the irrigation official who had blamed the 'madness of the times', I could not believe this gentle, gracious man capable of wielding the knife; but I could not see him without thinking about it.

Lacking people of our own, we had quickly acquired substitutes. In Bayu there was no place for strangers, and like other incomers we had been fitted snugly into village life. But our circles hardly overlapped. Apart from the headman, whom I saw every day, I spent little time with the neighbours. Mercedes was on intimate terms with them. She spent her days with Misti and Jona, or talking to Bu Lurah, visiting the farm at the back with Sofía, or up at Sumbersari, the hamlet next to the village shrine. At prayer-meals and weddings, she sat with the women in their finery or helped in the kitchens wrapping sweets and weaving the leaf parcels for sticky rice. There were always too many hands to help: one showed up and took a turn, a stir of the pot. It was enough to be there.

If pleasure entailed work (to host a feast was 'to have work'), not all work, by any means, was pleasure. Yet even in the fields there was a steady hum of commentary, a current of laughter, as the planting gangs, shin-deep in brown water, retreated in line behind the advancing blanket of green. Away from the fields, work took on a recreational feel, with talk and laughter the constant backdrop. As a sideline, Jona, who lived at the back of our house, employed neighbours to shell peanuts. They would sit in her yard all day, their worked heaped around them, cracking and chatting, earning peanuts. And among them sat Mercedes and Sofía, blending in physically in a way I found impossible. Unlike me, they were never spectators.

The women were open and humorous, without rancour. In this, as in much else, Bu Mari was the exception. Jealous of Mercedes' friendship with Jona (the only neighbour who could stand up to her), she took every opportunity to put her down. Jona, we understood, came from bad people; her first husband had been killed as a sorcerer; she had quarrelled with her brother-in-law, and so on. But, in groups at least, there was never malicious gossip. Instead, a constant banter, a stream of frank jokes and teasing that only sharpened when a man approached.

'How long do you do it for?' asked Jamsa, who wanted to know about the West.

'How long do you?' said Mercedes.

'Two minutes, like a chicken!'

Tiny, pale-faced Jona gave a red smile and adjusted the plug of tobacco in her mouth. Then she emptied a tray of peanuts into a sack and looked across at Misti.

'Misti likes big bananas, don't you?' she said.

Noto the carpenter walked in on this discussion and quickly caught the drift: 'How big?'

A shy woman, Misti giggled and held her hands wide apart.

'In that case, I can't help you,' said Noto. 'Mine are about *that* long' – holding out his little finger.

'If they are so big, how many can you eat a day?' Jona persisted.

'Four!' replied Misti, but she could hardly get the word out.

'Do you suck them or nibble them?' asked Noto, collapsing in laughter.

This joke ran for days.

Yet the villagers also knew how to be quiet together. Sometimes Mercedes sat on the verandah with Sofía and Misti and her teenage daughter in contemplation of the rain. And then hardly a word was spoken. These were among the best times.

I never found quite that acceptance, that sense of being utterly 'at home' (a Javanese concept), in our neighbourhood. But I had cast my net wider, across the village and beyond, in an effort to meet all types. The mosque official, the magician, the monsters and sprites of the dragon play, returned pilgrims (male and female), dancers (female and male-female): all these were important for my work. But I tended to return to the same few houses, and these people, simply because I liked them, became my friends. Of the regulars, there was one man whose company I particularly sought. Pak Lurah had introduced me in these terms: 'I want you to meet Man ["Uncle"] Warno. I go to him for advice. When you've met him you'll understand why.'

His house was in the west, at the junction with a dirt road to Delik, a village known for its firm adherence to Islam. During the 'troubles' of 1965, truckloads of Muslim youths had come to Bayu to wage holy war on the infidel. Standing in the road unarmed, Warno had reasoned with them and sent them back. He was not a strong man, but his calmness was powerful. Tall, thin, deliberate, with a dome-like bald head, he was about sixty-three. Under his sharp-brimmed, grey panama hat, which he wore indoors, his face was a dark slender oval, his nose thin and scholarly, his mouth precise. His gaze conveyed understanding and something for which Javanese lacks a word: compassion. He was good to talk to, and his wife made the best coffee in Bayu.

Min was his second wife. His first, the headman's aunt, had died giving birth. The baby survived and he had looked after her alone. Three years later, after the thousandth-day commemorative feast, he had married Min – 'a companion for my soul and body,' as he put it. 'It wouldn't have been right any earlier,' he said, indicating the bed-platform. 'Not quite legitimate while I still had obligations to the departed.' Another time, he told me how it had come about. 'A year and a half after my wife passed away, I began to think about remarrying. The girl needed a mother. A man needs a wife. I had heard that Min had lost her husband, and one day I went to her house in Pancoran and said, "I want you as a wife. My mind is made up. It's not a matter of finding a woman – there are plenty of those in Bayu. It's a wife I want. In a year and a half – after the thousand days – I'll come back for you." And so it was. I didn't speak to her between those two occasions.'

Sitting on the platform with her arms round her knees, plump and a little faded – it was hard being married to a philosopher – Min smiled approvingly, sometimes echoing his words. She had more or less adopted his idioms, as did anyone who shared much time with him. It was not that he was pithy or quotable, but his way of formulating the world got under your skin. The neighbours were 'those to left and right'; a spouse was 'the soul's neighbour'; the dead, 'those who have gone home'; the living, 'those who are clear'; divinity (not God), 'what nurtures'; the act of love, 'nature's duty'. And as I write this, in my head I hear his slow, clear, resonant voice, his perfectly formed, improvisatory sentences. Warno was one of the sanest men I ever met.

They had had no children together but Min was a good stepmother (the girl was now grown and married) and – in a way that was special to the mystics – they appeared a genuine couple. The marital bond wasn't simply a fact of life, more or less fragile. It contained something sacred: it pointed to something beyond.

'Ah! Sofía!' he exclaimed, as we walked through the open door with Sofía in arms. 'Sit down, Bu!' We took our places at his marble-topped table while Min prepared coffee. Warno, dressed as always in the smock-like black shirt and shin-length trousers of a farmer, beamed at us, then at Sofía, clucking approvingly like a proud grandfather. In an odd way, I felt we had done our duty.

The house was standard Osing: wooden, rather than bamboo-weave, and spacious, with a scraped earth floor. It was rather empty. At least it would have been empty any other time, for suspended from the rafters, darkening the room like a washing line in a city garret, was a pole hung with neatly ironed sarongs. They were heirlooms that Warno and Min wore on their Lebaran visits and hung up on display the rest of the week. (You visited in best clothes and received in rags.) The sarongs, like the festive food and the suggestively shaped parcels of rice, were gestures – not quite offerings – to the ancestors. When the dead 'came home' during Lebaran, it pleased them to smell the food and see their clothes on show.

Some people have so much stuff hanging up, you have to duck your head when you go in, said Jona. *It's like being in the market. I've just come back from Tari's. She's got her husband's new bicycle dangling from the roof, knocking people's heads off. And all those sarongs, never worn. What a waste! If the dead can manage to come to the house, surely they can peek in the wardrobe.*

But Warno did not have a simple view of such things. When I asked him about the sticky rice packets – the tube and the split diamond – he said: 'They are a reminder of our origins in male and female. Not just mother and father – *they* are only intermediaries – but the eternal male and female that compose us. For you are two, not one. Man embracing woman.'

'Embracing woman,' echoed Min, smiling.

There were levels of understanding, he explained. Take the Lebaran greeting, the request for forgiveness 'inside and out'. This was more than a handshake, as people commonly supposed, a mere claim on the other person's sincerity – though that was useful if one was to live harmoniously. 'The correspondence of outer and inner, of material and spiritual, is more than an idle wish, Andrew: it represents the way things really are. If you mistake this, you do so at your peril. It's like the great world and the little world, the cosmos and humanity: they are made the same way; the difference is only in scale. We have to learn to read the signs. But conversely, our thoughts and feelings have their forms in the outer world; our thoughts make sense to us through these forms. That's why I hang the tube and the diamond over the door.'

I wondered what Jona would make of that.

We had two more calls on our way back. Bambang had been introduced to me by Wan as 'the head of youth in Bayu'. 'If you want to get on with *them*, you'd better get on with *him*,' he had said. Youth was not simply a generational category. It was, in a broad sense, political, like 'the People'. Youth had been the vanguard of the anti-colonial revolution; in 1945 they had kidnapped Sukarno and forced him to proclaim independence, four years before the Dutch had finally been driven out. Muslim youth had led the pogroms against left-wing targets in the sixties. (The student leaders of that time became the leaders of today's reformist movements – a smart-suited counterpart to the shambling seminarists.) One of the village staff had been a nationalist youth leader, charged with secret missions across Java in the last days of Sukarno. Now stout and middle-aged, his security contacts from those days still gave him an aura of authority: he was Bayu's 'iron fist'. In Indonesia's generational history – 'the revolutionaries of '45', 'the anti-communists of '66' – Youth had been the constant force for renewal. But where was the generation of '93? Under Suharto's rule, politics had all but withered; idealism – left and right – had nowhere to go. And until Wan had spoken of 'youth' (a word his father must have used a lot), I had not thought of the young in Bayu as a distinct category, a political cohort. Indeed, they weren't. Until the next big thing came along, their energies would be channelled into piety and pop culture – or, failing these, petty crime and the rented thuggery of Indonesian politics.

Perhaps this was why Bayu's senior youth was not really a youth at all. He was in his late twenties and married, his wilder days long over, though the longish hair, the fashionable polo shirt and the racy smile perhaps made them seem nearer. He lived in a brick-built, town-style house not far from his parents, who were prominent members of the mystical sect. They had a board outside their house saying *Sangkan Paran: The Way of Perfection*. 'I'm not yet ready for that,' he told me. 'I'm not a serious person.'

Bambang was originally engaged to a gandrung – dancing was his passion – but she had jilted him, 'so I had to make do with *her*,' he said, indicating his wife. 'The house is hers.' He made an upraised fist. 'I'm just the cock!' At this his wife, Sal, slapped him on the arm and went out, laughing, to make drinks. Like him, she belonged to an extended category of youth that fitted awkwardly in the village. She wore a town-style frock, not the sarong of a matron, and she had the loose, shoulder-length hair of a younger woman. When she came back, Bambang continued in the same jokey vein and I saw that his frankness and her tolerance were part of what made them 'matched', 'a couple'. Childless, they had stayed together for six years whereas others would have remarried.

'I was once engaged to the daughter of Haji Sartono. Both our fathers are harvest brokers, and they thought it would be a good alliance. So they betrothed us as children. Right through adolescence we didn't speak to each other. Didn't even say hello. Why? Because I was shy. Still am. People think of me as brash, but I don't like calling out, shouting across the road as some do. Like now, when you passed, I felt some reluctance to hail you, "Hey, Andrew, Mercedes. Drop in!" Anyway, the engagement was called off when I was discovered with someone else. So eventually I was able to marry whoever I wanted.'

Despite this experience, he didn't think arranged marriages were any weaker than love-marriages. People divorced because they quarrelled over who was in the right, and that could happen with anyone. It could be the most trivial thing, like whether you tramped mud into the house or left your sandals tidily on the doorstep. 'Your ways and her ways don't match. That's why people madly in love can split up straight after the wedding: the sandals.' More often it was infidelity. 'Seventy-five – no, eighty per cent of men go whoring or philandering. Why should the woman put up with that?' He looked mischievously at Sal and she snorted and shook her head.

Sal said: 'Love grows through familiarity. People are attracted because of beauty or politeness or because they like somebody's ways. But often they aren't in love when they marry. It comes through habit. Love takes patience and forgiveness.'

A bit uncomfortable with all this sincerity, Bambang wagged his finger at me and said: 'I saw you going into the mosque this morning. Better be careful. They'll have you praying next.' Then, as if unsure of the impression he wanted to create: 'I couldn't make it myself. Too many Lebaran visitors.'

'I wanted to hear the sermon,' I said, 'and see who was there.'

'We heard it over the loudspeakers.' He put his fingers in his ears. 'Aris. Try visiting *him* on your way back!'

So I did. What better moment? Sofía had become restless and Mercedes took her home, but I wandered around the little bay of houses opposite Sae's, hoping to find a welcome, and came upon Aris sitting glumly on his own.

'Yes, come in,' he said, unable to prevent me and disdaining the Lebaran greeting. 'The wife's out. Gone to the People's Park in town.'

Aris was small and undernourished, with a black cap and a white shirt that showed thin forearms and large wrists, like those of an adolescent. His sad eyes expected bad things of the world. He faced me with an expression that was defensive and slightly abashed, as though he could not be held responsible for his unfriendliness. I saw him every morning cycling to work in town and pushing his bike back up the hill in the evening – a lonely figure, ill at ease, like a missionary ignored by the natives. But it was he who had led the mosque service; and his name was one of three or four that cropped up in any discussion of religion.

I sat opposite him, a row of plastic jars between us, and tried to think of something friendly to say.

'I heard your sermon this morning, on the subject of forgiveness.'

'I know. I saw you too. It's the Idul Fitri theme.'

Idul Fitri rather than the Javanese *Lebaran.*

'I was wondering why you spoke it in Indonesian rather than Javanese.'

'To mark a difference. The others use Javanese in their sermons; I use the national language. They say the Arabic prayers and quote the Koran but they don't bother to explain. I want to show that what we are saying is relevant to the modern world, to Indonesia. It doesn't matter that some of the old-timers can't follow me. The important thing is the young people.'

He didn't offer me a biscuit from the jars, as was customary, so I put a pack of cigarettes on the table, which he ignored. I felt disliked and wondered what I had done to deserve this – apart from being foreign, white, infidel, and a friend of the headman.

'The old-timers – Mansur, Sapiki – can't give sermons that interest people,' he went on, unafraid to name names. 'They only know how to read from a printed text; they can't develop ideas. They are too repetitive and boring. And their ideas are old-fashioned. It's the younger men like Tompo and Yusuf who are progressing Islam in Bayu: people who know the modern world, not the seminary folk who think the only thing that matters is memorizing prayers.'

I said – thinking of Jumhar and his embattled prayer-house – 'They're very down on custom, on the local way of doing things.' In the traditionalist view, custom complemented Islamic teaching; in the reformist view they were opposed.

'The problem is that people can't tell what's custom and what's Islam. Our sole guide should be the Koran and the Traditions of the Prophet. Anything beyond that is unnecessary, useless. It's *wrong* to burn incense, *wrong* to send prayers to the dead or ask their blessings – only Allah can bless – *wrong* to read out the funeral catechism to someone who is already dead, *wrong* to hold prayer-meals. These things are Hindu-Javanese. Muhammad didn't do them, so why should we?'

I thought of Tompo, the primary-school teacher, the man who wanted telegraph poles rather than trees with branches. Aris listed his points with the same impatience, the same schoolmasterly exasperation. I knew he could cite scriptural backing for his views. But in a mixed village there were other considerations.

'Prayer-meals make good neighbours.'

'They aren't *necessary*. Look at Mandaluko. They don't have prayer-meals or welcoming the Fast and all that nonsense, but they are just as neighbourly as we are. Bayu is miles behind villages like Mandaluko and Paspan. *There* religion is high, custom low. Here it's the opposite. The proof is that if you go to a wedding, nobody turns up to the Islamic ceremony; but they all go to the reception. But which is the more important?'

I said: 'From the point of view of village solidarity, the big celebration.'

'No. It doesn't *do* anything. It's just pleasure.'

'Is that a bad thing?'

Aris shifted awkwardly in his chair, his bony knees showing through his sarong. For the first time, he began to glare at me. His face, narrow across the temples, flushed briefly with anger. But he was confident of his arguments.

'Let me spell it out for you,' he said very slowly. 'There is a simple test. What was right for Muhammad is good enough for me, good enough for any believer. That's all there is to it.'

This was plain speaking. 'Muhammad', not 'the Prophet Muhammad'. 'Right' and 'wrong', not 'better' or 'fitting'. Rules not reverence. Utility. But no questioning of the ultimate grounds or reasons. That was for the mystics.

'What about mysticism, the Sangkan Paran people?' I said, ready to be hung for a sheep as for a lamb.

'Nothing to do with religion. Those people are beyond repair. In a generation they'll be gone.'

We continued in this way for a few minutes longer, facing each other irritably over the biscuit jars. I had not defended a position – that of the traditionalists, the gradualists or the mystics; I had merely put the questions. But I had a strong sense of my irrelevance: in a moment I would be gone, and nothing I could say would matter. Aris would carry on the fight against the unbelievers, the backsliders and compromisers. He had the missionary's security, the tone of righteous complaint. He knew that I could not possibly agree with him (although it was not my place to disagree). Yet he carried on, not wanting to talk to me, but telling me all the same. It was the least Javanese conversation I had had in Bayu.

'Look, there are two views. The mosque official thinks that you bring people to Islam by sugaring the pill. That's what the nine Javanese saints did. That's why he clings to tradition. But all these things mislead. Buyut is *not* the guardian of the village. A tiger-man! Only Allah can watch over us. Praying to spirits is a sure way to hell. If you want to be safe from hell, you must fast and pray five times a day: it's as simple as that. If you want to go to heaven, you have to obey the rules.'

'Do you think a lot about the afterlife?'

He looked at me resentfully and said slowly: 'One should be aware of it, afraid of it.'

I said – this time thinking of Noto astride the prayer-house roof, cigarette in mouth – 'Isn't faith the important thing, and being a decent person? If you believe in God surely you'll be recognized.' It was Noto's phrase.

'Huh! No merit in that! Even the devil believed in God. Belief without worship is worthless.'

I had intended a friendly call, but he had no small talk and the interview – for such it was – ended awkwardly. I put out my hand and said – not meaning it – 'Drop in some time.' At which – not meaning it – he nodded. Hypocrites!

Aris – I had no need to ask – would not be attending the seblang in the neighbouring village of Krajan. The seblang was a sacred dance, a fertility rite at which a nubile girl went into trance and channelled local spirits. In recent years, the authorities had moved it from harvest time to Idul Fitri. The idea was to domesticate it within an Islamic festival. But the effect was to boost the non-Islamic part of the celebrations, underscoring the division of ritual labour: the spirits for this life, Islam for the afterlife. The seblang was a Trojan horse.

On a fine breezy day, we walked with a party of villagers through the fields to Krajan to witness the event. The girl, aged fifteen, had been chosen by the spirits to be a seblang. Two weeks earlier, a medium had voiced their wishes: she could not refuse. And though she would perform every day for a week, doing the steps perfectly, she had 'never learned the dances' and 'would remember nothing'. (Yet she spoke to me afterwards of being led across a golden river to a palace – perhaps the village shrine.)

We joined the crowd that had formed in the middle of the village, in a dry dusty space among red gables and whitewashed bamboo walls. Under a canopy draped with vegetables and sugar cane, a small percussion band – slightly weary and wry, in the way of musicians – had assembled. The girl came out: white socks, sarong, bells on her ankles and wrists, and a fantastic headdress of flowers and weeds. With crinkly ribbons of long grass almost covering her face, she looked like a nature goddess or an enormous rag doll. A stout matron – one of the singers – stood close behind her and pressed three fingers over each eye. The band began to play and the woman rocked the girl's head from side to side. Hidden by her green tresses, the girl held a winnowing tray in her hands. In front of her, a man in black with a Javanese head-tie revolved a censer under her face, muttering spells into the white smoke.

After a minute of this queasy rocking and smoking – the fat woman swaying with the girl – her movements became independent. The doll had come to life. She dropped the tray – in sign of trance – and for the next two hours she danced, as a succession of local spirits animated her youthful body, tossing her head from side to side, jerking her hips, swinging her bare arms. At one point, she mounted a table and threw her red scarf into the crowd. Whichever boy was hit had to climb up and dance with her, shamefaced and proud. Then, goaded by one of the attendants – 'Swing those hips!' – she ambled and swung round the arena, letting the crowd touch her headdress, sometimes stopping to give them a strand or a flower to be put in the ricefields as a charm. Three hours of this before she collapsed, falling prone onto a mat, to be brought slowly round, relieved of her headdress, restored to herself.

Like the dragon in Bayu, the trance dance was a reminder of old Java, mute but expressive, a minor challenge to the official faith but protected by cultural bureaucrats and the majority for whom it was still sacred. Absurdly – or perhaps not: it helped rid the area of pests and evil influences – the military-minded headman of Krajan regarded it as a branch of village security.

This year, among the crowds and the schoolchildren taking notes, there was an Indonesian film crew. With their cameras and furry microphone booms they invaded the arena. The men had long hair. They wore sunglasses and the patch-pocket waistcoats of photographers. The director was a young woman in a black gown and full Islamic headdress – brown and plain beside the seblang's flowery crown. She strode back and forth before the entranced dancer, framing the action, capturing the primitive. She was smiling and confident.

One evening after Lebaran, my social duties over, I strolled up through the village towards the west. It was that comfortable hour before the moist closeness of the night when the air becomes breathable and the earth releases the day's heat into the sky. The soft tarmac road was still warm, crusting at the edges. There was a faint breeze, a restless settling down. Lighted doorways disclosed a relaxed, end-of-party scene: men smoking in sarongs, women laughing, their hair loose. And on the evening air, amid the usual chanting and chatter, the laughter and songs, a different sound: from one of the prayer-houses an impassioned speech.

It was the mosque official's nephew, the young man who had attended university in Malang with Sri. I turned off the road towards the haloed building, intending to enter, when I heard the words, 'slaughtered like sheep, our brothers and sisters in Bosnia'; then 'Christian warriors'. As I stood back in the shadow: 'our obligations as Muslims' and 'jihad'.

Strange words, a new voice. What would his audience think? Unlike Iraq with its totemic leader or Egypt, of the camels and pyramids, Bosnia was nowhere, not even a landmark on the villagers' map. It was merely a name, the faraway victim of a monstrous crime. But what was that to Java? Villagers knew all about neighbourly killings: they would sympathize, but they would forget. Other phrases – 'struggle', 'strife', 'blood sacrifice' – recalled the warcries of the 1960s, things put out of memory. But ordinary words, used in a new way, can have a special force. The young man spoke of the *ummah*, the 'congregation of the faithful'. In Bayu the *ummah* was rarely mentioned. It excluded – and therefore offended

– the non-active majority, the people for whom community meant neighbours or village, not the ties of faith. Even the pious did not speak of the *ummah*. But the speaker meant something more: a worldwide congregation to which Java and Bosnia, remote points on the globe, evidently now belonged. Here was an awakening, or an attempt at awakening, and it wasn't to the diverse faith that brought Muslims together in Mecca. It evoked an international brotherhood under threat from Christendom and the infidel West.

I shuddered and walked on.

9
The Sanctuary

Can't recite, can't pray, can't even read. What I can do is plough and plant, said Ramelan. *My religion is rice. I thank God when my belly is full.*

In rural Java, where almost everyone is Muslim and officially so (all Indonesians are required to subscribe to one of five recognized religions), non-Islamic practices are tolerated as 'custom' but not as 'religion'. Depending on where you draw the line, prayer-meals, grave-visiting, healing rituals and spirit seances pass as local expressions of Islam, traditions with an Islamic sanction, or permissible custom. (To reformists, always clear where they stand, they are simply idolatrous superstitions.) But such practices may not be seen independently as 'Javanese religion', since in law there is no Javanese religion; and the quickest way to get into trouble is to claim this status for your tradition.

In any case, Javanese traditions, including those persisting from the Hindu period, have, over the centuries, become so intertwined with Islam that they can no longer stand alone. They enriched the dominant faith – or mined it from within – Javanizing Islam as Java, in turn, was Islamized. So, to identify oneself as a Muslim or an adherent of Javanism was not necessarily to make a stand or stake an exclusive claim, but rather to emphasize one or other aspect of one's cultural heritage; or even – a step further in relativism – to recognize the superior claims of Islam or Javanism in different situations. Weddings and funerals followed the prescribed Islamic forms; but they were embedded in an older cosmology of place spirits, ancestors and guardian deities. And in the prayer-meal, with its brightly coloured offerings and cosmological symbolism, the rival elements of the Javanese mix had come together, beautifully balanced, in a kind of truce. You could read the symbols several ways – as ancestral, Islamic, or mystical – and all of them, at different levels, could simultaneously be true. The dish of five-coloured porridge – blobs of red, yellow, white and black, oriented to the cardinal points; a multicoloured blob (their combination) in the centre – derived from Hindu-Buddhist cosmology. In the pre-Islamic kingdoms, this was the colour scheme of the four quarters of the realm clustered about a sacred centre, the royal palace, which was the axis of the world. But the four-five porridge also represents the Companions of the Prophet, the four passions of Islamic psychology, and the four spirit siblings that accompany every human being into the world (the Self being the middle blob). Or, again, the layout joins microcosm to macrocosm: the human person as world symbol. For the mystics, four-five symbolizes the human faculties grouped around *rasa* – a Sanskrit word meaning intuitive feeling or consciousness, the seat of divine indwelling life. All this from a plate of porridge.

Given such complexity, it was hard to tease apart the strands and say you were one type of person or another – Muslim or Javanese. The one implied the other. Instead, the strain was towards unity, an embracing – not an erasure – of difference. Village religion wasn't exactly a synthesis, rather a kind of horses-for-courses ecumenism. For weddings and funerals you needed Islam; for earthly blessings the ancestors; for magical protection the village guardian spirit. And just occasionally, as in the prayer-meal, it all came together. There was even a folk etymology – *manungsa* (human) = *manunggal ing rasa* ('united in feeling-consciousness') – proving that sectarian differences were superficial: all human beings were one; all part of something bigger. Only a minority – the Arises and Tompos – saw their religious identity as total. Watchful but unwatched, alert to openings, they posed a threat that was persistent but – for the moment – tolerable. Their time would come.

In Indonesia, where religion is regulated by the state, a question about religious affiliation is, in a broad sense, political, and the safest response is a shrug. But the more thoughtful Javanists –

usually those with some mystical training – have several possibilities. They can universalize Islam, as the old headman Harsono did when he told me that I too was a Muslim because *islam* means 'welfare and prosperity', something all human beings seek. Or they can turn Islam inside out, fitting it to a pantheist scheme. Or, conceding its practical importance, they can make of it a worldly affair, scarcely related to spiritual matters.

Religions are political parties, said Rupo. *Things of noise and crowds and red tape. The broadcasts from the mosque are pure propaganda. You won't find God there.*

Only a few diehards refuse the compromise and yearn for the lost, misunderstood time when Java was still *buda*.* They argue – in private – that Islam is an alien faith, and that what they themselves practise is indeed 'Javanese religion'. 'No Arabic oaths here,' boasted the caretaker of a shrine in another village. 'I won't say them. I'm *buda*.'

We were cheated, said a man in Bakungan. *The Arabs colonized our souls. Then the Dutch encouraged Islam to keep us stupid and exiled those who knew Javanese philosophy. But why should I pray to the ancestors of the Arabs and forget my own?*

Most ordinary folk, deploring controversy and happy enough to acknowledge themselves Muslims (what else?), have quietly made their own pact with orthodoxy. Village Islam offers many ways. But equally they dislike being told what to do.

They say you've got to pray, got to recite, got to fast. If you don't do the prayers, when you die you'll come back to earth. But look at Pak Iyar who died last month, said Jona of her father-in-law. *Never prayed in his life. Did he come back? Of course not. Listen, I couldn't pray if you paid me. But if I come back, so be it. Don't worry about me. I'll plant, I'll shell peanuts again. I'll be fine.*

Ramadan had been a crash course in Religion: how to do it, how

* *Buda* is the word Javanese use for the Indianized pre-Islamic civilization, a blend of native Javanese, Hindu, and Buddhist elements. Most of Java was *buda* until the sixteenth century. Banyuwangi held out until the end of the eighteenth century when Dutch conquest ended the last *buda* realm.

to impose it, how to avoid it. For a whole month it was literally in the air. Yet there were other kinds of Islam – *our Islam*, in the carpenter's phrase – that did not conform to the official variety. This popular Islam was propagated in the fields, in the cemetery, in the home and at the village shrine. It had more to do with worldly blessings, good harvests and domestic peace than religious merit and obligation. It would usually include a brief Arabic prayer – the opening words of the Koran or the 'I seek refuge' formula; but the important thing was the ritual gesture: the gift to the ancestors or vow to the guardian spirit. It could not be taught, much less enforced; indeed, it couldn't be formulated as a creed or a code for it was simply the way things were done, an aspect of everyday life. Yet it had its own sanctions. Neglect of the ancestors, the village guardian and the rice spirits – not to mention one's neighbours and kin – could bring illness and misfortune, even death.

Did I tell you about when Sunar put a spell on me? said the headman's mother. *He came to the house one day and asked for rice seed – he was going to plant. I said we'd run out. I was sick for a day and a night; could hardly bear anyone to touch my head; then I went all floppy and weak. My husband wore his hands out massaging me. Took me to God knows how many healers, but nothing worked. Finally, Ran* [the local healer] *went to consult Buyut and divined the cause. Old Sunar had slipped a piece of paper under my sleeping mat with words written on it. We found it and Ran said it was a hex. Another time I was possessed by the ghost of my own father. I'd given permission for his house to be dismantled so we could sell the plot. I fell ill and he began speaking through me!* 'It's my house. No one told me about it. I'm angry!' *My husband heard – said the voice was just like Pa's – and that night he held a prayer-meal and sent blessings to the departed.*

After Lebaran, I went on a coach trip to the Surabaya zoo and the saints' graves, said Ramelan the ploughman. *On the way, we stopped for a drink and I took a leak in a field. Suddenly I heard this high-pitched scream, like when you step on a cat, and realized I had pissed in a haunted spot. I fell down, frothing, and they had to drag me to the bus. For three days I was shivering and out of my mind. It was Buyut who saved me. Pak Ran carried me to the shrine and blew incense over me. That's when I woke up.*

I wanted to meet Buyut, this hidden prelate around whom so much of village life eccentrically revolved. I had heard so much about him, witnessed his effect on the villagers, seen their fear. At the dawn climax to the dragon show, I had run from his avatar, stumbling with the crowd, not sure what I was fleeing. That small, urgent, thrusting head, menacing but somehow vulnerable, a swimmer bobbing in rough waters: was it a tiger, or a man in a mask pretending to be a tiger, or a man who thought that he was a tiger? And then the aftermath, the bruised and dazed figure slumped on the ground, not yet himself. Who was he? Unmasked, drooling the leaves he had gobbled, he looked like a child who had been whirled about and set dizzily down. He was Mul, of course, the boy who had seen his father chopped up like a fish; but he was also the villager whom the spirit had chosen, the man-tiger who rode the surge of ancestral power. It was an odd conjunction of political weakness and supernatural force. But that, I had decided, was the real point of the drama: for Buyut's world – his show and his shrine – was also a sanctuary. This sanctuary was what the dragon men, dispossessed of everything else, had managed to hold on to. And while the drama defiantly signified nothing ('It's about man's cruelty to woman,' the headman had gamely suggested), its cast of rejects had lent it a special significance, like *Godot* played in a prison camp. Amateurish and clunky, the play was a showcase of supernatural power – an outing for the deity and his pet monster; a reminder that its handlers could not be ignored.

The guardian spirit was feared but also revered. He belonged to the night, to the powers of darkness, but he was on 'our' side, the bright daylight world of men and women. So it was right that the dragon men, victims of a great crime – a national crime – should be his chosen crew, the unlikely guardians of the village. They had outlasted the purges of the sixties and the 'mysterious killings' of the eighties. During those dark times, sorcerers and political radicals alike were demonized as 'figures of the left' (the *sinister*, one might say). It was Buyut's triumph that somehow Bayu's rebels had endured and had even, through the powers of the weak, attained a certain grey eminence, like the shaggy beast himself.

Buyut's gentler side was on display in the prayer-meals held at his shrine. During the Fast, I had attended one such event. It took place on a Thursday afternoon, at his regular surgery, when villagers waited outside his wicker shrine to present their respects and request his help. I had gone there with the headman, who had troubles on the domestic and political fronts. Pak Lurah lived next door to one of Bayu's six prayer-houses, a newish concrete building different in style and tone from Jumhar's Light of Paradise down the road. During the week, he had been attacked in dawn broadcasts by Mustari, one of the regular prayer-leaders, who had declared through the megaphone, *People who don't pray aren't fit to be leaders*. 'That was for me,' said Pak Lurah. 'I hate the man, but what can I do? If he names me, I'll charge him with criticizing a government official, but he wouldn't dare. Those megaphones –'

He made a snipping gesture with his fingers and grinned at me conspiratorially. Perhaps he needed Buyut's help: a tiger on his side.

I was invited to the meal because I happened to be around: such things were never announced. 'I'm going to Buyut's,' Pak Lurah had said. 'Want to come?' It was more like a jaunt than the usual slightly solemn occasion; almost spontaneous, though of course he would need a specialist and a handful of 'witnesses'. We first collected the diviner Ran, and walked the back way across the fields, meeting Bu Lurah and Mercedes with Sofía as they came up via the old cemetery. The carpenter Noto and Jan, the headman's son-in-law, would bring kettles and leaf parcels of food. Altogether there were nine of us.

The reason for this spirit picnic was not made clear. People held prayer-meals at the shrine to obtain Buyut's blessing before weddings and circumcisions, and afterwards to give him thanks. (Muslim rites of passage were framed by something less than

Islamic, or at any rate local and Javanese.) But Pak Lurah expressed no such intention. I had a sense that there had been a domestic row and reconciliation. He had a cut over his brow which he kept fingering in a wounded way but would not explain. Bu Lurah was breezy and triumphant, artificially cheerful. But as we made our way there over the stubbly fields, Pak Lurah mumbled something about having 'got over a cough' and wanting to thank Buyut.

'You probably think it's *primitif*, don't you?' he said, cheering up; 'putting chickens' claws on Buyut's headstone, speaking to the spirits.'

'Yes, quite savage really. Why can't you be modern like Aris? Prayer-meals aren't in the Koran.'

'I knew you'd say something like that,' he cackled.

The diviner, grimly forging ahead, looked back with a puzzled expression. We had taken a roundabout route to avoid the straggle of houses at the back of Dusun – Ran's devout neighbourhood. But our baskets of food, and the aroma of cooked chicken and fried coconut, gave us away. For a headman it was undiplomatic to be seen heading for a daytime feast during the Fast. And so when we passed the mosque treasurer at work in his fields, the old man took full advantage of Pak Lurah's discomfort. He leaned on his hoe, pushed back his brown felt hat and said in a knowing voice: 'Where are you going?'

It was the standard greeting.

'Pak Andrew's having a prayer-meal at Buyut's – for the baby. Next week is her Descent to Earth. I'm just observing.'

The man nodded sceptically. But it could have been true. Sofía was well over six months and overdue her infant graduation. At her Descent, she would officially touch down and be introduced to Mother Earth.

We reached a clump of palm trees on the village boundary and entered the picket-fence compound. The men began sweeping the dusty yard with twig brooms. Bu Lurah and Mercedes spread out banana leaves for the food. Sofía was playing with a neighbour's boy, feeding him a sweet. Over the fields floated a strident, amplified voice, its harshness muffled by the wind. The village felt far away.

In dappled light, under a sparse tree, stood a thatched hut about the size of a shed in an English suburban garden, and around it, little groups of petitioners waiting their turn in the shade. In purple sarong and black cap, Ran knelt at the door and murmured a prayer. I watched through the loose wicker weave as he entered and bent to embrace the headstones that marked the resting places of the guardian spirit and his consort. From a fold in his sarong he produced betel nut and clove cigarettes which he placed on the stones; between them he strewed pink flowers.

'Come!'

The headman ducked inside and there was a brief whispered discussion as they crouched in the fretted half-light. Then, to the unseen audience, Ran conveyed the headman's request – for health, prosperity, and a harmonious household. While he spoke, he burned the incense that would carry the wishes and the scent of the food upwards to the spirit.

I picked up one side of a telephone conversation: 'Yes, Buyut. It will be done . . . It's all here, Buyut . . . No, I didn't.'

More than prayers, then: answers; but not for my ears.

Flowers and incense, murmured formulae – in Javanese not Arabic; then they withdrew, shuffling backwards, leaving a chicken's head and claws on the stones.

While we ate, another caretaker – the dragon keeper – ministered to petitioners inside the shrine. A woman was complaining loudly about the boils on her belly and her husband's spendthrift ways. Outside the shrine, he smiled affably and gestured to us politely to enjoy our meal. In Bayu there were no secrets – at least with a wife like that. Pak Lurah was lucky.

Did I tell you about how we got hitched? asked Pak Lurah one day. *I'd had my eye on her for some time. In those days she was the pick of Dusun: long black hair, slim and graceful. One night, at a gandrung show, I spotted her in the crowd. I bought a bag of oranges and tied it with a handkerchief. An old widow was the go-*

between – passed her the oranges. She smiled at me, and we slipped out and walked home together. I didn't know we were being followed by Basri, her betrothed. On the way, I told her that Basri had a mistress, a widow in another village. I slandered him, see, so she'd be happy to leave him! When we arrived at the house, her parents were asleep at the back so we had to be very quiet; we just sat there quietly, hand in hand. There was a knock at the door. I dived under the bench and she went to answer it. Basri said: 'Where is he?' 'Gone home,' she replied. Basri made a commotion and the old folks woke up. I managed to get away unseen. A week later I kidnapped her. Her parents had to agree and the wedding was performed on the spot. For the next four months I slept in her house, on my own in the front while she slept with her parents. We didn't sleep together until after the full ceremony, which they delayed until she'd finished high school.

We chatted and enjoyed the fresh air, the food, and the indiscreet requests. ('Ah! Was she *your* cousin or his?') It was like having a Catholic confession box installed in an English teashop. Sighs and complaints within the shrine; raised eyebrows and giggles without. In the mild, inconsequential cheer, weighty matters dissolved, sins were forgiven. Distance from the mosque – half a mile, no more – allowed a relaxation of the usual codes, a decorous informality. A fresh-air faith. This was the first prayer-meal I had attended where women and men (and children) were seated together. Bu Lurah, plump and smiling, knelt beside the rice mound, doling it out like Mother, or turning to slap a neighbour at some teasing remark. Noto, his hat tipped back, gestured with a chicken leg: 'You know, Bu Sofía [as he called Mercedes], I'm sure Sofía will pick an onion at her Descent to Earth. She'll be a farmer, I predict. That's why she's so at home here. Won't want to go back to Inggris.' Jan, who had abandoned the fast after breaking a tooth, tore off a great hunk of meat with un-Javanese glee and spoke through a crammed mouth. 'Get her to marry here, Bu. Drus's son would do nicely. Then you could have Drus as your in-law! Ha, ha!'

Pak Lurah leaned across and whispered to me: 'Have you seen

Siti today? Beaten black and blue by that brute. We heard the shrieks in the night.'

'Why doesn't her brother protect her?'

Siti's brother – the husband of Misti – lived opposite her. He was a tough character and no friend of the pious Drus.

'He would but Siti won't let him. Pride.'

Bu Lurah looked across reproachfully and the headman shut up.

We cleared away; then, with a parting nod to Buyut, filed home.

It was all pretty tame; nice work for a guardian spirit, I thought, but hardly the thing for a were-tiger. I couldn't connect the violent dawn eruptions with the quiet procession of petitioners, the night terrors with the day job. Back home, I told Wan of my concerns. 'If you want to *talk* to Buyut rather than just present a request,' he said, 'you have to do it through the medium. You can find out who is bewitching you or put a jinx on your business. But it has to be in the dead of night. Other people can't hear these things. They shouldn't even know you have gone.'

'I don't think anyone is bewitching me.'

'You never know,' he said vaguely in his slightly muffled voice. 'But I have some questions of my own. And I'm going as soon as I can fix a date. Come along.'

Actually, he hadn't said 'the medium'; he had said 'Uncle Pin' – one of the caretakers. You didn't specify the occupation: that would be too explicit; just as Ran was never openly referred to as a magician. In Muslim Java, one preferred to speak of 'old folk' or 'wise men', avoiding the challenge to orthodoxy; or one simply named them. Pin (short for Arifin) was far from wise, but his calling qualified him to impersonate the tiger-oracle to ordinary villagers; and his nocturnal performances were generally convincing enough to overcome their doubts. About ten years ago, he had fallen ill and for a week lay 'between life and death, stiff as a board, eyeballs bulging'. In the classic manner of a shaman, the illness was interpreted as soul abduction. It served as his initiation. The deal with Buyut was that Pin's soul would be restored to his body, and the whole man restored to health, if he agreed to minister at the shrine. Buyut would 'borrow my body and speak through me'. But – unlike a shaman – Pin himself would not become a master of spirits, merely their passive vehicle. That was why he had to have his assistant, Poniman, on hand to burn incense and put the questions. Poniman was like the girl who is sawn in half every night by the conjuror, who marks the cards and substitutes the white rabbit. He knew the score. But he treated Pin with a certain awe, a respect for his office.

The day before our interview with Buyut, we called on Pin to make arrangements. He was sitting on a bench at the back of his wooden house smoking a corn-leaf cheroot, his wide splayed feet – the soles whitish with dried mud – dangling above the ground. In the late afternoon sun, the yard was half in shadow.

Pin's land, eroded by rain and sun, sloped down to a gully that was slippery with trashed leaves and coconut spathes. At the bottom of the gully was a stream. On one side of the yard, abutting the next house, a chicken coop was loud with black bantams and ornamental hens. Around the edges Pin grew herbs, beans and chillies. A bicycle, upside down and missing a wheel, stood under the eaves. You had an impression of industry. But the house was quiet, without children.

As we arrived, Pin's wife – pinch-mouthed and put-upon – came up from the stream with a bucket of water and a basket of laundry on her head. Pin took us inside and closed the door, then went through to the front door and closed that too. He was a small man with an alert, nervous face, and a surprisingly deep voice, low and resonant but with a sharp edge, like that of an Irish priest. With his wife suspiciously hovering in the background – 'she has forbidden me to introduce you to Buyut in case I make a spectacle of myself' – we whiled away the time in magician small-talk: the latest witchings and unexplained deaths; how to distinguish a poisoning from an evil charm; the 'colour' of a sorcerer's invisible missile (green at the moment of entry). Pin began to boast about his week in the spirit world – how he had been taken to Mecca (one of the few foreign places in the ordinary villager's cosmology) and had met there his deceased father wandering about in pilgrim's robes. Buyut himself had taken Pin's father to Mecca and made him a haji; the local godling conferring the Islamic distinction.

'I was lowered down near the Grand Mosque, dressed all in white like a pilgrim. That's when I ran into Pa. I was so happy to see him. But he said not a word; just nodded in greeting. When I tried to address him he got angry. Buyut told me: *Your father is now a spirit; you are still a person. The spiritual and the earthly cannot mix. Only I can speak for you.* I was there a week; and I've been back twice and confirmed what the hajis report. I've seen the black stone, and washed in water from the Zamzam well. I stood where they throw stones at the devil.'

In the usual Javanese manner, he included directions – what was northeast of what; and later I checked on a plan of Mecca in a pilgrims' handbook and found them to be roughly correct – or as accurate as one could hope for on a spirit flight. Clearly, he had done his homework. But when I questioned him about seances at the shrine and what was revealed there he disclaimed all knowledge. 'I'm in a state of forgetfulness; I'm not there. I only know what Poniman tells me afterwards.'

Perhaps this was politic. When you were spilling the beans on fellow villagers, it was important not to be accountable.

After the Mecca trip, Buyut had taken Pin on a tour of the power points of Banyuwangi – the coastal crags and volcanic peaks, the surf-gnawed southern cape, the sunken shipwrecks. He had met the resident spirits of each sacred spot.

As if he had spread before us the proof, Pin said, 'I know it all yet I've never been there in person.'

I nodded, impressed, and he added sharply: 'Wan doesn't believe!'

'*I do*. I believe.'

I was sure that Wan didn't believe: he was along for the lark. Soft and sleek, squinting through his smoke, Wan was a sceptic who, in a famous phrase, lacked the courage of his lack of convictions. And yet others who were far from being simple peasants (a rare enough species in any case) had 'gone through Pin'. Among his clients were the district army commander, a Chinese merchant, a mystical policeman and a Catholic schoolmaster. Through Pin, the mosque official had asked Buyut about the origin of various Bayu rituals: which bits were Islamic and which mere custom. He had questioned Buyut on hats – the origin of the head-tie and the Javanese turban. Were they worn in the old days in Arabia?

After his spirit flight Pin had returned with the gift of divination. He had been able to supply the authorities with the names of sorcerers in the district.

'Were they arrested?' I asked. Sorcery was a criminal offence.

'No, but after I named them they died in mysterious ways. Some fell from trees or dropped dead in the fields. One was found in a ditch covered with ants.'

I felt he wanted to claim credit for these 'bad deaths'; but he raised his hands in innocence and said: 'I only named them.'

When his wife had disappeared, Pin gave us the instructions. We were to meet at the shrine at midnight, bringing clove cigarettes and betel nut. Pin would provide the incense – not the usual benzoin used in prayer-meals, but a white resin exuded by a tree that used to stand next to the shrine. The tree had long gone, but the caretakers always found a nugget of resin under one of the headstones.

Around midnight, Wan and I crept out of our house and walked in pitch darkness – no torches – through the tree-roofed cemetery, across the stream and up the hill towards the hamlet of Sumbersari. The village was silent: more than that, exhausted. After the clamour of the Fast and the rebounding jollity of Lebaran, farmers had gone back to being farmers. Days were for work, nights for sleep. Even Drus's dog, curled up in front of his shuttered store, was asleep.

We passed through the hamlet and out into harvested fields – not long ago flooded rice paddies, now dry and crunchy underfoot. As always, at night one felt the intense peacefulness and security of the village, the little close-packed houses, the sense of people all around you asleep, the enfolding darkness like a warm embrace. And this utter calm – so different from Nias, with its lawless trails and deep wilderness – extended into the countryside, the sleeping fields and gently swaying palms, the isolated fieldhuts where people kept vigil over their fruit trees. It was hard to remember that, in Java, when bad things happened, they happened at night.

Out in the open, under a big sky, the steady pulse of insect noise was much louder. The moon was new but there was enough starlight to keep on the track and find your way. As we neared the shrine, Wan gripped my arm and pointed to a black object moving very fast from the west. It could have been a dog running – light on its feet; no sound. It moved swiftly along the edge of the field, then changed direction and made straight for us. Suddenly Pin came into view – it was he – hopped over the fence and vanished into the shrine.

'Has he seen us?'

'Of course. What do you want him to say?'

From within we heard fumbling sounds, then the crackling of incense and Pin's soft crooning. *Peace be upon you! Pin is here!*

I felt a hand on my shoulder and turned, with a start, to hear Poniman: 'Approach. Don't speak to him until you're called.'

We crouched beside the open door. Through the white smoke that leaked out and hung in our faces I could dimly make out Pin. He was hunched over the headstones, rocking back and forth. I had set up a microphone just under one wall but had brought no camera. At the four dragon performances I had witnessed, each time I had shot the dawn break-out, the tiger-trance, either the camera had failed or the picture had fogged, showing a ghostly white spot where Ran was wrestling on the ground with Mul. (*What did you expect?* they said.) In one picture I had caught the greenish mask ploughing through the crowd. What my camera couldn't capture was the terrible urgency, the collective panic, the life in the paste-board thing.

Buyut did not like to be photographed but perhaps I could catch his voice. How different would it be from Pin's tobacco baritone? If there were more than one spirit, how would I distinguish them? The procedures of invocation and handover were important: clues to the cultural logic. But the first sound we heard was a soft thumping, followed by grunting and buffeting as Pin tumbled about inside the shrine.

Wan murmured to me, 'Possessed.'

In four and a half years of fieldwork in Indonesia I saw many trances ('spirit possession' was an *interpretation* of trance) but – like other onlookers – could rarely be sure whether they were genuine or faked. Fakery, taken to the limit, becomes real, like the prisoner who, feigning madness, goes mad. In a famous essay, Lévi-Strauss tells how an Amerindian apprentice shaman is disillusioned when he learns the tricks of curing, but the efficacy of his magic – his success at curing – finally compels him to believe in his own powers. In spite of himself, he becomes a great curer. In any society, there is a distinction between an acceptance of the worldview within which spirits (or gods or saints) communicate with humans and a measured belief in the abilities and honesty of an individual practitioner. Pin might be faking, but almost no one doubted the existence of Buyut and his capacity to intervene in village affairs. Not even Pin.

Whether he was faking the gruff voice that broke suddenly from his body or it came to him unbidden was something clients might argue about. I wasn't convinced, and I sensed that neither was Wan. The performance lacked what the Polish anthropologist Malinowski called the 'co-efficient of weirdness', the authenticating frisson that distinguished the really unreal from the put-up job. There was too much back-story and self-justification; the spirit voices were too similar; the handovers too awkward. What Pin needed, rather than his dogged apprentice, was a good radio producer, a man who could conduct in the dark. And yet if there was one thing weirder than a man in a remote hut in the middle of the night incarnating a tiger spirit, it was a man *pretending* to do this. At the very thought, the hairs stood obediently on the back of my neck.

The rumblings stopped and Pin – or rather Buyut – began to speak, shortly to be interrupted by Lundoyo, another were-tiger and star of the barong, the dragon play.*

BUYUT: Come, Lundoyo! This is the path from the grassfields: leave the animals grazing – the forest recedes – the mountain slopes away. I shall borrow your body, Pin. I'm weary from the road. I have not eaten [a request for incense]. What do you ask of Buyut? Ask and it shall be told. Come Poniman, ask them what they want.
PONIMAN: They ask about the barong, Buyut. Where is it from?
BUYUT: From the time of kings, to order the people, not to oppress them. There is no king in the barong, I will not permit it. *Barong* is from *rong-rong* [holes, orifices], regulating the body, so that male and female are different, so that man marries woman. *That* is its origin.
PONIMAN: I beg you to tell them, Buyut, where you come from.
BUYUT: Buyut comes from Tegal Magelang [in central Java]. He fled in the time of the wicked kings. He would not be ruled by others. He hates tyrants. Ask more! What is your guest's concern?
WAN [entering the shrine]: Peace be upon you, Buyut. I have a request: Where in Bayu can I find a wife, a woman who is patient and kind, pretty and a virgin?
LUNDOYO [interrupting; in a lower key]: Eh! Ask, ask again! That's clever. Your elder brother Lundoyo shall answer. I too have come to the village for a wife. Eh! This is not Pin: this is Lundoyooooo!
WAN: Indeed, Sir.
LUNDOYO: You want a wife, but you are afraid of your mother.
WAN: That I am, Sir.
LUNDOYO: She says, 'Wan, don't marry, don't leave me!' But I will show you how.
Look northwest of here. Who takes your fancy?
WAN: I cannot find anyone suitable. I want a wife who is patient,

*The spirits speak Low Javanese in the standard form of the language, rather than in the Osing dialect Pin himself normally speaks. Poniman and Wan address the spirits politely in High Javanese.

kind, pretty –

BUYUT: Then govern your mother! Tell her, 'I won't abandon you, Ma.' Ask help of Buyut.

WAN: I will, Sir.

LUNDOYO: This is Lundoyo. Listen, you are being thwarted. That's why you have no success with women. Your cock is shrivelled by your rival. You will get nothing until you deal with Aryo. Find the charm buried in a little packet in front of your house.

BUYUT: Ask more!

WAN: My work doesn't prosper. What can I do?

BUYUT: Beware Aryo! He has put a spell on you. Go to his cattle shed. Take soil from it. Put it in water and drink it. Who drinks that soil drinks the placenta of Aryo. A great evil will befall him if he persists.

WAN: But what can I do? I want to learn carpentry. What would suit me?

BUYUT: Forget carpentry. (Ooh! I am hungry.) Bayu has too many carpenters. Poniman, have you no questions?

PONIMAN: What happened with my application to be a civil servant, Buyut? It's already six months and there's been no reply.

BUYUT: It will fail until you give up gambling and whoring. (Ah! My joints! This cold weather.) Don't think I haven't seen you in Krajan! I've followed you and spied on you. You're destroying yourself. Do you admit it?

PONIMAN: I confess, Buyut.

BUYUT: Give it up! Pin can't have a frivolous apprentice . . .

And so it went on for the next hour: homely advice mixed with dubious local history; whiffs of supernatural danger; a shuffling among the spirits; noises off. All pretty much what Pin himself might have said. I was disappointed. There was no poetry, no peek at the spirit world. (*But what did you expect?*) Instead, a mundane dialogue; a counterpart to the official creed, but more worldly and immediate. Perhaps that was the point. If you could eavesdrop on ordinary silent prayer you would probably hear similar requests – for a job, a partner, a cure, the destruction of an enemy. Yet for such everyday concerns the mosque had no answers. That was Buyut's advantage. Indeed, Buyut knew just what you wanted.

PONIMAN: Have you something for Andrew?
BUYUT: His daughter hates loud noise. She cries in the night. But she will be a queen one day in her country – that far land where everything is expensive. Stay here, Andrew; you're at home. Buyut will watch over you. Don't talk to Ran. I don't like him. He tells lies . . . And Wan, drink that soil!
WAN [obsequious, mumbling]: If there's anything I've done to offend you, I beg your pardon.
BUYUT: Humans are prone to error; all are sinners. But you won't die at the hands of men. If your sins only amount to that, well it's not much. You have nothing to fear.

With these encouraging words, Buyut signed off.

Poniman sent us away – Pin's revival a secret matter – and we headed back across the fields in starlight, each lost in thought. As we approached the house, bulking black in the dark, Wan said to me:

'That thing Buyut said about Aryo. It's true. I *was* his rival, and I *did* have problems with women. How could Pin know it?'

He quietly fastened the door and put a finger to his lips. 'Don't tell Ma.'

Next day, Wan stopped by Aryo's compound and dropped something near his cattle shed. Bending over, he took a handful of soil and put it in his pocket.

He didn't find a wife – at least not during our stay. But, against the advice, he took up carpentry and began to make a fair living at it. Noto, son of a were-tiger, was his teacher.

One shouldn't believe everything Buyut said.

10
Genesis

The headman's daughter was pregnant with her first child – seven months pregnant, to be exact – and the family was in a spin. Dewi had already had one miscarriage, but at seven months a foetus was complete and could survive if steamed over the rice cooker. That was the theory: I never came across one of these premature, half-cooked children. But leaving nothing to chance, Dewi's parents were planning a big celebration and a protective ritual, the Seven-months Prayer-meal. Unusual in the long history of the Javanese peasantry, the baby would be born into privilege. At twenty-two, Dewi was already well off, with a big house of her own (built by the headman) and four or five hectares of prime rice land. The father-to-be, Jan, was the son of Bayu's third biggest landowner, a man with a rice mill and fifteen hectares of land to his name. Only child of an only child of an only child, the baby would be rich.

Just fifty yards up the road another family was preparing for a similar event. The expectant father, Joko, was a messenger in the district office; in the evenings he sold lottery tickets from a hatch at the side of his house. He owned a green uniform and a bicycle. His wife, Eti, who came from another village, taught in secondary school. They had a daughter of six, a beautiful, graceful creature who, with fan, gold sash and ankle bells, was already an accomplished dancer. (Eti, slow and matronly, had never danced: dancing was Joko's passion. He had performed in national competitions and was a devoted instructor, Noto's likely successor.)

The two families – Joko's half a generation older than Dewi's; his grandparents long since dead – had moved apart economically, as had many households since the green revolution of the 1970s when, quite suddenly, people who had grown up in similar circumstances found themselves belonging to different classes. At least that was how it looked from the outside. The bigger harvests, now three per year – the soil, chemically cleansed and replenished, was inexhaustible – meant that minor differences in landholding and accidents of family size and fortune multiplied differences in wealth. The more you owned, the more you cultivated (or farmed out to sharecroppers) and the more land you could buy. The cycle of feasting and prayer-meals told people they were still the same – that was the point. But their varying scale and elaboration said otherwise. At Dewi's wedding, the headman had received four tonnes of rice in donations from over two thousand guests.

But there was more to it than a simple economic calculus. 'I am on a downward path,' said Purwadi, Joko's father, in Lear-like tones. 'My grandfather belonged to the gentry – he had a title – and was a courtier in Solo. The Dutch sent him into exile. He came to Banyuwangi and founded the village of Tamansari where I was headman: yes, only a headman. And take my wife: I'm not saying I made a mistake in marrying her, but she's on the same steep descent; her family has been losing land for generations. If you marry someone who's going up it can correct your own descent. But I sense our decline is bottoming out. Neither of my children [he meant Joko and Eti] works hard but they are doing all right. Perhaps it's the spirit of my ancestor coming back. The wheel of reincarnation.'

I was glad he saw things that way. I never called on him without feeling pinched and a little dismayed at his poverty. He deserved better.

Whereas the headman and Dewi occupied spacious adjacent houses, bright concrete buildings (though still preferring their homely bamboo kitchens), Joko's family lived together in an old-fashioned, dirt-floor bamboo house. The front room or parlour, which was also the bedroom for the middle generation, was no more than twelve feet wide, too small for the usual sprawling bed-platform on which casual callers could sit. When you visited, you were literally fitted into place and somebody usually had to step out to make room for you. It was like living in a caravan: within its confines any movement required a corresponding shift elsewhere, a constant awareness of mutual position, of height and width. The family, especially the men – slim and precise, rather stern, where their women were plump and kindly – had cultivated a physical neatness and restraint like that of accountants or solicitors. Father and son would sit straight-backed with their hands on their knees, smoking frugally, taking up as little room as possible. They spoke in turn as if words, too, took up space. And their sentences were matched, similar in diction, *fitting*. This was something I had noticed in other houses where adult men lived together. Between a father and son there was supposed to be a certain reserve, a strict inequality – they were never seated together at feasts; the son never contradicted or interrupted the father. But restraint and consideration made cohabitation possible.

There was an obvious analogy: the tiny, delicate rice terraces that moulded the hills in tiers and looked from above like the scales of a fish. Planted right up to their scalloped edges, leaving only the narrowest of walls to walk along, they showed that many could live from little. Properly ordered, space could be infinitely subdivided.

The new arrival would enlarge the family, bringing new demands on resources, practical problems. Mother and infant would sleep together, the parents separated for the next one or two years. The grandparents would move further back into the kitchen, the old retreating before the young. For Purwadi, however, birth was less a practical matter than a conundrum, an insoluble mystery. Whereas the headman spoke of heirs and land, Purwadi spoke of Male and Female, of Life, of existence. He was a mystic.

'So tell me, Andrew,' he began one day, 'how is it – according to the English way of seeing things – that we exist, that there is anything at all? Where, indeed, does the baby come from?' He laughed at the phrase and went on, not waiting for an answer: 'Don't tell me from the father's sperm and the mother's blood – that's obvious. What is in those ingredients? When you made Sofía, did you wonder how all those marvellous things came together to make a human being? From where: the legs, the hair, the voice? Who gave her that smile? Not you or Mercedes. You were only the bearers. All those things were contained in a single drop. That's the mystery: the tree, the leaves, the fruit are concealed in the seed; the tree dies and sprouts again and somehow it's still the same thing, over and over. Tree and leaf. You and Sofía. See, it's more than sperm and blood: there's what exists between a man and a woman, the feeling of one pitted against the feeling of the other. Without that contest, that spark of desire, nothing would come of it. The Almighty is within that feeling. God is in *rasa*.'*

Joko placed before me a plate of fried bananas and a glass of coffee. 'Drink up!'

'That's why we say of life, *It comes without origin; it leaves without destination*,' said his father. 'Remember you were asking me what the name of our association, Sangkan Paran, means. That's it: the origin and destination of Being.'

He bit into a banana. 'Take this fruit. Where is its sweetness? In the banana, you'll say. Or in me perhaps. But it lasts only in the moment of eating; it disappears with the banana. Without me it would have no taste, no sweetness: I could not really say it exists. In the same way, Man and Life – what the Muslims call Allah – exist together or not at all. Without humanity no God; without God no humanity. Here, eat!'

I ate – and swallowed, unasked, my questions about land holdings and class.

The headman's preparations for the Seven-months Prayer-meal were in full swing. All day long, women arrived with baskets of rice and eggs, sugar and vegetables. They stayed and stirred; they wrapped, chopped, and washed; they talked a great deal. Mainly they ate. Bu Lurah, brisk and sprightly, served them coffee and glutinous sweets fresh off the production line. Their children, faces smeared brown with goo, sat glumly on the ground, drugged with sugar, or hung limply from their mothers' slings, chewing abstractedly in a glucosal

*Rasa, a Sanskrit-derived word, means 'feeling', 'sense', 'consciousness'.

stupor. As soon as they emitted a sound they were crammed with more sweets. They were the quietest, best behaved children I had ever seen.

With so much activity and staff turnover, each section – sweets, vegetables, sauces, meat, rice – needed its own overseer. Panji, Bu Lurah's girlhood friend – a transvestite – was in charge of sweets. He was back from a spell in Bali where he ran a food stall for construction workers, Javanese men building hotels for tourists.

'The things those tourists do! Australian women *pay* Balinese boys to sleep with them.'

'Why? Don't they have husbands?'

'The husbands are drunk.'

'Ooh, I don't believe you!'

'And they have massages on the beach, in full view; get their hair braided. It takes half an hour and they pay fifteen thousand rupiah – three times what our men earn on the building site in a day.'

'It can't be true.'

'Honest, it is, I swear.'

Misti took charge of the rice, which basked in conical steamers over clay ovens (and not a foetus in sight). Over two days she and her fellow section-chiefs fed the workers, the donors, and the forty or fifty men who came in the evening to make cash contributions. That was all apart from the actual feast. The sacred dishes of the prayer-meal – each dedicated to some spirit or prophet – required special care and were the responsibility of an elderly woman, someone past sexual activity and therefore 'pure'. In everything concerning the ancestors, purity and wholeness were the principles. The festive chicken had to be a white unmated male, with flawless beak and wattles. The firewood over which the chicken was cooked had to be washed and dried before use. Even the flowers sprinkled on the pillow-altar should not have been smelt. *The spirits are pure and accept only what is pure. If someone lends you a shirt, would you return it to them dirty?*

Pregnancy and birth were not female-only affairs. As attentive to his wife's cravings for green mango or bitter papaya leaves as any anxious Western father, the Javanese husband goes a step further in devotion. Hedged by taboos and sympathetic symbols, he avoids anger, refrains from slaughtering animals (violence could rebound on the child), never sits in the doorway (blocking an exit) or wears a sling (it might twist the umbilical cord), and tries not to curse or swear – something Javanese villagers rarely do in any case. Some men experience labour pains.

On the afternoon of the feast, husband and wife make the ultimate switch. It happens quickly and furtively and is not for public entertainment, though it cannot be omitted. I saw it done only twice and managed one blurry photo. But how often do you get to witness the moment of conception?

At the back of Bu Lurah's house – away from the bustling kitchens – the headman had removed three slats from the bamboo bench. On the ground was a winnowing tray containing seven cones of white porridge wrapped in jackfruit leaves. Jan and Dewi rushed through the house laughing, half a dozen women and children after them. Then Jan squatted beside the bench and held his cupped hands beneath it while Dewi picked up the cones one by one and squirted their contents through the gaps in the bench. Each gobbet Jan caught and let fall to the ground. Someone said, in blessing: 'May the birth be as easy as the conception!' So easy, indeed, that male and female roles were reversed, the woman fertilizing the man's womb-hands. (When I told a friend in Banyuwangi about this he winced: such things should not happen, nor be spoken of.)

And then a further regression. The couple carried a plate of cooked rice into the yard and force-fed one another, pawing it into mouths, plastering the rice roughly onto each other's faces, spluttering and laughing. What did it mean? Mutual feeding is part of the wedding ritual ('sharing'); to be fed is to be childlike and dependent. (Sick children of twelve are spoon-fed by their mothers.) But the yelps and screams of the onlookers said something more: it was a celebration of joy. Life as laughter.

Every man should assist when his wife gives birth, said Untung gravely. *When you've seen what she goes through you can never bring yourself to hit her. We lost our firstborn – twins – straight after the Seven-months Prayer-meal. My wife had been in labour for two days before we fetched Pak Ran for help. He gave me something – it was like a nutmeg seed – and told me to put it in a glass of water and cover it. When it bloomed, the child would be born. We were hours in the kitchen with the midwife and forgot all about the seed. When the twins were born dead I suddenly remembered and ran into the house to look. I took off the cover and the seed had bloomed.*

Of course birth takes a long time, said Bu Mari. *Only a man could doubt it. Have you ever known a woman be ready to go out in only five minutes? The make-up, the hair, the finery. A long labour means the baby is getting ready to face the world. Of course it takes time.*

Two months later, I was again sitting with Purwadi in that tight hot room beside the road, hearing him lecture on human ontogeny. His daughter-in-law was giving birth in the next room, but he hardly modulated his tone – even, rational, with a hint of shared excitement, like a man showing a boy for the first time the wonders of creation. 'It can't be born until the elements outside and inside are in perfect balance. See, the little world – that's us – and the great world are the same. Earth, wind, fire and water become flesh, breath, heat, and blood. The baby sucks them in through the mother's blood as it later does through her milk: hence coconut milk in the prayer-meal. Then when the moment comes, *pramana** descends from the fontanelle' – he sat erect with closed eyes and lowered his hand, like a veil, before his face – 'through the eyes, ears and mouth, endowing the senses, sinking downwards in the diamond shape of a rice packet. Think of it: a child sees before he hears, hears before he speaks.'

We heard the cry. Purwadi opened his eyes and a smile spread across his face. 'Ah! There it is, just as I said.' (He would almost have taken credit for it.) 'Excuse me now; I have something to see to.' And he rose and passed through the curtain into the kitchen.

*A Hindu-Javanese concept denoting divine life.

I remained where I was and waited until they came back. Behind the curtain there was a flurry of activity, muted voices. And then I confronted the scene with which this book begins. It involved a further switch – identifying father with daughter – as Joko powdered his face and put on the sarong and jacket of a traditional Javanese woman, male becoming female so that the child should grow up with the feminine graces. I hardly knew how to react: I was not supposed to be there. 'Look at Pa,' said his daughter shyly as he knelt and buried the placenta inside the front door. 'He did it for you too,' said the grandfather, glancing at me with a smile, 'and you've turned out all right.'

This time there was no laughter, no audience. 'May she grow up a true woman, a real woman,' said Purwadi before stooping to insert a charm in the folds of the placenta. 'May she be cool like water, fragrant like flowers.'

That's not the end of it. The husband has to wash the birthing mat. Why? It's a special mat of pandanus with a red border, said Supandi, who travels every year to the island of Bawean to buy them for the village. *Red and white: the waters of the female and male, like the red and white porridge of the prayer-meal or the Indonesian flag. The white centre is reddened with the wife's birth blood. The husband takes it to the river to wash it clean. Not many people will tell you that. It's something between husband and wife.*

I returned later that evening to attend the banquet. Joko, back in his green messenger's uniform, was selling lottery tickets from the hatch. The old white-haired headman, Harsono, gave the prayer-meal address – a little fuller and more philosophical than usual with High Javanese polysyllables and an extra dose of numerology. He had joined Sangkan Paran in 1953 and considered himself the senior member, even if Purwadi knew more. But it wasn't an event just for mystics: that would defeat its purpose. Though he disavowed orthodox piety ('A pious Muslim is like a man who bumps his head on the air and trips on a smooth path'), Purwadi had invited Mustari, a conservative Muslim, to speak the closing Arabic prayer. 'Strictly it's not necessary,' he told me afterwards. 'Some people like to say that the Muslim frame encloses and protects the higher Javanese wisdom, so both are necessary. Not true. Mustari is my neighbour. Our wives are cousins. It's as simple as that.'

Fortune-bloom-goddess – for that was her name – was born in her mother's kitchen after an hour of labour. The other baby – Dewi's, the headman's first grandchild – was delivered in hospital after a long and difficult birth. (Expensive too: Rp350,000 in hospital fees was about as much as a middling farmer could earn in a month.) 'I was so drunk with the medicine I hardly remember anything of it,' said Dewi gratefully. But Hari, the baby, bore the scars. On the back of his head was a blood-filled lump the size of a grape where the rubber sucker had pulled him out.

From the beginning Hari was destined to be different. Home from the maternity ward, he was put on display in the back room while Jan held court at the front. They had laid him on a bed, his forehead covered with a blanket, wrapped and gloved like an Eskimo. 'You never know; he might catch a chill.' Around the bed swarmed relatives and neighbours, fanning themselves against the heat, speaking in hushed voices. No one dared disturb the starched sheets to pick him up. 'He must be left alone unless he cries,' the doctor had ordered. So Hari was the first village baby not to be passed from hand to hand, mother to mother, in the usual Javanese manner. When he was hungry, one of the women would lie stiffly beside him and hold a bottle above his mouth. Unable to resist, he glugged it down until it was empty.

Dewi had been told in hospital that her 'milk hadn't come out' and that she couldn't breastfeed. But no one had helped her try, and the grandmothers were happy to take charge. 'She doesn't want the trouble of it,' said Bu Mari, inviting criticism. 'She'd rather others wake up and feed him.' The grandmothers slept on the floor either side of the little bed. Dewi, looking rather lost, hovered awkwardly in the background.

When Dewi was a baby, said the headman's mother, *I took over. A granny knows best. Her mother let her fall one day and I was furious, snatched her away and took her home with me. She used to sleep with me and I'd only let her home to be fed. I used to carry her in my sling on the hip until she was six or seven years old, and then, when she was big, I carried her on my back. I wouldn't let her play with the other children and get dirty. She'd cry a lot. Still does.*

After a day and a half, Pak Lurah declared that Hari ought to be picked up more: it wasn't normal to leave him in bed; it was a torment to onlookers. Besides, his soft head was becoming flat at the back through lying down all day. 'See, look at that: flat as a board!' he said, holding the baby against his stiff palm. 'Sofía's is flatter on the sides because she lies on her front.' (He slumped forward, imitating the posture.) 'To get the right shape, one should turn them every twenty minutes. It's a form of cooking.'

If the head was wrong (and he worried about that grapeish lump) so was the name – Jan's choice. 'Harikurniawan is too heavy for a small child to bear,' said Pak Lurah. 'You can see it weighs on him.' He consulted the diviner and persuaded Dewi to change it to something lighter. But this never caught on. A neighbour, who had stepped in aggressively as a substitute mother and began to carry the baby around in a sling, chose a third name. Eventually, they settled on the abbreviated *Hari*.

After a week, Hari went to stay with Bu Lurah's mother, his great-grandmother, who said she would keep him until the feast at forty-four days. 'By then he'll be out of danger. He'll be a child.' (A newborn is called by the same term as a foetus.) But a week later Jan's parents, who lived in the west end, came down on a moped and bore him away. This tussle lasted about a month.

The two new babies were not supposed to meet for three months, nor were their mothers. Individuals in parallel positions – doubles – can be dangerous to each other; in some sense they are competing for the same space, fighting for the same air. For this reason, the children of brothers do not marry; they are counterparts, like brother and sister. In cases where it happens – love prevailing – somebody close to the couple will die. When I pored over genealogies with Ma Witri, the headman's mother, and we found instances of parallel-cousin marriage, she kept saying, 'Ah! That's why so-and-so died, then.'

The reserve between a father and son owes something to this competition for life: the son replaces the father, they are one and the same, but the father is still around. So, too, the avoidance between people at either end of the life cycle – great-grandparents (*buyut*) and great-grandchildren (also *buyut*). The young should have seen off the old, and the baby's cry gives its living ancestor the hiccups – a nudge towards the abyss. (I have seen an old man whimper at the cries of his great-grandchild.) This did not deter Hari's maternal great-grandmother, Ma Witri, a formidable woman not much over sixty; yet if the new mothers or their babies had come face to face, there would surely have been a mystical stand-off, an 'overheating', as they put it, and one or other party must die. Better to keep a distance.

Fortunately both thrived.

The milestones of a Javanese child's life are marked by rituals that interweave practical wisdom with humour, a little philosophy (depending on who is interpreting) and the necessary quantum of weirdness. As always, one wonders how these things ever began. Who, for example, could have invented the Empty Prayer-meal? This takes place a few days after the child's navel scab has dropped off. In the afternoon, the midwife Scratches the Ground (a separate ritual) with a fieldknife, pierces the infant's ears (if a girl: a needle through the lobe pressed against a slice of turmeric), and threads a bit of umbilical cord around the child's neck. (The cord represents one of the spirit siblings: dunked in oil it provides a cure.) Then, in the middle of the night, a group of men assemble solemnly for a meal. The covered dishes are brought in – baskets with lids, mounds covered with banana leaves. A prayer is spoken; the lids are lifted and – Look! They are empty! All feign surprise; all laugh. (At 3 a.m. you have to laugh.) And then the host returns with the real thing, the brimming bowls of food. 'Symbolizing,' said Harsono, 'that woman is empty until filled by man's seed. First nothing, then something.'

I had recorded the litany of the Empty Prayer-Meal, and when he heard the recording, Hasan, the part-time teacher in Banyuwangi who transcribed my tapes, was again shocked. (It was he who had baulked at the porridge-squirting.) For him, a city-bred Muslim of mixed descent, it was obscene. The mystery of the universe could not be contemplated through procreation, only through the authorized word of God. Javanese symbolism was a perverse error or a joke.

Harsono – ready, even at dawn, to ponder ultimate things, his appetite for the infinite undiminished by half a century of talking – said to me after the ritual charade was over, 'That moment of conception: why do I, an old man of seventy-five, harp on it? Because it leads us back to our origin, the source of everything.'

I must have looked puzzled, because he suddenly cracked a smile and said: 'Here's the mystery. Father and mother produce the child, yet they do so without intention or will. They are mere intermediaries. For the world to exist there must be something more. Without that hidden thing, there would be no result. Equally, without the red and the white, nothing. Eternity is in that combination of three. What is it that brings life? It can't be grasped, but without it nothing happens.'

Purwadi had been half-listening, his long solemn face slightly averted as he gazed at the opposite wall, his elbows resting on folded knees. Now he turned to me, and said, probing my ignorance: 'What do the English say about all this? Where is God for the English?'

I stammered something about heaven and the English believing that God made man in his own image.

'That's true enough, so long as you don't imagine God *preceded* creation. Man is indeed God's image, his material form. Your God is from your head to your foot. But what about Nabi Isa [Jesus]? Is he God or the son of God? I've never quite understood.'

'Neither have I,' I said. 'But he's supposed to be both.'

'Well, if Jesus is a symbol of how we come into being, that fits – more or less. God in man; a man-god: it's almost Javanese.'

'But Jesus was a unique case.'

Purwadi sighed. 'Ah! There's the error.'

*

The babies were launched. The Scraping of the Ground, the Empty Prayer-meal, the Forty-four Days. The red and the white and the something-extra; the twelve constituents. Miraculously, they had come into being. (The jargon was infectious.) Both fathers had provided the midwife with a chick, matched to the sex of their child. Mistakes could be costly. A female chick for a male child, and the boy would turn out a man-woman, an androgyne. This was how Panji, the transvestite, explained his fate. 'Pa didn't have a male chick at the time and took a chance on it.'

But the grape on Hari's head had grown and Bu Lurah was worried. On Pak Lurah's motorbike – she riding side-saddle, the baby in her lap – they took him back to the maternity clinic, and then to a doctor, but nothing could be done. So they went to see a diviner – not Ran, but someone more powerful, someone they didn't know. They took a parcel of betel ingredients concealed inside Hari's clothes, wrapping the whole thing in banana leaves. ('It looks like the clown's parcel in the dragon play,' joked Pak Lurah.) The diviner opened the package and 'chose the good' from the ingredients, using the pieces to grind a paste to be smeared on Hari's head. He consulted some calendrical tables and made a diagnosis. The problem was that Pak Lurah had planted red flowers in front of the house and these were forbidden to Hari – a kind of personal taboo. They gave the diviner Rp1,000 and came home to uproot the flowers. Next day the lump had gone.

11
Mystics

The way into mysticism for the ordinary villager was not through books or lessons or meetings with remarkable men. It could begin with a baby's cry or a plate of red and white porridge. It lay before you, half-concealed in the routines of everyday life. The merest question could open the way. And once you had made the shift of perspective, things genuinely looked different; and there was a logic which told you how to proceed, how to deepen your understanding without fear of getting things wrong. For all its wordplay and extravagant numerology, Javanism is a philosophy grounded in experience.

This is something Western scholars miss. They begin among the manuscripts of the royal courts in Solo and Yogya or the oriental collections of Leiden University, sifting the yellowing texts for Indian and Arabic sources. (Java is always the terminus of cultural diffusion, never the origin.) They hunt for systems and conceptual networks. What they are after is an abstract spiritual geometry, a metaphysical pass-key giving entry to any text, however cryptic – which would be fine if Javanese mystics were scholars like themselves.

At my first meeting with Purwadi I had asked him whether 'the knowledge', as practised in Banyuwangi, was homegrown or transplanted from Central Java, its traditional heartland. Was I getting a garbled version of things better understood in Solo? Purwadi had hesitated, as though the question were wrong or perhaps unsure whether to choose the difficult reply or the simple one. Yes, it was true, he said, that the great poet-mystics like Ronggowarsita were from Central Java. But they were passing on wisdom that was available to anyone. 'It's already there when we are born. People say it goes back to the Hindu sages or the Nine Saints who brought Islam to Java. But the Nine Saints are really the nine holes of the body which regulate our life in the world. Everything 'outside' in the world is also inside, part of our make-up. These teachers were only mediators, not the sources of knowledge.'

Javanese philosophy, as Purwadi described it, wasn't something to be taught, like Islam or constitutional history; even less imposed: it was found within. Everything you learned had to be tested, tried out and fitted to experience ('fitting' was a favourite word). It was the opposite of the rote learning of the classroom or prayer-house. Nothing was taken for granted; nothing accepted on authority.

One Friday I was sitting with Warno, the old-fashioned black-suited farmer who lived in the west end of the village. The bench in front of his house, shaded by a broad and leafy tamarind tree, stood a little back from the road. The corner plot, a bare yard devoid of flowers and unnecessary plants, was bordered by a picket fence. Over the loudspeakers we heard the call to prayer and watched as the faithful streamed down the road towards the mosque. In their crisp shirts and dark sarongs, prayer-mats folded over arms, they were proud and purposeful, conscious of setting an example. Daily prayers were unobserved, but congregational worship marked a difference: it was a display of piety, what the laxer Muslims resentfully called an 'exhibition'.

Warno watched them calmly and said, with a sigh: 'When you don't understand things, they seem very far away. As a young man I used to do that.'

'You mean go to Friday worship?'

'I used to do the call to prayer. And then one day, in the middle of the call I suddenly knew that there was nothing out there, just my voice in the air. I was standing there shouting at nothing.'

He turned to me with a frank stare, knowing that I would be surprised at his words. It was not the sort of thing people said – not in the village of Aris and Tompo; not anywhere in Indonesia.

'At the time, I was a Koranic instructor, and after this I began to wonder about the meaning of the words. What did they refer to? It seemed to me that I knew the *name* but not the substance. You can know someone's name but if you've never met that person you wouldn't recognize them if they walked into you; you might even be sitting talking to them but wouldn't know. That was my position. And perhaps the words were empty, just air. I came to realize that to make sense of them I had to *locate* them in what I already knew. Do you follow me, Andrew?'

'Yes. I'm trying.'

He picked a slice of mango from the plate which lay on the bench between us. 'For me, the first step was to ask what these really meant – the prayers, the turning to Mecca, the pilgrimage, the names of God, his Oneness. If there was nothing outside us, what could they mean? *Oneness*, in that case, could only refer to common humanity, to something inward and shared. And then you wonder: How do I act on that?'

Warno's search for the meaning of things went beyond a simple loss of faith or a crisis of doubt. Who was to say *faith* had anything to do with it? Yet when he told me about his final call to prayer (how strange the walk home from the mosque must have felt that day), I was instantly taken back to my own last communion, aged seventeen. I remembered kneeling at the rail as the priest handed wafers to the row of supplicants and suddenly finding myself outside, observing, no longer belonging. I remember, too, my surprise at feeling no regret. At that moment I wasn't disturbed but absorbed in a different way, aware of the oddness of things, the robes, the trusting upturned faces. Guiltily but joyfully, I swallowed the wafer for the last time. It was a first step towards anthropology.

Warno had taken a different step. The world – the Javanese world – was to be recognized, not changed. Islam could not be ignored or left behind: it was a part of everything, and there was no alternative. But an Islam which no longer matched experience could still make sense if properly interpreted. It was a matter of fitting the words to the reality rather than the other way around.

In the coming months, as I got to know the mystics better, I found that they shared Warno's self-reliance, his independence, and it gave their words a solidity which was unlike the simple received faith of the pious or the brittle certainties of the zealots. I never felt that I was hearing a dogma repeated. And because they were men and women with different histories and personalities, they showed me different aspects of Javanism. Warno was ethical, Purwadi metaphysical, Rupo sceptical. I also discovered that the habit of referring everything back to the self was quite unlike the individualism of the West, which was a cultivation of difference and separation. Individuality was an illusion; knowledge a matter of finding what joined one to others, the Self beneath the self. Dogma, religion, and politics were what got in the way.

Religions have nothing to do with spirituality, said Rupo. *They are things of the world, political parties. Parties have bosses, religions have gods.*

For this reason, Bayu's mystics were content to see their association, Sangkan Paran, legally disqualified as a religion. Orthodox Islam, fearing an exodus of nominal Muslims from its ninety-four per cent majority, had lobbied hard to prevent Javanism gaining recognition as an official religion. Bizarrely, the many Javanist mystical societies were classed as 'Belief Streams', answerable to the Ministry of Education and Culture, not the Ministry of Religion. 'Belief' was not a word the Bayu mystics ever used: nobody was required to believe anything they had not experienced for themselves. But in a spirit of rendering-unto-Caesar, they were happy to play the game and periodically surrender their official booklet to the police chief and the Religious Affairs Bureau.

Last month I gave a talk to two hundred members at Gambiran in the south, said Purwadi. *I had called people to the village office using the public address system, but I spoke to the meeting using a microphone that wasn't broadcast outside. After a few minutes, a man came in and handed me a note, stamped and signed by the headman and the mosque official. They demanded that the meeting break up because it was an attempt to spread a false religion. At that point I switched on the outside loudspeakers and told the whole village that I wasn't preaching religion but knowledge of humanity and that I couldn't accept this unreasonable demand. I carried on for an hour, but next day I was summoned to the district office and faced the police chief and the army commander. I explained again and my opponents had to back down.*

Of all the Javanists in Bayu, Purwadi was the most accomplished. He had studied Ronggowarsita and the *Book of Centhini* – Javanist classics of the nineteenth century. He had copied out, longhand, the secret manuals of Sangkan Paran, of which he was regional head. He went on retreats and meditated in caves in Alas Purwo. He made visits to the palace in Solo and was on familiar terms with the association's national leadership. He could talk entrancingly of the symbolism of the shadow play, the Descent of the Absolute and the principles of the 'serpent power'.

Seeing Purwadi return from the fields with muddy feet and perspiring brow, or trotting under a milkmaid-style yoke (the steps in rhythm with the bounce), was always a shock. I felt a pang of embarrassment for him, guilt at my own clean hands. With Warno, this was never the case. In him, farming and philosophy were perfectly complemented. He tended his ricefields, mending and making, with the same unhurried care that he brought to conversation. He spoke of planting ideas and weeding errors, trimming and grafting. And it was Warno's earthy rationalism that most attracted me, his steady methodical voice that compelled. His philosophy had nothing of the magical; nothing untried. In this he was different from some of the other mystics. The old headman, Harsono, was happy to use a sonorous phrase without knowing what it meant. He was concerned that I should think *him* the cleverest, that he had more in reserve – more than we, his dull companions, could ever understand. (After I told him about Hindu prayer-meals in the south of the district, he began to use Sanskrit jargon in his own addresses, basking in baffled respect.) Rupo, another veteran, was, by turns, a serious sceptic, even a solipsist ('Have I ever prayed?' he scoffed. 'Prayed to *what*?'), and then – unaccountably – a dabbler in magic. But Warno, more than anyone, was concerned that I should understand, and in explaining things to me, he would go over them hour after hour until he had them perfectly straight in his own mind. At the end of our discussions, which I usually taped, he would say, with a slow grin: 'So how do things stand for you now? Broader or narrower?' To which there was only one reply.

Javanists liked to talk. Into the small hours they would sit up under a dim lamp, 'rubbing together' ideas, the men in hats, smoking and sipping coffee, the women with their legs stretched out on the bench, chewing tobacco. They mostly belonged to Sangkan Paran, but neighbours and fellow-travellers would call in, nodding sagely or chiming in with some aphorism. Any reputable visitor from another village would be gently grilled, his brains picked, to see 'what matched' or 'what made sense'. They wanted to know about Western cosmology, the planets and stars, the English explanation of Life. The Hindu formulas I brought back from the south were checked for similarities and tried out like new tools. Common to both traditions were the law of karma, the heroes and villains of the shadow play and the language of mystical power. They listened to the tapes I had made, clucking at the litanies and temple chants. But Balinese cosmology was too fantastic and the Javanese Hindu converts too literal-minded. The mechanics of reincarnation were preposterous: in the era of birth control the dead outnumbered the living and souls had to queue up for bodies. But what could survive death? Strictly there was no personal soul: Javanists spoke of a 'shift of realm' as the constituents of the body returned to the elements. But this was closer to Buddhist extinction. Death was dissolution, not the portal to an afterlife.

It was axiomatic that things could be understood at different levels: even the diligent pious understood that. What made sense at a low level might be contradicted by higher knowledge. Experience and aptitude imposed limits and one could get stuck on the lower rungs. Orthodoxy was like the knowledge one acquired at primary school: useful for starters, said Warno; but if one had learned how to read and add up one could graduate to secondary school. One could throw away the abacus. After all (to extend his analogy), it was no use parroting the two-times table when a problem called for algebra.

'There's nothing wrong with praying,' said Hadi, whose son was married to the headman's daughter, 'so long as you *understand*. But most religious people don't. They don't know why the hands are held to the chest, why sunset prayer has three repetitions of the postures, or why some people stick out the left forefinger when they take the seated position.'

'Why?' I asked.

Hadi laughed, and looked at me half-seriously. 'What is it that points? Ah, well! That's for a later discussion. When you've understood all those things, you'll know that you've performed your act of worship without moving an inch. Sitting here drinking this coffee. Or doing what you like best.'

Sex as prayer (the 'true worship', they called it); the world as a cipher. Such symbol-mongering infuriated the pious, including Hadi's own son. He always mocked my interest: 'All that riddling talk,' said Jan. 'What does it mean? What can they teach you?' But to Javanists, orthodox literalism was endlessly amusing.

For seven years Ismail scoured the wilderness seeking God, said Harsono. *He climbed mountains, crossed deserts, swam rivers. Finally, he lay down exhausted on a boulder and fell asleep. He woke to a thundering voice. 'Why do you seek God far away? Where you are sleeping, there is God's place.' Ismail blinked and looked in astonishment at the black stone that had been his pillow. He declared it to be the house of God and built a shrine. The black stone became part of the Kaaba in the great mosque of Mecca. When I tell that story*, Harsono continued, *I always remember what Joyokusumo* [the founder of Sangkan Paran] *used to say to hajis: 'You've been to Mecca, seen the Kaaba. Now where is* your *Kaaba?'*

But it was possible to talk Javanism without raising hackles. The ingredients of ritual, the stock of symbols, the shared values – life, love, neighbourly solidarity – created a common language. Nobody raised an eyebrow at 'the red and the white', 'the three-in-one', or the 'four things', since at some level they meant something to every villager. Everyone had learned their times tables. And when a pious neighbour walked in on a late-night Javanist brainstorming, conversation would ramble on in much the same vein – it would be rude to stall – and the neighbour, having taken his place at the table with perfect ease, would depart, an hour and two coffees later, none the wiser; or perhaps would drop off to sleep, lulled by familiar words and near-meanings.

One evening when I was passing Purwadi's house he called me in. Around him, against the background wailing of the mosque, life was being busily pursued – Joko selling lottery tickets at the hatch, Eti filling the baby from a huge pale breast, Ma Purwadi pounding rice. But Purwadi was studying. He sat stiffly in a high-backed chair by the open door, holding a large notebook at arm's length. Formal and dignified in black cap, batik shirt and square spectacles, indifferent to the heat, it was as if he had dressed to read. The book – old-fashioned copperplate writing, the ink brown against yellow paper – was, it turned out, his own composition, his own version of The Knowledge. It contained all he intended to pass on to Joko before he died.

'But he still follows the dancers,' he said with a note of regret. 'He's not ready yet. See, it's not like –'

He waved his hand, suggesting easier paths, the words unsaid.

'It can't be forced, and the young have other preoccupations.'

Joko was my age, the age his father had become interested in mysticism. But times had changed. Bayu's mystics – the hundred or so members of Sangkan Paran – were mostly over forty. Somehow it had become accepted that the younger generation, Suharto's children, had never grown up. Unlike their parents, who had lived through revolution, independence and political massacres, they had never learned to think for themselves. Knowledge – delivered through megaphone, textbook and television – was unquestionable. Unsurprisingly, young people, even old young people, were 'not yet ready' for Javanism.

With an aloof casualness (but he had been waiting for me), Purwadi pushed the book across the table. I handled it like the treasure it was, knowing that I could not borrow it and certain I could remember no more than a couple of sentences. Under such headings as 'Descent of the Essence' and 'Dying into Life' there were mantras, quotations, numbered descriptions of the stages of death (the passage of divine life from the left foot through the limbs and trunk: a route-map to extinction), and diagrams, clumsy beside the neat, rounded script. Some of the drawings were of humanoid figures, like a child's pictures of aliens, with arrows pointing to nodes and organs. The labels were Sanskrit as well as Arabic. The text was high-flown and poetic: words I recognized but could not understand. When, much later, I made my own laborious handwritten copy – old technology the proof of secrecy – I had already learned that Purwadi's manual, and the ever more secret books to which it referred, were only clues to a fuller unwritten text whose ultimate incontrovertible source was individual experience. Labels, in the end, didn't matter.

Purwadi folded his glasses and dropped them into his batik-shirt pocket. Then he locked away the book in a cupboard (a glimpse of files and manuscripts) and said: 'Let's call on Warno. He's been asking me about something.'

Sitting outside the house opposite, smoking a corn-leaf cheroot, Harsono, the old headman, grinned and got up. He ambled towards me, bandy-legged, and said, 'Going to Warno's? I'll come along. *Rubbing together*, ha!'

At seventy-five one could still learn.

We walked the length of the village, a self-conscious delegation, Harsono – his bandy legs giving him a slight roll – pleased at the glances we attracted, Purwadi, upright and firm-chinned, eyes fixed straight ahead. Seeing us, two or three others fell in along the way, and we arrived at Warno's already a small crowd, Purwadi to the fore. What he wanted to tell Warno about was breathing. The circulation of breath could be an aid to meditation. By drawing one's breath down to the navel and holding it while silently reciting a mantra one could begin to detach oneself from the world. When the senses were stilled, *rasa*, feeling-consciousness, could be drawn upwards from the genitals through the navel and solar plexus, the throat, between the eyes and up to the fontanelle. The sounds and sights and smells that were granted were not those of the outer world; the voice that one heard was not one's own voice. 'All these are Allah.'

We sat around the coffee table watching Purwadi as he demonstrated. He had folded his arms across his chest and shut his eyes, tilting his head slightly back, his handsome face composed in a grave mask. When Warno's wife, Min, brought in plates of hot, sweet porridge, wincing as they chinked on the marble table, Purwadi didn't seem to notice. We watched him through the steam. Every few minutes he would give some commentary, indicating where he had reached. 'Ah, see now the breath has begun to revolve in the lower regions.' Or: 'Now a gentle ticking as *rasa* rises through the spine.'

Our coffees grew cold and Purwadi was still breathing. Some of the men had shut their eyes. I glanced up and noticed, totem-like above the door, the Freudian rice packets, male and female, under which every visitor to the Warno household had to pass. In the big empty room, the still air had the faint warm smell of wood.

Finally Warno plucked up courage and leaned forward to sip his coffee. His older brother, breaking the spell, said: 'So you're pulling *rasa* up inwardly?'

'While breathing,' said Purwadi, opening his eyes with a smile.

It seemed a big achievement. The men were impressed. But Warno slapped a mosquito against his cheek and sighed.

Rupo had just come in and was sitting on the platform at the side. 'Ah, working the *rasa*!' he said. He closed his eyes and lay back.

Rupo was one of five brothers and sisters, all now in their seventies, who had been personally initiated by Joyokusumo. In the 1950s they used to walk to Joyokusumo's house in a remote plantation district to the west, a distance of thirty miles. Sometimes, after meditating with the master, they would find themselves back in the square in Banyuwangi as the town clock struck one in the morning, not knowing how they had got there. Rupo was one of the original members; but he had learned other systems as well and had made his own synthesis. He was white-haired but strongly built – he still worked in the fields. His face bore an expression of stubbornness.

Purwadi said: 'You shut down each of your senses, so your eyes don't attend to what is outside, your ears hear only what is within. It's like the Muslim washing his eyes and ears before prayer: a separation from the world, what in English is called marking a "distance". Which way you face doesn't matter. There's no fixed point, no turning to Mecca.'

'East, west, south and north are in you,' said Rupo. 'There's nothing outside.'

'No need to go outside,' said Min.

We drank our coffees and Warno replaced the empty porridge dishes with a bowl of red, hairy rambutans while we waited for someone to take up the thread. Despite Purwadi's initiative, there was no leading voice. If someone had something new to say, or to repeat, they said it. 'Rubbing together' was the right expression for this mild conceptual friction, a gentle game of wits with no winners or losers.

'Let's see if he knows where he is,' said Rupo, who had now moved to the table. 'Which way is east?'

Sheepishly, knowing I was being set up, I pointed with my left hand down the road towards town.

'And the limit of east?'

'What do you mean by *limit*? Isn't it the same?'

'The limit of east, for you, is here,' said Rupo, patting my right side. 'So the limit of west is where?'

Wrongly, I pointed west.

'The limit of west, for you, is *here* –' this time tapping my left side: my *east* side, as I now saw. 'For me, of course, sitting opposite you, the limits are reversed. But it's simple: all the directions originate from you.'

They laughed at this little exercise, no doubt often repeated with beginners. But it proved the point. As you moved through space, the directional planes moved with you. There was no fixed compass, no God's-eye view. And this dogged anthropocentrism – so contrary to orthodoxy in its relativism – explained many things, not least the

Javanists' refusal to reject others' views out of hand.

'Up, down, above, below, it all starts here,' said Rupo, brushing his frame with a stubby hand.

'Pious folk say *God Above*,' said Min.

But this too, like other religious terms, could be recast in human terms.

Putting the orthodox position, I said: 'Aren't you simply twisting the meanings of words, turning religion inside out?'

Rupo said, 'The words in themselves don't matter. We say Monday, Tuesday and Wednesday; but in reality there's no difference – they are all just days. What matters is the reality, not the name. Of course, some people are impervious to the truth. So there are simpler ways for them to understand, places to go and pray –'

And then Min, who had taken her place on the platform, away from the table, said: 'On the temple is written: *Do not enter if you don't know what is within. Stay below if you don't know what is above.*'

Prepositions again: they oriented you to the world – in Rupo's words, they showed you where you were. Javanism was all about staying where you were but changing your point of view, which, I suppose, was the point of the insistent wordplay. I had not thought so carefully about prepositions since coming across John Donne's 'To his mistress going to bed':

> *License my roving hands, and let them go*
> *Before, behind, between, above, below.*

That sly and sensual elegy would have appealed to the Javanists. (The temple, as I later found out, was a stupa-shaped building called the 'place of emptiness' erected over the tomb of Joyokusumo.)

Warno had hardly uttered a word since we arrived. I could see that he was unimpressed by Purwadi's demonstration of meditation, but he seemed more disturbed by Rupo. Or rather, he wanted to frame the argument in moral rather than purely metaphysical terms. And when, at Purwadi's prompting, the conversation turned to the make-up of the human person (the English, as ever, providing the straw man), he said, in his slow and allusive way:

'Listen! Man possesses God entirely; and if one is conscious of that, one must comport oneself properly. You've been given this sight, this speech, this hearing. How, then, can you then mistreat them, how can you waste them on impure things? How can you see *red* and say *green*?'

He held up a rambutan and laughed.

'We have eyes and ears, but without Life they see and hear nothing,' said Rupo, resuming metaphysics. 'Seeing and *what* sees are two different things. *What* sees is Life. We call it the Hidden because it can't be grasped in itself; only its effects. A stillborn child is the same as one born alive except for that one ungraspable thing. But would you deny the difference? For me it's simple: without God no Life, without Life no God.'

I said, 'So there is no God outside the self?'

CHORUS: No!

AB: But what makes Life?

RUPO: Life. *Who makes is who bears.* The rambutan makes the rambutan. (Taking one.)

HARSONO: But only man has consciousness and knows it. Man is the highest.

MIN: Children are taught that God came first: God made us, as we make sweets.

RUPO : If that's the case where is he? Where is his house?

AB: So this is very far from what the pious say.

WARNO: Two different stories.

AB: But I've heard you say, *Thanks be to God.* What does that mean?

RUPO : In the sense of a God that walks about and makes people, there's no such thing.

WARNO : If you say there was a God before there was humanity, you then have to explain where God came from. If God is in humanity, the problem doesn't arise. To ask which comes first is

like the chicken and the egg.
RUPO : The cock crows inside the egg.
CHORUS: They are together.

We broke up at two in the morning, Rupo fast asleep on the platform, sheeted like a corpse, Warno still in his grey broad-brimmed hat, swirling the coffee grounds in his cup.

12

The Suitors

Over the months I had lost touch with Hasan, my occasional assistant of the early days. I no longer needed his help with transcriptions – my Javanese had caught up with his – and I rarely went to town without Mercedes and Sofía. But in Ramadan he suddenly took to visiting us.

Thick-bodied, hairy and bespectacled, Hasan was about as far from the Javanese ideal as possible, though had his temperament suited his appearance he might have served for a minor shadow-play warrior. His personal heroes, both coincidentally hirsute Englishmen, showed different sides of his character. They were heroes of war and peace. In an Indonesian history of the Second World War (a book I borrowed from him, curious as to its angle), he had read about Orde Wingate, the maverick commander who lived behind enemy lines in occupied Burma, marching his men – the bearded Chindits – through the jungle to attack Japanese units. Wingate showed you could live close to your enemy, kill them by stealth, said Hasan. His other exemplar was John Lennon, whose utopian slogans he would drop into conversation like mantras. There was one particular song he liked to quote. But he could not imagine a world without religion. He laughed at the sheer daring, the insanity of it. 'How could John say such an amazing thing!' No, it could not be imagined. And then, with the same note of shocked admiration: 'You know, John gave away ten per cent of his wealth, just as the Koran instructs. There aren't many Indonesians would do that.'

An unemployed teacher – he could not pay the price of a job – Hasan had spotted me in my first week in Banyuwangi and had latched on, eager to show me around. He had approached me in the market and struck up a conversation that was unlike the usual requests for an English lesson or a photo. An outsider attracted to another outsider. I was grateful for his friendship and we travelled about the district meeting local experts, talking to headmen and eating at dusty roadside stalls. Hasan knew basic English but we always talked in Indonesian. His Javanese, though less than fluent, was good enough for my purposes, and in the early months I paid him to transcribe tapes of prayer-meal addresses and wedding ceremonies.

His parents came from far-flung regions of the archipelago – Lampung and Borneo – which, I suppose, made Hasan and his five or six siblings proper Indonesians. Banyuwangi, like other ports, was full of such people – Mandars, Bugis, Madurese and Malays: the seafarers, merchants and retired pirates of the Java Sea. In the urban back streets, with their ethnic flotsam, their stranded migrants, so local and yet so rootless, mosques provided a substitute community, a sense of belonging. In the bigger cities – and in Indonesia whole cities could be backwaters – Islam was the lingua franca. Whenever I penetrated the warm warren of alleys that led to Hasan's house, the loudhailers were always blaring, the prayer-houses lit up with a warm yellow light, full of children rocking over Korans.

Hasan's father was a pensioner who had been invalided out of the army in 1976. During the first weeks of the East Timor invasion, the Indonesian troops, ill-trained and terrified, had walked through the bush shooting at anything that moved. Hasan's father had been wounded by a comrade's grenade, his shout directing the throw. Only a tree had saved him. Now he sat at home scowling and irritable, speaking in a slur, making awkward, angry gestures from his wheelchair. It embarrassed his son that he spoke to me with a note of contempt.

A useful attribute in a guide, Hasan was able to move in different circles. With villagers he was friendly and teasing; with officials he was polite, even deferent. Yet Suharto – from whom all power and title flowed – he regarded as a criminal and dictator. This was a factual description for a president who had plundered the country for thirty years and murdered a million of its citizens, but at the time you could not say the word *dictator* without breaking the law. In the Orwellian regime that Suharto had built, Indonesia was a *demokrasi*, a 'legal state' with an elected president. Posters depicted the Father of Development in a conical hat, bending to plant rice, or, latterly, making the pilgrimage to Mecca. Television showed him breaking the Fast with Islamic leaders: 'playing the Muslim card', as even the newspapers dared to suggest.

Despite his lack of any formal position, Hasan knew a great deal about which businesses in Banyuwangi were controlled by the president's family. One of Suharto's sons owned miles of prawn farms all around the coast. Vast areas of pristine mangroves had been destroyed in their making, coastal dwellers made homeless, fishermen grounded. Suharto himself took a percentage off lucrative timber businesses in the area. 'Just think. If they own half of Banyuwangi, which is hardly on the map, imagine what they own elsewhere!' But Suharto, of course, was only the top of the pyramid. At every level there were concessions and private monopolies. Every job had its price; every contract and court judgment its backroom deal.

Hasan seemed to know the details – how the deals had been done, the size of the rake-off, how much or how little compensation had been paid. He told me about the compulsory burning of cloves on plantations to keep the prices high, a practice condemned even in colonial times. He knew about the arrests of students and local dissidents, the beatings of detainees. He knew things that were not reported in the newspapers, laughing nervously as he fed me the information. And when he began to speak of informers and placemen, people paid or forced to spy and entrap, I wondered whether my new friend, so full of criticism, was playing a double game, or perhaps even warning me of what he was doing. I did not doubt his hatred of the system, but I could not trust his confidence. Still, his candour was admirable. I wanted to help. If he settled down and found a job maybe he could be happy: a quiet, modest life with the domestic satisfactions that Java offered. Difficult for one who knew so much, but in Indonesia there was no other way.

So I introduced him to Sri, the girl with whom we shared a house, the adopted daughter of Bu Mari. Her father, Sae, back from one of his working trips to Bali, had asked me if I knew anyone in town, some honest young teacher or civil servant. 'It doesn't matter if he's poor, as long as he's got a good heart and will look after her, make her happy again.' I knew Sri aspired to something better than the country boys of her childhood. She had lived in Malang, studied for a degree. She had turned down Tris, a trainee teacher who had given up applying for jobs and started a watermelon enterprise. How could she marry a former classmate, a mere farmer like her father? Each time Tris called in he would bring her one of his outsize tasteless melons. 'Where's Sri today?' he would hopefully ask, stroking her melon as he sipped his coffee.

These days Sri was often out. With the daughter of a Catholic schoolmaster who lived in a house at the back, she had enrolled on a computer course in town. 'Computing and Accountancy', like ELT, was a newish thing in the provinces, a promised link to a wider world. It attracted the same well-groomed, optimistic young people – the generation of would-be white-collar workers, children of peasants and labourers who could not pay for government jobs and who lacked the capital and commercial skills of the Chinese population. Sri's course was held in a hot cramped cavern – temporarily filled with noisy machines and fans – between a cycle repair shop and a Chinese grocery store (pyramids of tins, umbrellas hanging from the ceiling, and a stand of turtle eggs, soft and dented, like collapsed ping-pong balls, in a bed of sawdust). In the afternoons she and her friend set off on mopeds, freewheeling downhill, hair streaming in the wind, away from the village tedium.

Sri and Hasan, we thought: yes, a good match.

For all his attachment to John Lennon and his guilty talk of 'worldly temptations', Hasan was a good Muslim. His religion was orthodox, but he had the Javanese tolerance of difference. He was mildly scandalised by some of the tapes he transcribed for me (he had scribbled 'porno' in the margins of a litany), but Javanese syncretism – the mixing of traditions – amused him and flattered his sense of Indonesia's cultural wealth. He had read about the Hindu past: it was what made Java special: syncretism was its legacy. Like most townspeople, however, he had no inkling of what the mystics talked about (or that they practised a scepticism John Lennon had only imagined), and by the time I became acquainted with them I no longer needed his help. So his renewed visits came as a surprise. I had nothing for him – no more tapes – and I had only vaguely suggested that Sri was entering the marriage market. But I soon realised that, like the melancholy Tris, fruit in hand, it wasn't me he was coming to see.

Wan and his mother, catching on, began to take an interest in my visitor, commenting on his town sophistication and his superior knowledge, ignoring the disadvantages. 'Pak Arjo would have approved,' said Wan, paving the way. 'You can see the quality.' Bu Mari, with a rare politeness, referred to him as Pak Hasan. Flustered and girlish, she boasted to neighbours of his tremendous prospects, his contacts with government people; but she knew better than to interfere. And so, when he visited, they withdrew behind the curtain to the back of the house, leaving Hasan and Sri with us in the front room. We drank tea together, and then Mercedes and I withdrew in turn, leaving them sparring, he teasing, she laughing or clawing the air in mock irritation. But I wasn't convinced of his interest. The pretext of his visits meant that his intention was never declared. Sri was pretty and charming, highly educated by village standards. Her family was well disposed. What more could he want? What was he waiting for?

And then, when Lebaran came and he paid her natural parents a formal visit, it was clear that something was wrong. Shaved, barbered and laundered, like a man attending a job interview or a trial (some people cannot be themselves when they are smart), he was suddenly overawed, baffled by the parents' simplicity or perhaps afraid of the strange world opening to him, the world of porno prayer-meals and endless relatives and weird heretical rituals. With much nodding and modest gesturing, they welcomed him in, placed before him coffee and biscuits, and let him talk. And as he talked on and on, growing nervous and incoherent, their mouths fell open. Sae told me afterwards, 'We didn't know what he was talking about. We couldn't say anything back. Just smiled.' Then, gripping my arm suddenly: 'Did we frighten him off? He's a good man, isn't he?'

But Hasan had frightened himself off and Sri had another disappointment to add to her recent failures. Then came salvation.

A friend of Wan's – a family friend from years back, before Wan had come to Banyuwangi to be adopted by Arjo and Mari – visited from Surabaya. He arrived one morning with a bag and a briefcase, stepping uncertainly out of the Colt pickup right in front of the house, his creased trousers and shiny shoes untarnished by the journey. He had a little moustache and a tentative smile. He wore a pale shirt tucked into his trousers. His name was Benny.

We were busy at that time with events in other parts of the village, so we did not see much of him. But Benny's mild, modest presence impressed so lightly on a gathering that one hardly knew he was there. He spoke quietly and little, laughed only when others laughed and generally kept out of the way. With Wan he was amused and conspiratorial. Bu Mari's ironic prodding and slaps he took in good part. In a way I could only envy – remembering my first conspicuous month in the village – he fitted in.

We heard little of his quiet conversations with Sri (Malang and Surabaya often featured), but he had an immediate effect on her. She seemed more grown up; calmer but happier. And seeing him go to the prayer-house in the evening and stay on for chanting, she began to do the same. In the evenings, her father Sae would wander over and sit on the bench, observing from the sidelines. He watched Benny with an approving grin. One day – his glowing eyes fixed on Benny – he said to me: 'You know, I don't think Hasan would have been right for Sri. Too serious. She likes to have fun.' Then he said: 'Benny is going to do well for himself. He's only got two more exams to pass then he can be an optician. I've seen his kit: cost a fortune. He's going to work in Jember. Shame it's so far. Shame for Sri. Do you like him?'

'Yes, I like him.' After Hasan I did not trust myself to say more. And the truth was, I did like him and I hoped these good people would get everything they wanted. I hoped Benny was what he seemed.

Within a couple of weeks they did indeed get what they wanted. Suddenly, and for no declared reason, it became urgent that Sri and Benny should marry. The mood in the house turned unpredictable. Wan was his usual casual self, relaxing into the Surabaya dialect with Benny, staying up half the night with him smoking and talking. But Bu Mari wore a frown and had sudden fits of anger; then the frown would give way to hysterical laughter; shrieks at Sri; more of the prodding and slapping; big plates of food for Benny. It was the same with Sri's parents. They were agitated but resolved, pleased at last – and with so little planning – to marry off their daughter. The full customary wedding could wait; that took months to organize. But the Islamic ceremony must happen at once.

Marriage is usually planned by the girl's parents when she is still a child, wrote the headteacher Rapi'i in one of his newspaper articles, *although elopements and abductions are common. Often the parents look for a candidate among the girl's cousins. Every Lebaran, the candidate calls on the girl and presents her with two bottles of syrup. In the evening, her family returns the visit and is welcomed by fireworks and homemade rockets. The wedding takes place one month after the Islamic ceremony, and the boy rides a horse, the girl is carried on a litter.*

You don't believe me about the bottles of syrup, do you? said Untung. *Just wait till I fetch them from the back. Here, look: untouched after fifteen years. They're black now and probably solid. But my wife wouldn't dare open them. Enduring love.*

A week later, at eight o'clock on a fine sunny morning, we gathered under the eaves of Sae's house. It was a small crowd: parents of the bride and groom; Bu Mari, her father and Wan; the mosque official;

Sri's great-uncle Harsono; the headman and Bu Lurah; Mercedes and me. Presiding was the *penghulu*, the district religious official, a brisk humorous man, like a schools inspector used to dealing with fools. Unusually for a Javanese, he was bald. Some of his jokes concerned his baldness.

Benny's parents had arrived from Surabaya the evening before. City people, they were hardly different from the poorer villagers of east Bayu (but only the poorer), with the same small stature and apologetic, careworn faces. Their neighbourhood – to judge from the photos they had brought – looked like Hasan's in Banyuwangi: a jumble of whitewashed miniature houses; alleys choked with trishaws and tented drinks stalls: a village – less than a village – in a city of four million. Benny's father, a dark-faced, wrinkled gnome in a black cap, was, by profession, an entertainer, a music-hall clown. His mother, sallow and wordless, worked in a clothing factory. Before the self-confident Bayu folk they visibly shrank.

The penghulu seated the participants around a table in the open air, Sri and Benny together, Sri's father on her left.

To her mother: 'You sit here; no *there*, Bu: can't have you interfering with the bride! Pa, over here please. Don't forget you're giving away your daughter today. Look sharp! Don't worry, you only have to say Yes.'

There being no engagement, this was the first moment that Sri and Benny were officially together. They looked abashed but happy, quietly certain, Benny in a shirt and tie, Sri in a pink headscarf, her face lacquered with make-up, big dark eyes, yellow cheeks.

Forms were signed, and two passport-like marriage books. The penghulu questioned bride and groom in turn, and made off-colour jokes about their names which had them looking down (but the mosque official laughed). Was the marriage payment ready? Yes: Benny placed a thousand-rupiah banknote (about a dollar) on the table and Sri picked it up. Then all parties joined in the opening of the Koran, and the Confession of Faith. The penghulu then turned to Sae, as the bride's representative – Sri was not required to speak – and made him repeat, phrase by phrase, the terms of the marriage contract. Bride and groom changed places and the groom went through the same routine, this time holding hands with the penghulu. An Arabic declaration, to which the groom replied: 'I accept'; a brief general prayer (all with cupped hands raised), and it was over.

The penghulu said: 'Now you can marry. But not before you hear my words of wisdom.' Aside: 'Haven't I said this somewhere before?'

His advice, laced with innuendo, concerned the mutual obligations of spouses: of fidelity, kindness, and respect. He turned to Sri. 'You, my dear, must be ready to serve husband day and night. And what does that mean: *at night*? No? Oh well, no doubt *he'll* explain everything. And don't forget, not more than one baby every five years. Java is filling up. We can't have you young folk . . . Listen, mothers and fathers, it's all set down in the Koran. So the golden rule is not to transgress your *Rel—*?'

'Religion,' they all replied.

The mosque official, who had giggled throughout this interview, slapped my knee and said, 'Ah, Pak Andrew! Ah! Ah!'

The penghulu turned to Benny, who bit his lip in apprehension.

'Finished school?'

'Yes, Pak.'

'College?'

'Er, yes, Pak.'

'Can you read?'

'Yes, Pak.'

Turning to us: 'See, it's easy, isn't it, getting married in Indonesia.'

To Benny: 'Well or badly?'

'Not badly,' said Benny.

'All right. Let's see. Read this.'

And Benny read from the marriage book he had signed, stumbling over the odd Arabic word, which he was made to repeat, and reading out the conditions of divorce. It was businesslike, a contract with the same Arabic terms as any other contract.

A round of handshakes. Photographs (my function). Then the inevitable, ever-welcome prayer-meal – mounds of rice, multicoloured offerings, incense, betel, unguents – which Harsono explicated in a circumlocuitous Javanist-tinged litany. I sat on the ground next to the penghulu and was impressed by his generous appetite.

A job well done.

I told Hasan on my next visit to town. He smiled ruefully. 'I hope they are happy.'

And I hardly saw him again until three years later, at the beginning of our second period in Bayu, when he called in with his new wife. The girl, once a shop assistant in town, now a clove sorter, was already pregnant. Hasan told me he had abandoned his teaching plans and found a job on a clove plantation as a foreman. 'See, I've got responsibilities now. I can only leave there with the boss's written permission. You should come one day. You wouldn't believe it. Every minute of the day is planned, every aspect of life organized. You can live and die there. *Brave New World*,' he said, in English. 'A good subject for an anthropologist.'

13
Incense

The newly-weds moved in with Sri's natural parents. Sae and Sutri emptied their room, a hot cell eight foot square, and slept on a bench in the kitchen. The kitchen was also the bathroom; in a corner beside the well, behind a wattle screen, was the squat-down latrine – Bayu's prototype, installed by Arjo. The plumbing was crude – a pipe leading to a stream – and the kitchen smelt: you would not want to sleep there. But they had managed before. Twenty years earlier, brother and sister – Sae and Mari – had lived in the same house with their spouses; and it was a common solution, the old making way for the young. When Benny had qualified as an optician and had served a term in Jember he could look for openings in Banyuwangi and could build a house in the village. The cramped living arrangements – the young couple in the tiny shuttered cell, the slightly awkward meals, eaten separately – would be temporary.

Sae and Sutri continued to go to the fields, working harder than ever: the customary wedding, still some way off, would be expensive. Sutri, small and energetic, as volatile as her husband, joined planting gangs or shelled peanuts. (But a day's shelling was worth only a single packet of cigarettes.) On slack days, when the paddy-fields could be left to ripen or soak – they had plots at different stages – Sae worked on building sites in town, returning late, his face dark from the sun.

Sri stayed at home with Benny and watched television.

'Hasn't he got work to do?' said Bu Mari, poking in. 'I thought he had exams.'

'He has, but he doesn't need to be there all the time,' said Sri. 'You don't understand about these things, Bu.'

'I know when someone is trying to earn a living.' And she stalked off angrily.

The headman said to me: 'Do you think Benny will make it? I'm not one for pushing, but if I were Sae I'd be worried. If things come too easy, you can't force a change.' And he remarked on Jan, his son-in-law who, four years after marrying, still depended on him for food. 'I built the house and set him up – not that he was short of money, with the rice mill and all that. But my wife still cooks for them, takes their food next door every day. What can I say? It should come from him but he doesn't seem embarrassed.'

Benny and Jan had become friendly. They attended the prayer-house together and talked flatteringly of Jan's ambition to do the pilgrimage. They were part of the group of seven or eight men who chanted on Thursday evenings. So too was Drus, another would-be pilgrim; but Drus, with his rings and amulets and scary talk, made Benny, the trainee optician, nervous. Benny's wariness with Drus – he lowered his eyes, almost in shame, when the other man talked – made me wonder whether I had underestimated my sorcery-obsessed neighbour. Or perhaps he knew something that could not be passed on.

Benny liked to go round to Jan's to watch the boxing on television, each backing a winner. (The American boxers, with their meaningless names, they identified by size and colour, like fighting cocks: 'the fat one', 'red shorts', 'the white', 'the black'.) They had this much in common. And both men, young and consciously modern, 'progressive' and Muslim, had 'followed the wife' and settled with their in-laws. But Jan owned a great deal of land and helped out in his father's mill. He didn't need to work. Whole days went by when he did little but get ready for prayers or chanting, combing and oiling his short curly hair, adjusting his sarong and cap, gazing for minutes on end at his reflection in the full-length mirror (Mercedes, who spent time with Dewi, had told me this), before walking ten yards to the prayer-house or up the road to the mosque: this sequence repeated three or four times a day.

'What can I do?' said Pak Lurah. 'He's my son-in-law. And Dewi is still like a child; she won't be separated from her mother.' He lit another cigarette and, as if consoling himself, said: 'As long as Dewi is happy. As long as he doesn't take a mistress or a second wife. You know women can't stand that.' And he glanced backwards, with a pained grin, to the kitchen where Bu Lurah was working.

Perhaps stung by overheard remarks, Benny spent the next ten days in Jember, leaving Sri moping in the house, married, but more of a daughter – doubly a daughter – than a village wife. She still went off to her computer course in the afternoons, but without the girlish carelessness, the sense of escape. Now, as Bu Mari kept saying, she had got what she wanted. But unexpectedly life went on the same. The only difference was that she had moved from one mother to another, from Mari's ambition to Sutri's bewilderment. When Benny came back – Sri, affectingly, yelping with excitement – it was to announce his failure. Either his exams had gone wrong or his sponsor had pulled out; it wasn't clear. His expensive equipment (his 'capital', as he called it) he had had to sell back at half price. He would have to find work in Banyuwangi.

Grave, shuttered family conferences; late-night visits from the headman; solemn impractical advice (no doubt of a rambling and Javanist strain) from Great-uncle Harsono; and Bu Mari marching up and down the road between her house and theirs. It was a difficult period.

One morning, around ten, 'half the day gone', Bu Mari stormed up the road and hammered with her fists on the shutters of Sri's bedroom, screaming, 'Get up you lazy bastards! Get up!' I heard this from the headman: other reproaches could not be repeated. She walked back crying and distraught. We hid in our room unable to face her.

The crisis revived other, deeper conflicts. In the story of Sri's adoption there were at least two versions. In one, the two mothers, living in the same house, had from the beginning taken turns with the baby, and when Mari and Arjo set up on their own – the young childless woman and the ambitious schoolmaster-politician – it was easy and natural to take Sri with them. (Mari sometimes boasted she had borne Sri away 'when still red'; in fact, she and her brother were still one household.) In the other version, Sutri had surrendered her daughter to her scheming sister-in-law when the baby was already several months old, a loss from which she never recovered. She had had to take medicine – water blessed with magic words – to quell her yearnings, and had gone away for a week, or a month, to break the tie.

Sutri had also let her son, Sri's older brother, be temporarily fostered by a neighbour; but Busono had always come back to her: his foster-father was more of a godfather (to use our term) than a substitute parent.

'Why is it', said Sutri one day to the transvestite Panji, 'that people always want *my* children? I'm sure if I had ten, they'd all be taken from me.'

'You only have the pleasure of making them, dear,' said Panji with a smirk. 'I'm surprised you haven't produced a dozen more. One for each of the neighbours.'

Sutri slapped him, scandalized: 'Ooh, how could you! Listen to him, Andrew!'

One day, many years ago, when Sutri had gone off to the fields, Mari had looked in on their old shared house. She had waited for the boy to come home from school, fed him and swept up afterwards. When Sutri came back, she exploded. 'How dare she do that! As if I can't look after my own son. As if I can't keep a tidy house!' And later, Sae had run to Mari's house with a machete and had sworn to kill his sister. Their father, even then laconic, had stood between them and said, 'I hope you've got plenty of money, Sae.'

Over the years, incidents of this kind and other, lesser slights had led to periods when the two households were not on speaking terms. Nothing unusual in that: in a crowded and sociable community, 'not speaking' was the commonest way of dealing with conflict. Harmony meant that some voices had to fall silent. Women could be working side by side in the fields, or in the communal kitchens before a feast, and blank each other out. Only those in the know would know. The original offence – it might be trivial: an oversight or careless remark – could almost be forgotten as the invisible barrier became permanent. And then only something big – a birth or death – could restore relations.

After our departure, at the end of our first period of fieldwork, there was one such freeze. It lasted until just before our return three years later when the birth of Sri's son made the peace. Maternal rivalry had much to do with it. But not only that. Mari had wanted something better for her adopted daughter: she, the first woman in the village to read newspapers, the first to be fluent in Indonesian, the wife of a politician – Arjo, the saviour and educator of Bayu; she, the mother of Bayu's only female undergraduate. Then there was the matter of a veil.

A month after his return from Jember, Benny found work as supervisor in a prawn farm, one of the new ventures owned by the president's son. Much of the time he was away, but when he came home it was an event: laughing, presents, prawns all round. The family was happy; Sri less so; Mari was pacified; Benny restored to good grace.

*

In the middle of the month, two men died on successive days: a 'bad death' and a 'good death'. The leader of the *kunthulan* percussion group, Sugito, was electrocuted while changing a lightbulb in his house. It was eleven in the morning and the road was unusually busy with people coming back from the fields. A Colt pickup, a kind of covered wagon, happened to be passing – labouring uphill at ten miles an hour – when the calls rang out. The Colt shuddered to a halt in front of the house and a paramedic who was on his way to the plantation at Licin for his weekly surgery got down with bag and stethoscope. Instead of pronouncing Sugito dead, which might have shocked the family, he had him carried to the Colt and 'taken to hospital' (the Licin passengers with their chickens and baskets dumped beside the road). Halfway there, he told the driver to turn back.

By the time Sugito was brought in, the house was already crowded with the sympathetic and curious. At the sight of the Colt pulling up outside, a soft moaning broke within. Businesslike, knowing the routine, men lifted out the bamboo facade, opening the house to the street, and laid the corpse in state on the platform, head north, feet south, in the Islamic orientation. Under the batik sarong which covered it entirely, the body was naked. As people arrived, they lifted the corner to see Sugito's face. There was no queasiness in touching the dead. Pak Lurah, who had driven the hundred yards on his motorbike, sat on the platform and felt Sugito's arm, commenting that it was still warm. 'I saw him play only two days ago. The *kunthulan* will be dead without him.' *Kunthulan* was a tambourine group, though 'tambourine' sounds too limp and folky for the fierce, thrilling percussion: fifteen youths beating variously sized goat-hide tambours at incredible speed, crossing and multiplying rhythms, spurring each other on, sweat streaming down faces and arms. Sugito was the founder and leader of the Bayu group.

Kunthulan had its origins in Middle Eastern Sufi drumming groups, and in West Java drumming still went together with magical feats of endurance and Sufi chanting. Here it was strictly secular: Sugito's youths were the drinkers and gamblers, the all-night dancers, the motorbike boys. Sugito had brought them together, taught them discipline; and when they played – raising the temperature at weddings, the bride and groom approaching amid thunder – they forgot the crowds; as they boiled to a climax their gazes were interlocked, their faces ecstatic.

Inside now no one was crying. I could not see Sugito's wife; the children would be at school. The opened-out front room and the yard were busy with men; at the back, women prepared drinks, cooking the rice that would feed the mourners. By the head of the corpse was a small bench with offerings: a brass dish with betel on one side, a flask of water on the other, and next to the body a small brazier with a nugget of crepitating incense. Incense: the smell of life and death.

I was talking quietly with Pak Lurah when Sugito's wife came in.

She had been at a neighbour's house, being comforted away from the busyness. Now the neighbour led her in: she looked upset but not smitten; she could walk and speak. But at the very moment she entered, her father arrived – he had rushed over from his village three miles away. And as he faced her – a peasant in his work clothes – his prepared grimace melted and he was taken by a violent seizure, falling to the floor, thrashing, growling and grinding. Pak Ran, the healer, who had been tending the brazier, topping up the incense, said: '*Possessed.* A bad death.'

They carried him into the yard, rigid and foaming, his skin grey. The two elders took charge, Harsono cradling head and shoulders, reciting mantras, his brother Ran blowing on the crown, the spirit's point of entry. When he was calmer, they carried him, log-like, to a dark room at the back, and there they left him, alone but for a brazier (now two were needed, the dangers doubled), stretched out on the floor with his arms sticking up vertically, unconscious but quivering. No one paid him any further attention – I went round at intervals, half expecting him to have died – and apparently he woke up later in the day and remembered nothing. I know not what story lay behind this trauma, what guilt or frustration could fell the father-in-law or cause Sugito, scarcely dead, to possess him. Was it the horror of the moment, meeting his daughter on the threshold, composed but abandoned, four children to feed; or shock at the unnatural reversal, the young preceding the old into death; or something in the past that I would never know about: random death, home from the fields? 1965?

This was what fieldwork was like. Sometimes you grasped everything: the stories developed as you expected: character unfolded as plot; plot defined character. Then something happened that threw you. And before you had time to investigate, to fill in the picture, the scene had changed and it was too late; the events remained opaque and you would never know. There remained only the experience, the mark.

The young wife was now on the platform, bent over her husband's body quietly sobbing, her mother sitting behind her with her arms around her waist. Through the gate, women came from all over the village bringing tubs of rice on their heads, small children slung on their hips.

I went into the road to breathe, hardly registering the blinding sun: all this had happened in less than an hour. And then I realized it was Friday prayers, for smartly dressed men in sarongs and caps were filing down the road towards the mosque. Even-paced, purposeful, they passed the stricken house in their immaculate prayer-garb, not pausing to look to the right. Facing the flow, I met the village secretary, a man of my own age, and he shook my hand and smiled, as on any other day. He was fluent in the Indonesian governmental jargon, a man known to be 'progressive', a diligent Muslim. He glanced at the crowd, gave a fixed smile and passed on. My neighbour Untung, who had been carrying firewood to the house, said to me: 'They can pray at the mosque next week. But help with the dead can only be given now. Next time it might be their turn.'

Was it because Sugito, in their eyes, was a reprobate; or because his death was awkwardly accidental, a 'bad death' (or perhaps not accidental at all, but fated, a punishment), or because the 'intention', a part of the formula for worship, could not be broken, that they glided past? Like Untung, I was appalled.

And then, in a painful echo of his words, next day it was Untung's turn, or rather his father's. Arsad, the older brother of Warno the mystic, had been ill for a week. He had gone to the fields as usual and had collapsed in ripening knee-high rice. ('He won't see the harvest,' said Untung.) And while the mortuary rites were going on at Sugito's – the first of seven funeral feasts, spread over three years – a slightly larger crowd, less agitated, more orderly, gathered at Arsad's.

Again the routine took over. Women bringing rice; men smoking in the front room; the house folded out to publicize the death; the shrouded corpse lying in state; betel, a burning lamp, flowers in water; a glimpse of the face under the raised sheet; streaming incense.

Man consists of body, breath and soul, said the mosque official (who, as head of Islam, conducted funerals). *The soul is what survives: it's the soul I address at the graveside. For forty days it hovers about, clinging to the world. After the Forty-day Prayer-meal it enters the realm of the grave. At the End of the World, it is called to the Almighty. I don't believe it can bother the living, though some people say so. When they come to me saying they've been 'visited', I recite a prayer over a glass of water, they drink it and are cool again; but it's their conviction, not magic, which has cured them: thanks be to Allah. Nor can the dead come back in their grandchildren, as the Balinese say; though, it's true that if you tie a thread to a placenta before burying it, the thread is sure to reappear on the placenta of the next child; and so on up to the fifth. What possessed Sugito's father-in-law? Surely not Sugito himself. It must have been an evil spirit.*

Untung, the only son, the only surviving child, was solemn but composed enough to go off on a borrowed motorbike to give the news in another village. Warno, who had lived next door to his brother all his adult life, was – almost – the same as ever. Only Arsad's wife seemed upset. But why should one grieve for a completed life? One simply let go. Death, as Warno explained, was a change of realm. One 'returned to eternity'. This stuff, he said, pinching his arm, was a temporary housing. It would dissolve into its elements leaving nothing.

'Nothing,' repeated his sister.

To Arsad's wife this was a poor consolation, but she had heard it all before. Of the four siblings – three brothers and a sister – only Arsad had not joined Sangkan Paran, the mystical association. 'My religion is rice,' he used to say, like several of the villagers. 'And there's an end to it.'

To rice he had returned.

It was too late to bury him, so we sat around the corpse and talked. At midnight I went home with Mercedes and then came back again after an hour's rest. I wanted to see everything; more than that, I wanted to show solidarity to Untung. He was one of the people I liked most, admirable in his plainness and decency: a kind of Javanese ideal. The strength of Javanese civilization was not just in its most developed products, the glittering dancers and strong, independent women, the mystics and philosophers, but in its ordinary types who combined mildness with resilience, duty with a kind of cheerful poise, a simple acceptance of life. What Misti, next door, was for Mercedes, Untung was for me: the good Javanese; someone whom, in another life, one would like to be. What did it take to make a Misti or an Untung? That was what I had to find out.

The night was warm, the village quiet. Far away, in another village, someone was celebrating: a wedding or circumcision, the violin and the singer's high voice carrying across the fields. 'That's Ituk,' said Noto the carpenter, who recognized her style.

About fifty people remained in the cluster of houses around Arsad's, filling his yard, the benches and tables fitted between houses and fences, spilling out onto the path. Sitting up, 'staying awake', was something learned from childhood when you sat (and snoozed) through the dragon play; later you served at neighbours' events: two, three or four nights in a row without proper sleep. There was nothing worth doing that didn't last all night.

Conversation, or at least the tone of conversation, was not very different from that of happier occasions. People talked about death, but in a detached, even amused manner. (It was different at Sugito's.) They wanted to know whether the corpse in the West was dressed or just shrouded. One man said he had seen Christian corpses equipped with spectacles and shoes. It was wasteful but made sense, he thought. After all, you wouldn't go to meet the district officer in your sandals, let alone the Almighty.

Another man said it took up to thirty years for a body to rot away, depending on the soil. He had dug graves and found partially decomposed bodies that were already fifteen years old. All that time waiting for release! Warno said that it hardly mattered: what was gone was gone. That was why people only concerned themselves with the recently dead: but even they were as nothing. Pak Lurah began talking about Dayaks and cannibalism: how people in Borneo stored their dead in jars and ate morsels of flesh as a kind of penance. He had seen it on television. At this Warno raised his hand to his mouth, perhaps masking nausea. But it was an aesthetic response, not a moral one.

Warno's surviving brother, Taji, said that what one did with the dead in a practical sense was unimportant, as long as proprieties were observed. He himself had no fear of the ancestors: they were in us or they were nowhere. There was no separate realm of spirits, no afterlife. 'Only the living are eternal: we live on in our children, that's all, just as we existed before our birth in the mutual desire of our parents, and of theirs before them.'

'So why do people say prayers for the dead?' I asked. 'Why have commemorative feasts?'

'Well, of course, only the living actually hear. It's a kind of remembering, an acknowledgement of origins, of what we owe to our parents, to male and female. The words, like the food, are for us, the living. The ancestors can't hear, can't be helped. They don't exist.'

Rupo said, 'Strictly, if one believes they exist, then they do; if not, no.'

Harsono said, 'The funeral feast is symbolic, like everything in this world. But not everyone knows how to interpret symbols. The Muslim clerics don't.'

Purwadi, who had been listening with approval, said, upbeat: 'You know, Javanese are now surpassed by Chinese in the understanding of Sangkan Paran philosophy. I even know of Islamic teachers who have joined.'

'Is that possible? Do they give up praying then, doing the "five times"?' said Taji.

'No they carry on – so I believe. But they *understand* what they're doing.'

'Ah, so *dubbel*,' said Taji, reassured. (As a boy he had known Dutch.)

At intervals food was served; rice and meat, coffee; Untung ushering and taking care of everything, thanking visitors, making sure they had drinks and cigarettes. I played chess with Pak Lurah and beat him. Then Wan played him and won more easily. 'I hate chess,' said Pak Lurah, pushing away the board. 'I've always hated it.'

The funeral took place in the early morning. They had washed the body in seven kinds of water, the mourners supporting it on their knees, letting the water drench them. I asked the mosque official to explain.

'Charcoal water, to "wash the hair", to remove bad thoughts. Coconut water: "*Thus far is my life,*"' he sang. 'It's a leavetaking. Tamarind water: it cleanses. Water of *wedoro* [a cemetery plant]: so the dead are forgiven. Lovers' water: so the dead will be happy in the grave, like the time of lovers. Incensed water: happily installed, he is there for eternity. Fragrant water: so his name is fragrant.' The names and the effects were linked by puns and rhymes. The occasion, the ritual frame, was Islamic, but the technique and the sentiments were Javanese, the words 'fitting' in their rhymes, soothing in their rhythms. Arsad's wife, listening, was pleased; after the talk of ancestors and nothingness – talk she had passed in and out of – she looked relieved. The mosque official had hit the right note.

In the new cemetery, to the north of the village, twenty men took turns in digging the grave, the red earth flying up in spadefuls from both ends. As many men stood around smoking or offering helpful advice. 'More on this side.' 'Slow down to the south: he'll be sloping downhill.' 'At least you won't be digging anyone up here.' Not like the old cemetery with its layers of dead.

Under a rising sun that was hotter by the minute, the mourners who had attended the wake sat among the headstones and stunted, knotty trees; Untung between his mother and her sister; Arsad's brothers and sister overlooking the cavity. Nobody was weeping: 'once the mosque official arrives one may not cry.' Those who were not close to the family settled down in the shade of shrubs and low trees at a distance from the grave, content to wait. A warm breeze blew from over the fields and a treetop windmill whirred. The cemetery briefly freshened. At a signal from the mosque official – it was his domain – his assistant jumped into the grave, only his black cap and raised hands visible above the rim, and chanted the call to prayer: for Arsad himself, lest he forget. Then the shrouded body – no coffin – was lowered into a niche in the side of the pit, balls of clay under the neck, the midriff, and the feet; the shroud opened at the head so that the cheek touched the earth; facing Mecca. Under a parasol, squat and solid, oriental with his goatee, the mosque official read out the formal address to the dead, then the interrogation by the Angels of Death: *Who are you? Who is your Lord? What is your religion?*

A boy distributed flowers and coins, a kind of blessing, which we sniffed and returned. Then the mourners – everyone in the village who was around on that day – dispersed or walked back to Arsad's. His wife would not be left alone.

Everyone was satisfied. No matter what one believed or disbelieved in – angels, elements, Nothing – it was possible to take part, to give of one's best, to console and support, and to feel that the ritual, the mosque official's calm words, and the gathering had been right. It was hard to imagine a better solution to the needs of kin and community, the diversity of belief and the practicalities of death. It was what village Islam could do. In neighbouring villages that had come under the uncompromising rule of men like Aris and Tompo, things were different. The dead were beyond communication, sealed off in their torment or bliss. No graveside speeches, then, or requests for ancestral blessings; no symbolic ablutions (the lovers' water, the cleansing tamarind), and no room for the waverers and sceptics. No incense.

I had spotted Sae in the cemetery, hanging back, avoiding contact. Wan had been there too, uncharacteristically silent, chipping nervously at a stone. I had been out of the house all morning and had missed a row. When I came back, Mercedes told me that Sri had put on a veil and had shut herself in Sae's house. Her mothers were in tears. Sae had threatened to throw her out. Benny had gone off to his prawn farm in Bali.

14
The Spring in the Cave

The road south to the forest led away from the uplands through shelving tiers of rain-fed paddyfields and down onto flatter, drier plains watered by dikes. The countryside was entirely artificial: the rice terraces with their plots colour-coded by age, some straw-yellow, some brown and muddy, some bright green, set in mirror-like pools; the lines of shaggy coconut palms, oddly black and white in the harsh sun; the thatched huts on stilts; the cream-coloured stucco minarets planted at intervals across the fields, squat like Spanish windmills; the paved streamside bathing places; the stands of fruit trees shading yards; and then the clusters of red roofs and whitewashed bamboo houses. Lowland Java went on like this, list-like, endlessly accumulating, for hundreds of miles.

Towns were ugly and functional, the meeting place of power and commerce. Hardly varying from island to island, they showed a different face of Indonesia: concrete markets and government buildings, motorbikes and trishaws, army barracks (compounds of dark-green trucks), Chinese hotels and shops, roadside billboards advertising vampire movies, canopied stalls selling tofu, tangled posts of electric cables. We passed through Rogojampi – small but choked with traffic (the villagers held their mouths) – and then out again into balmy ricefields, a glitter of green and gold. I commented, thoughtlessly, that it was beautiful. Hadi, not bothering to glance to the side, said the land was poor, with lower yields than Bayu. He owned a rice mill: he knew the figures. A hectare in Bayu was worth two in Rogojampi: the soil needed more chemicals; the costs were higher.

The countryside, like the town, was functional: a workplace, not an object of contemplation. Only the courts – the palace cultures of

Yogya and Solo – were still devoted to art and beauty, things of leisure. But they had been in decline for two hundred years: Dutch conquest had seen to that. Change, new ideas, came from the towns and cities. But the strength of Javanese civilization, its cultural and human diversity, still lay in its villages.

I thought of the dragon show, with its painted backdrops of town and forest, its formally contrasted worlds of humans and spirit-animals. The village was somewhere in between: drawn by the glamour of town (such as it was), but prey to the tigers and spirits of the forest. Village life was robust, enduring; yet in the dragon play it seemed fragile, endangered: sunlight fringed with darkness. For as soon as you stepped outside the village – into the fields, the cemetery, the night – you were within reach of a hidden world. At midday too, when the demon Kala, son of the Hindu goddess Durga, stalked his prey. No one was foolish enough to work in the fields at noon.

Behind the house is a thicket of trees, said the carpenter. *Haunted: they may not be cut down. One night I was keeping watch over a durian tree – big fruit ready to drop – and I was lying back smoking a '76' when I heard this Grrrr. The bench began shaking, almost threw me off. Old Sumo heard the roar from his house and ran out shouting: 'Noto, get away! You'll be eaten!' It was then I remembered the advice to light a fire if you're on watch in a haunted spot. So I made a fire and challenged the spirit to show itself. Nothing. I stayed awake, just counting the durian as they fell, not daring to pick them up until daylight. But next day Sotelip went there to ask the spirit for lottery numbers. He burned incense, sat with his eyes closed like this, and the third time he asked there was a tremendous roar. Sotelip opened his eyes in terror and saw the tiger, the jaws more than a metre wide. He couldn't run. My wife found him unconscious when she went to the spring.*

There was a Java *within* that you couldn't see from a train window. Shadowing the workaday world, this inner world was only a step away, in trance, dream or possession. And between the parallel worlds, ritual operated as a kind of border control: keeping danger at bay, securing blessings, confirming order. The place spirits and ancestors, the rice goddess, the were-tigers, the legions of sprites and demons led by Kala: all could be controlled through the proper performance of ritual.

None of this was visible to the traveller. And if the land away from the volcanoes seemed an endless straggle of villages and fields, without direction or purpose, in reality life in the village was focused, concentric. You moved within circles, each circle sanctioned by collective ritual – the rotating prayer-meal invitations and neighbourhood work groups; the village-wide circumcisions and funerals; the inter-village weddings with their air of local competition and pride. There were also, of course, the daily trips to the fields; rarer visits to town; and the annual Lebaran bus journeys to saint's shrines, Surabaya zoo, or Bali-in-two-days. But to the village you always returned.

In the outermost circle, almost beyond reckoning, was Alas Purwo, the Primeval Forest. And it was there that we were headed, twenty-seven of us in a Colt pickup that hot May morning.

Our visit had been reconnoitred and, in a sense, scripted in advance, by an octogenarian named Tarsika. Tarsika had recently done the trip to 'prove' the contents of his Sangkan Paran handbook. He had gone there alone, with nothing more than a walking stick and the book as his guide, using its cryptic poems as map references. Standing in the middle of the forest, he had read out: 'Desire north, Essence to the south', and had known which way to walk. The directions must be correct because Alas Purwo was the place of First Things, and to go there was to return to one's origins. With a pure heart one could not go wrong. Moreover, Joyokusumo, the founder of Sangkan Paran, was now its guardian spirit. 'When my time comes, look for me in Alas Purwo,' he had told his followers. Back then, in 1956, men and women from Bayu had prepared his body for burial, washing the corpse on their knees. 'Not a drop touched the ground; we drank it all,' said Suyit, who had been one of the first initiates. Two days after they buried him Suyit had inserted an iron rod into the grave and it came up clean. The body, perfected, had vanished. *Look for me in Alas Purwo.*

'You have to remember that everything in the forest is symbolic,' Purwadi reminded us in a loud scholarly voice, as we bounced along in the Colt. 'The king of the forest, the tiger [*macan*] means "reading" [*macaan*]. So to enter the forest is to read it, to live its text. It's a place of spirits, so we must sift the material, the worldly, for what is refined and spiritual. That's how you read the forest.'

Tarsika had read his text very carefully. Like the other members, he knew the praise-songs and mantras by heart. He had wanted only to 'verify them', to 'apply them'. And his report on Alas Purwo, repeated and embroidered as he went from house to house in the days preceding our trip, made entertaining listening. The forest he described was straight out of Javanese mythology: steamy grottoes, temple-like banyan trees with dangling aerial roots; maze-like false trails; gibbons swinging from creepers; overgrown Hindu ruins; impenetrable thickets of bamboo. Following the book he had come to an isolated house; and as he approached he was met by a crone who greeted him with the Sangkan Paran salutation. 'It was then that I wondered *what* she was: hermit, spirit or vision? I answered her in kind, and she put her hands on my shoulders and said, *My child!* I sank to my knees and wept for joy.' It was hard to credit: she had lived there since the time of Sukarno, Indonesia's first president, perhaps since 'sixty-five'.

But she was not alone. When Tarsika had asked to stay the night, she replied: 'You must ask my companion. He's gone to the market for food.'

'Market! What market?' said Tarsika, looking round at the forest. 'But that's how it is in Purwo. It contains everything. You are hungry and suddenly there's a starfruit tree and you eat your fill. Or you wade through a pool and your pockets fill with fish. Or you might get lost – if you are the kind to get lost – and die.'

The old woman had shown him a tree watched over by Siti Jenar, and under it he had slept.* When he awoke, he followed the words

*Sheik Siti Jenar, one of the early Javanese saints, a mystical exemplar, was denounced as a heretic for proclaiming the identity of Self and God.

of a praise-song – *Attributes west, Being to the east* – and found himself at a cave. The entrance was concealed by bushes; the way within was narrow and slippery; bats clung to the roof. 'And there I saw Mother and Father: the dripping of the roof, Pa: the dark cavity, Ma.'

But it wasn't all sex. He had had to fight his way back through a tangle of bamboo and creepers. 'A metaphor of the historical struggle,' said Tarsika.

His meandering, didactic narrative had provoked curiosity and some scepticism. Who was the crone? Was she real or some kind of apparition, or the childlike fantasy of an old man? How had Tarsika come out alive?

'What you are privileged to see depends on you,' he said. 'I don't say you will find the same things.' He held out his hand and closed the fingers, making a flat-topped cone. Then he opened them, the fingers different lengths, pointing different ways. 'Human beings are the same but different.'

When I heard his story I was with Bambang, Bayu's 'head of youth'. Bambang had listened with a smile. But his father, the Sangkan Paran treasurer, had said, laughing: 'You can't believe it; but you can't disbelieve either. Perhaps Man Tarsika is right: each of us will find his own. You have to go there and see for yourself.' And so they did. Indeed, the whole clan – mother and father, grandfather, Bambang and his brother – now sat in the covered truck.

In the last village before Purwo, we stopped at the house of a Hindu mystic – a convert – known to some of the elders. He took his time getting ready to greet us: we heard the cranking of a well as he took a shower. This was a sign of respect, noted with approval. But he could not be persuaded to accompany us. 'It would be wrong. You must find your own way.' When he told us that his wife was a descendant of Joyokusumo's wife, there were nods and significant glances. From now on, you felt, everything would happen as it should: good or bad, nothing would be recognized as chance. And as we reached the forest – till then unknown to most of us – the feeling was of familiarity, not discovery. It was the same, when, a month earlier, I had accompanied a group of villagers to Baluran reserve on the northeast coast. The warthog that came up to be fed they had called Bagong after a clown in the shadow play who can assume the shape of a wild pig. They had held out their rice and bananas fearlessly, as though feeding a pet. And when we came to the savannah, with its herds of wild Javanese oxen, there had been no hesitation in crossing. After saying a mantra, the villagers had walked straight through them as though they were domestic cows. 'Yes of course they are dangerous,' they said, as we looked back at the white rumps, high horns and flicking tails. 'But not if you know the right words. You are recognized.'

The Colt trundled away, leaving us at the road's end; and there we had the first of many picnics: the parcels of compressed rice that tasted like cold potato, hardboiled eggs, chilli, and betel.

We followed a path through sparse woodland out to the ocean. Grajagan bay curved away in a white ten-mile arc. It was the longest, certainly the emptiest, beach I had ever seen, the end dissolving in haze. The forest came right down to the shore, which was banded white, ochre, then grey, sloping steeply into the sea. Unbroken from the equator to the Antarctic, the ocean was massive and fierce, the dark breakers thunderous. Under a looming grey sky the pilgrims made their way in little clusters around the bay, stopping now and then to examine some object thrown up by the surf or to rest for a moment and comment on the vastness and loneliness of the ocean. It was recognizably a village outing: men in wide-brimmed hats and baggy shorts; women in sarongs, some with cloths wound round their hair in rough turbans; everyone barefoot.

After an hour, at some landmark invisible to me we struck off into the forest and followed a track that led gently upwards, away from the booming surf. The treetops were low, the air damp and still; the leaves beaded with sweat. At frequent intervals there were rests for a cigarette or a betel chew; foreheads were mopped, bottles passed around. And then we moved on, sometimes only a line of women's baskets visible ahead, bobbing above the green. Not far into the forest and unexpectedly real, a long low hut came into view, smoke rising from its thatched roof. An old woman – no apparition – emerged to greet us, blessing us with a Javanist formula. It was all as Tarsika had said: even Bambang was impressed. One by one we moved forward and knelt, pressing faces to her hand. She may not have been a spirit, or even a saint, but only a special person could live so far from society: she deserved our respect. I too stooped and felt her hand on my shoulder, heard her words of acknowledgement.

The brothers Warno and Taji, in their customary black, were last to greet her. They bowed like the rest; but after they had taken her aside and talked to her for a while, Warno turned back to us with a broad smile and we understood. Tarsika had been overawed by a couple of eccentrics.

Dinner, however, was all that one could have imagined: hornet soup – two-inch-long insects floating in a transparent glue – followed by frog stew; the frogs whole, in a lapping spawn-like gel. (One for *The Anthropologist's Cookbook*, I thought.) Suyit, at seventy still boyishly enthusiastic, said: 'One bowl of hornets is equivalent to twenty-five injections. No tonic more powerful.' And he made an upraised fist. Ma Suyit, fifty years his wife, rolled her eyes. Taji swallowed a whole frog and said, choking: 'Makes you feel hot. Muslims can't eat this stuff. *Haram*.' At which his brother laughed. 'I don't want to feel hot. I'm quite hot enough, thank you. Min and I have brought our own rice cakes. Here, anybody want some?'

While we ate, the old woman's companion came in with an armful of firewood. ('Back from the market,' some jested quietly.) Again the exchange of formalities, now less extravagant; and then we went out to bathe in a freshwater lagoon, not far from the shore, women among men 'like brothers and sisters'.

The rocky margin of the lagoon, a purplish lava, granite-hard, extended outwards just below the water so you could walk seemingly on the surface of the sea. Bambang followed me out, Christlike, to look at hand-sized starfish that clung in the hollows. As we made our way back to the hut, Bambang said, 'I've noticed that Westerners in films like to stroll by the sea on their own, don't they.

Why do they do that? Is it romantic?' Some days later he told me that he had seen spirit men out on the ocean, calling me, and he had followed in case they had lured me away. His father had seen them too: they could not believe that I hadn't. What, then, had drawn me to the sea?

Back at the hut the old couple pointed out the best places to sleep. Their bedstead held only four. But there was room on the floor for half a dozen more. And outside there was the banyan tree watched over by Sheik Siti Jenar. The snakes wouldn't dare bother us.

Under the tree, now wrapped in their sarongs, though it was hardly cool, the elders swapped stories of things they had seen in sacred spots, visions they had been 'granted' in meditation. Purwadi remembered meditating in one of the caves with his guru, Dasip from Tembakon. 'That was before I joined Sangkan Paran. We sat in the cave in total darkness – stark naked, mind – and meditated for twelve hours. Dasip could go on for days like that: he didn't feel the cold. At one point a cobra reared up in front of me. But I didn't panic. I held its gaze and it backed down. Dasip had put a pot of slaked lime beside me to ward off danger, telling me to dab some on whatever confronted me. So I did, putting a blob on the cobra's head. Next morning we compared notes; told what we had seen. When I mentioned the snake, Dasip said: "Look under your sarong; what do you find?" And there on my manhood was a white streak of lime. A sign, said Dasip, of what was tempting me: "You can't go far on the mystical path until you give up womanizing."'

We slept under the stars and at dawn set off through dripping bamboo forest for the caves. It was hard going, every muddy overgrown trail leading nowhere. The old couple had given us directions, but the sun was barely visible, there were no landmarks, and we got lost. After about two hours of climbing and slithering, Hadi said: 'I'm sure I've passed this tree at least twice before. We are going in circles. Who has brought a boiled egg?' 'Not me,' said Elan. 'I ate mine on the beach.' But he looked guilty. Boiled eggs being round, one walks in a circle.

We opened our bags, checked for eggs, and had another picnic.

On all sides, big-leaved plants, soaring trees, creepers, bamboo as thick as drainpipes, no hint of a trail. I doubted we could even retrace our steps: the forest had closed behind us. Bambang took the initiative and began slashing a path with a machete. Perhaps the trail was concealed and he would find it. On inauspicious days one was blocked, stymied. There were roots that formed slip knots, tripping the unwary, catching at the feet. But you had only to pull them and they unravelled 'like an empty rice parcel'. The paths opened if you hit on the right form of words, saw things in a proper context. There was a way to finding the way. Tarsika had said, 'As in meditation, you have to surrender yourself; let the forest lead you.' But a sense of resignation had spread through our party, a collective shrug. We had not yet reached that dizzying state known to Javanese as *keblinger*, when one has totally lost a sense of direction. One man pointed to a leaf and said 'north'; another indicated a fern and said, 'Or shall we go west?' But we were as good as keblingered.

Seated on a fallen tree, leathery and sprite-like, Suyit took a photo from his breast pocket and began saying a mantra. The photo was of Joyokusumo. He beckoned me over and I saw a tall, pale young man in a Javanese turban, dark jacket and sarong, his hands loose at his side: a colonial-era portrait. Suyit turned the picture over. It was the same man in similar clothes, now old. 'He changed with the moon, see. In the waxing phase he was young, in the waning phase old. He was male and female. Look at the hands: the right is like yours or mine, the fingers of the left are flush, like a woman's parts.' The holy man as hermaphrodite, a symbol of completeness, the complementarity of male and female. 'But he never had children. His wife wasn't really a wife, just a companion, like the old couple in the house.'

'Miraculously' we were rescued. Two ragged men came upon us – sent by Joyokusumo, said Suyit; outlaws, said Rupo – a moment of mutual surprise, more pleasing for us than them. We made a line to greet them and they filed shyly past, touching hands, eager to be away. Again the question went round: what kind of men could live here, so far from the world, with nothing and nobody? And what a coincidence! 'Vagabonds and outlaws,' insisted Rupo.

Hardly a word was exchanged, but they showed us the way. It was all as it should be.

The Padepokan Cave was formed by a breach in a cliff above the line of the forest, the crevice black, fringed with bushes, against the limestone bluff. On hands and knees we made the final ascent, the trail now visible, thick with symbols. Warno, forging ahead, said we were putting the teaching into practice, proving Joyokusumo's words. The movement up to the cave suggested the passage of life-force from the heel along the limbs and up through the torso, the flight of feeling at the point of death. But the entrance, the narrow insertion, was Life.

From the Padepokan Cave it was possible to move diagonally down to the Palace Cave, but we retraced our steps with pedantic precision. 'You have to go in and out the same way,' said Ma Suyit. 'How you were made: how you were born. Understand?'

We had reached the climax of our journey.

The Palace Cave was unexpectedly large, dome-like; the air dank and acrid. Clustered on the roof, darkly visible in the mass, a moving layer of bats, their droppings falling around us like heavy spots of rain. With the air of a cathedral guide, Warno led us forward, crouching before unusual formations – a coral-shaped structure that projected from the floor 'like hands in supplication'; a swollen stalagmite 'like a pregnant woman'; a raised platform of rock, like an altar, on which lay the remains of offerings: incense sticks, ashes, petals. Bambang's father squatted before it and said a prayer to the guardian spirits, 'those who watch'. On the altar he left some straw cigarettes and coins. Others were absorbed in quiet contemplation. Rupo had lit a torch of leaves. He followed the gleaming wall, scattering sparks, his face red and cadaverous in the glow.

In groups of three or four we moved forward into the darkness, feeling our way, and then fell to hands and knees and crawled in wetness to the black interior, 'the inside of the inside'. At the end was a spring. And there, amid the squeaking and flapping of bats, the air tangy with ammonia, we splashed faces and drank, laughing and spluttering.

What was it, the spring in the cave? I think of the flower-water of the funeral; the drenching of children in a shadow-play exorcism; the dousing of the generations after a Retirement Prayer-meal; the making of holy water in literary recitals: water always the ritual lubricant, the instrument of purification. Lustrations, 'fragrant water': *banyu wangi*. To the mystics, the spring was something more: not an elixir – they were symbolists, not magicians – but an image of life, of generation. A return to the source of things – to the moment of conception when the universe came together to make an individual, 'the great world into the little' – was a moment of transcendence. Apprehended as a whole, or in miniature (the world in a grain of sand), life was always Life: unaccountable, beyond human reason, divine.

We returned to the house and bathed again in the lagoon, talking quietly, our voices small against the distant surf. Then we set off back through scrubland and secondary forest to the bay and the trail to where the Colt was waiting. As we motored back, people spoke of their experiences and what they now felt, as after a night of meditation. There were small things to 'take away', but no epiphanies, nothing extraordinary. Three of the party who had become detached from the group had spent the night in the forest and heard the roars of tigers, but luckily they had survived and made it back to the pickup. Bambang's father had come across a quartz crystal and was said to be 'granted' his treasure. We had been lost and were fortunate to be found. But that was all. Warno, who had slept under the tree of Siti Jenar after meditating half the night, had had a dream. He dreamed that his feet were placed one on top of the other as he slept. A piece of wood leaned against his soles and a boy climbed up the wood and picked a fruit from the top. When the boy descended the fruit vanished. It was a presentiment that next day we would have no mystical trophies, nothing to bring away. But this was no reason to be disappointed, said Warno. More important than any revelation, the whole party had proved what Joyokusumo had said; fitted experience to words. Alas Purwo was well named. *Alas* meant basis, *purwo* meant origin. So to penetrate the secret places of Alas Purwo was to know one's origins. There was no need to look for supernatural realities, said Warno; no need to go outside. The forest was inside us, as we were inside the forest. Its spooks and demons were our own; its springs and caves told the story of every human being. 'It's like the shadow play. People see their fears come to life on the white screen; but they are only shadows of the reality. They marvel at the heroes; they quail at Kala. But they carry their demons within them. The good and the bad, the brave and the weak. All are in us.'

15
Initiation

I found myself drawn to the mystics. In a simple-minded way, we like people who like us; and among the mystics I felt accepted and liked. But there was more to it than that. Added to the usual Javanese friendliness, there was an openness about them, a human sympathy that was hard to resist. They seemed to exemplify the Javanese virtues of social harmony, empathy and gentleness. It was these qualities rather than their esoteric ideas that first attracted me. In most respects, of course, they were like other villagers, including some of the devout Muslims with whom I was on good terms. But their attitude towards their ideas was different, and this led to a different way of thinking, a more tolerant, open-minded approach to life, a certain fix on the world that in the end made for a different kind of relation, perhaps even a different kind of person. To be attracted to the person was therefore, indirectly, to find something congenial in the ideas, the way of thinking.

As I spent more time with Warno and Rupo, I noticed that their way of thinking had got under my skin. When some odd comment – a phrase from a sermon, a peasant's invocation, a cleric's pronouncement – happened to lodge in my mind, I would find myself saying: *That sounds silly, but it makes sense from a Sangkan Paran point of view.* Particular religious dogmas and practices – the Christian trinity, the incarnation, Muslim saints, heaven and hell, prayer, the multicoloured offerings of ritual – seemed less parochial, less arbitrary, when seen as human symbols, even if practitioners themselves did not see them as such. Warno's relativism was not, of course, like that of the anthropologist, a suspension of disbelief, a sense that 'whatever they say or do makes sense in terms of the native logic and way of life'. His way of 'locating' meanings, putting things in a different context rather than simply dismissing them, allowed them an intrinsic value. Supposing the great religions, with their creation myths, heroes and villains, were ways of grasping the human condition, symbolic meditations on life and our place in the cosmos rather than the factual statements they purported to be, they could speak to anyone: Adam and Eve were Everyman and Everywoman; the prophets were exemplars, even bodily symbols; the scriptures were cryptic essays on the person. Supposing religious rituals were ways of enacting and deriving these insights, their weirdness, their historical contingency, no longer counted against them. A pilgrimage traced an interior journey, an anatomizing of the human spirit. The names and places in themselves didn't matter. Conversely, one could make the pilgrimage without leaving one's house. The mistake was to take the symbol for the reality, to bow down before symbols.

The humanism of the mystics, so different from orthodox faith in external authority, still depended on a certain attitude of reverence that was part of the religious outlook. But because the *object* of reverence was different – or rather the direction of gaze – the fundamental religious question – *Why?* – remained unasked. In the mystical perspective it was unnecessary, unanswerable. Without a transcendent creator there was no reason *why* anything should be as it was; no motive for creation. You contemplated the facts as they were. It was enough to recognize, to feel, to experience.

Western secular humanism has lost this capacity for reverence. To find anything similar outside conventional religion you have to go back to the nature-worship of the Romantics or – a closer parallel – Sir Thomas Browne and the Neoplatonists. Common to all is a thread of pantheism. Yet the fact that there is Something rather than Nothing – more importantly, that there is life – should be just as astonishing to the unbeliever. The mystery of life – what it is, what it depends on, how it is transmitted – ultimately is no less a mystery to the scientist. You cannot make it, observe it under a microscope, or reduce it to something else; but it is not a theological fiction. And when, back in Oxford, I asked a zoologist-turned-medic for a definition, he looked at me askance and then said: 'It's not a question we would normally ask. But I suppose life is the ability to reproduce.' A Javanist answer.

Boiled down to essentials, Javanism – and especially its philosophical flowering in mysticism – is a heightened appreciation of the facts of life, and in these terms I could come close to the Bayu mystics; I could learn from them. (Their ethics – a prudential self-reliance, a rejection of external authority, a harmonizing with the natural order – were less inspiring, if unobjectionable.) I was not being pious about their pieties (they had few); I wasn't pretending anything to myself; nor was I putting on the anthropological fancy dress. As a father, the witness of my children's births, I was privy to the same wonders that affected them. I was a man alive, made of the same stuff, asking similar questions.

Why, then, not go the whole hog and join the club? In part it was a desire not to be too closely allied with any particular group. My work depended upon neutrality, an ability to move freely about the village and listen to everyone. I could have friends, but not allies or enemies. I did not want to come away with a partisan view. There was also at the back of my mind the spectator's reluctance, a sense that it was not my thing, that I would be kidding myself. Yet if I did not quite believe in it for myself, to my surprise I believed in its possibility. It was only my Anglo-Saxon dullness that got in the way.

Nevertheless, to the mystics I increasingly turned. After late-night philosophical sessions I walked back through the silent village disturbed but elated. The 'rubbing together' of ideas, the making of connections, was exhilarating. The words stayed with me; but so too did the Javanist mood – light but somehow weighty, playful but serious, a gay science. I could not say why, but I knew that if I had personal worries, it would be Warno or Rupo whose steady voice I would want to hear. In this I was not alone. When Pak Lurah had domestic problems or quarrels with the 'fanatics' he would drive west for advice, sometimes taking me along. 'Come on, let's call on Man Warno.' We would drink Warno's excellent coffee and he would turn over the problem in abstract terms, never mentioning names or accusations, always deploring confrontation and magical remedies. 'There's no point in holding a prayer-meal unless you practise what makes for wellbeing,' he would say. 'A mantra is only to light the way, like a torch. But what's the point of a mantra unless you can ground the meanings in your actions?' He would end with a wry laugh: 'So how, then, do things stand for you now, Pak Lurah, narrower or broader?'

One night, very late, I was sitting with Warno in his big empty house when a large bear-like man entered in a hurry, a look of urgency on his face. He had cropped hair and a coarse, bruised complexion; he wore an army T-shirt over his big belly. It was Sarko, the village security chief, Bayu's 'iron fist'. I knew him from the early days of fieldwork when he had often come to see me, presumably to sound me out for suspect political opinions. Staring at me with bloodshot eyes, he would say: 'So communists have a better system of government, giving away everything to the people, do they? Ah, so *that's* what communism means! Is that what you think too?' And: 'So back home, are you a rich person or a poor person?' It was a curious role play – 'fishing', they called it – his affected stupidity, my refusal to take the bait. Wan, who watched us, would laugh and later repeat the dialogues to neighbours.

In the 1960s Sarko had run secret missions across Java for the Nationalists, and after the fall of the first president, Sukarno, in 1966 he had persuaded Arjo to jump ship and switch to General Suharto. Sarko was not a timid man. But that night he had been thinking of his old comrade when an owl had flown into his house and startled him. 'Its head was like a kitten's and it fixed me with its eyes before flying out.' He cocked his head to the side and made his eyes bulge. 'If it's a sign that something is going to happen, I need to know what.'

Warno took down his copy of the *Life of Joseph*, a version in archaic Javanese that was often recited at circumcisions. Although the story derived from the Koran, and ultimately from the Book of Genesis, it belonged now to Javanese literature, and it had a sacred value of its own, as did the book it was written in. Warno's copy was leather-bound, in his own handwriting, Javanese script. He contemplated it for a moment then let it fall open: he would divine Sarko's fate.

The key words between his thumbs – in red and black, on opposite pages – happened to be 'without power' and 'from his house'.

'Well?' Sarko was pale, awaiting the verdict.

'It means the owl had not intended to fly at you: hence, "without power". It was lost – away "from his house". For you it has no significance.'

After Sarko had gone, I said, 'Why did you use the Joseph story to tell him that? Did you need it?'

'Sarko wouldn't have believed me otherwise. He was convinced it was a sign. Besides, my copy always falls open at that page, and I knew the words would reassure him. Sarko isn't the type of person to whom unexpected things happen. He likes to be ahead of events. That's why he was worried.'

Warno and Rupo were the rationalists; but there was a different side to Sangkan Paran, and to Javanism generally, that was closer to the magical world of men like Noto, with his tales of tiger-spirits, to the omens of Sarko and the spirit visions of the headman's mother. It was difficult to reconcile this enchanted world with Rupo's scepticism or Purwadi's refrain that there was 'nothing outside'. Yet in the hands of veteran adepts like the brothers Suyit and Suhem, the spirit world became a playground, a kind of mnemonic for their mystical exercises. Through wordplay and etymology, number and allusion – difficult to convey in translation – they would leap from sign to sign, symbol to symbol. If the world existed, it was as an object of thought.

SUYIT: Listen, Andrew. The time for teaching is midnight, when the hands of the clock come together.

SUHEM: When male and female come together.

SUYIT: Then all is revealed.

SUHEM: When six and six become twelve. Six feelings; the

twelve constituents. Twelve into one: a new person.
SUHEM: When the flame of the candle is straight.
SUYIT: To tell it before your feast [initiation] would be to endanger you. The plate must be clean before the food is served.
SUHEM: Consider the betrothed: they can only go so far. Married, everything is permitted.
SUYIT: Listen, Andrew. What do the pious say? That God is *up there*? In oneself, we say: in the body, but where?
SUHEM: You're bitten by a mosquito; you feel it. *There* is God. God moves about. Have you scratched an itch? There! God itches.
SUYIT: How do you say *ngoyo* in English?
AB: Pisses.
SUYIT: Ah, that's it. God is in 'pisses'. God farts, God pisses. The whole body, the whole movement.
SUHEM: You don't need to go to the mosque to pray: you have prayed before you've set foot on the road.
SUYIT: *I am alive, I learn to die.* Not religion, not magic: knowledge of humanity.
SUHEM: Do not follow the words of the dry book. Follow the wet book.
SUYIT: The writing without a board. Scratch it and blood flows.

And so on.

And so I was initiated. Curiosity, congeniality, friendship had led me there. My preceptor came from another town. He was an irrigation official, a small, grey-haired man, missing teeth, with a kindly expression. There are no gurus in Sangkan Paran – 'the only guru is oneself' – and Joyokusumo, the founder, was as much a symbolic figure as a real historical person. But there were teachings that could only be passed on at initiation, 'when the hands of the clock come together'. To receive this teaching, these strong words, one had to be fortified: to the unprepared they were dangerous. 'You wouldn't pass a powerful current through a thin cable,' said Purwadi. 'It would burn out. Initiation is a kind of insulation.' Yet over the year I had already acquired the basics of Javanist thinking: the sanctification of life, the indwelling divinity, microcosm and macrocosm, the impersonal Self, the ethics of mutuality, the preoccupation with sex and generation, the techniques of interpretation, the relativizing of other traditions. These things I had learned over coffees and prayer-meals, in caves, at funerals, at all-night Joseph-readings, and in the endless small-hours debates whose voices still echo in my head.

So many words, but always joined to experience. And that was what distinguished Sangkan Paran from the esoteric classical tradition and from the other, more doctrinal, sects in which Java abounds: the fact that its ideas had to do practical service, like the tools of the field. It was as patient and tenderly practical as gardening.

The initiation was to take place at midnight, doors closed, in the house of the treasurer, Bambang's father. I knew roughly what was expected of me: to join the communal meal, undergo a ritual bath, a death-in-life burial, and then receive the mystical instruction. I would be asked for a sign, some token that the teaching had 'taken'; perhaps some illumination. This worried me. In the days before the meal a poem by Robert Frost kept coming to mind in which the poet looks into the reflected depths of a well, seeing treetops, clouds, sometimes his own face: but nothing more. What right has he to expect more? But once, as he gazes rapt into the water and waits for the ripples to calm, a lightness clears at the bottom of the well. A glimpse of eternity or a mere stone? He cannot say, but he has seen it: *For once, then, something.*

I used to be an active Muslim, said Suyit. *In 1945, I was part of Hezbollah, the Islamic force the Japs set up to repel the Dutch. I had to chase after people in the village to make them pray! I was a fanatic. My younger brother was the same. Suhem even wanted to go on the pilgrimage. He had obtained a passport, raised the money and everything, and then he heard about Joyokusumo. We went to Jati and talked to him, or rather listened to him – you didn't say much, as he knew what you were going to say anyway. At Jati we learned that Java had twice been colonized: the Dutch colonized our bodies; the Arabs our souls. We learned the true meaning of Islamic worship, the true location of Mecca; how to read the wet book. After Harsono I was only the second to be initiated. They all come to me for instruction before doing it – even Warno! 'What will I see?' they ask. I tell them (not many would dare tell): 'If you see red, that's mother; white is father; yellow, the Hidden.' Whatever you see, that will protect you. Not your own mother or father – they are only mediators; but the eternal Mother; the eternal Father; or the bright light that precedes all, the spark before conception, before the world comes into being.*

The meal took place at eleven. It followed two hours of quiet chat; then a long 'unrolling' of the mystical chant: men and women together, voices in unison. For the banquet, no offerings, no symbolic foods: only incense, a rice mound and fragrant water. But the chicken had to be my match – male, already mated, near middle-age; and I had to eat at least something from every part.

Under the porch, the preceptor's assistant doused me with flower water, a cold shock in the night air. Then, clad only in a sarong, I went through to the back room, now crowded with witnesses. I lay with my head in the lap of Tirta Utama, Flawless Water (the preceptor's ritual name), aligned north–south, like a corpse. He threw a shroud over me. Through the white fabric I saw the dark shapes of the witnesses, the preceptor's head bent over me, and the peak of his Javanese turban. In the silence, I felt the object of intense concentration and at the same time a curious detachment and lack of will: what would happen would happen. And then the oil lamp was extinguished and we were in total darkness. I was in the grave. Still wet from the bath, I felt a chill on my skin but also an exhilaration and warmth from inside as after swallowing liquor. Tirta Utama recited the list of twelve preceptors, from Muhammad and Siti Jenar through the kings of Java and on up to Joyokusumo. Twelve was completion, the human inventory, the date of Muhammad's birth.

He himself was grade thirteen; I would be fourteen. Then he pressed on my eyes – was it fourteen times? 'What do you see?'

I saw only blackness. 'Nothing.'

He tried again. 'Still nothing.'

'Better take him outside and douse him again.'

The assistant led me out past the remains of the meal and the mild, curious stares of the other participants. Under the porch he dunked me in the barrel of water and took me back again, shivering, into the dark room. The procedure was repeated in every detail. Again the gentle tapping on the eyes, the focusing of sensation, the peculiar bodily hot-cold feeling like the burn of snow. 'This time what do you see?'

I waited, expecting something, expecting nothing. 'Nothing.'

Too engrossed, too physically absorbed, to do anything other than concentrate on the moment, it no longer worried me what failure would mean. To cheat was unthinkable. But perhaps my intention had wavered.

Tirta Utama said, 'The return to one's origin must be pure, prepared' (or some such phrase). 'Take him outside.'

Again the dousing – this time more of a scrubbing – the smiles (a hard case, this one, perhaps hopeless), the wet feet on cold marble, the shroud, the darkness and the question.

He pressed hard on my eyes and said, 'Look at the point of your nose. What do you see?'

Impossible to look at anything: the darkness and isolation were total. I saw nothing. But I heeded his directive. In this nowhere there must be a point, a focus. And then, at the last pressure, a squinting flash. *White.* Gone before I could be sure, but the effect had been unmistakable.

'White,' I said, in a voice that sounded very loud. The life flowed back into my limbs and I sat up.

For once, then, something.

And so began a catechism which I recognized from the mosque official's graveside speech as the interrogation of the dead by the Angels of Death. Some of the questions were the same, but the prompted answers were different. Sitting opposite Tirta Utama, still shrouded – he held the ends, enclosing us both – I repeated the secret formulas, learned about the passage of life-force from the dying person (traced, electrically, on my skin by his hand) and made the solemn vows, answering 'Yes' or 'No' as required. Later, and to my shame, I remembered that I had replied in the ordinary Osing dialect, not the correct form of High Javanese. Tirta Utama had been unperturbed. His last action was to tie a thread around my right wrist. It recalled the umbilical cord worn as a talisman by infants in a locket around their necks. But the wrist cord was more symbolic than magical. It was a token of mastery (the same Javanese word means 'thread' and 'power'): not of individual attainment, but the human mastery of the universe which mysticism taught. 'It will drop off after a month, but it'll always be there,' Suyit had said. 'Don't try to remove it early: you'll go mad.'

Next day there were smiles of surprise at the thread. The neighbours were pleased. 'We didn't think you'd go through with it,' they said. 'When the baby's grown Mercedes must do it too.'

Pak Lurah held my wrist as if taking my pulse and said sadly, 'One day. One day. I'm too caught up in things right now.'

'Ah, all that talk and nonsense,' said his mother. 'All that matters is that you're good to the neighbours, left and right.'

There were a few mockers. Bu Mari said to Mercedes: 'What does he want to do that for? *Him*, supposed to be a Christian! He'll go to hell.' But Wan was impressed. 'I might start visiting Man Warno when you've gone,' he said. Things hadn't gone too well for him since our visit to the shrine: his carpentry had taken off, but there was no sign of a wife. The spirit's prophecy had failed.

I was a little nervous about how the pious would take it. The mosque official, ever jovial, slapped me on the back and said that now I must study Islam properly too. 'I already do,' I protested. But Jan, the headman's son-in-law, was scornful. 'What's that thread for, then? Back to babyhood? You'll be like Hari!' He and Dewi laughed and I felt their laughter was a little forced.

Pak Lurah said, 'Your father wore it twenty years ago when you were Hari's age. Hasn't he ever explained?'

'I don't want to know,' said Jan. And then a touch defensive: 'I only want to know what's right; what we are taught in the mosque.'

The initiation, so late in our stay, was more of a completion than a beginning. It released me to think of other things, to gather up the loose ends of my work and remember why I had come to Java. But it also tied me to a group of people in a far corner of the world. The thread would always be there.

16
The Veil

'Sri is like a ghost! A ghost!' whispered the girls, as a tall figure in a floor-length blue gown and white nun-like headscarf swept across the road and vanished into the house. The girls held their hands to their mouths in the gesture of shock. They could not recognize their childhood friend: she had become somebody else. There was something fearful in their whispered huddle, and seeing them close ranks I recalled a moment in an earlier period of fieldwork, years before, in the tribal society of Nias. The occasion was a wedding in which a girl had been married off to a much older man. I remembered the clumsy handing over of brideprice, the girl's sullen acceptance, the gay-sad wedding dance, and the row of stunned, resentful faces as the bride's friends watched her being taken away, knowing they might suffer the same fate. Sri was still with us, but how could she continue to live among her friends in the old way? The girl who would dance about the house, singing and tossing her hair, had been taken from them. A ghost.

Our neighbour, Untung, a man of simple modesty, said to me: 'I would never let Katri dress like that. She's a good Muslim, does the prayers – unlike me and her mother – but there I would draw the line.' I had noticed a sticker on the inside of his front door. Katri, his fourteen-year-old daughter, had put it there. It said *How to dress in the Muslim way* and it pointed out what had to be covered: the hair, the shape of the body, everything except the hands and face.

'It's only for the mosque,' said Untung. 'And even that's not strictly necessary. It's an Arab custom because of the desert storms. The men wear gowns too.'

Nobody in the village had ever worn the full headgear and gown outside of religious occasions. Even the mosque official's daughter –

unusually pretty with her long plaited hair and close-fitting dresses – wore the garb only in the prayer-house. It marked a separation, a distinction between sacred space where one was anonymous, an abstract individual before God, and the social world where one had personality, name, recognition. In Java there was no sharp boundary between domestic and public space, no concept of purdah. Within the village, a woman could move anywhere unhindered, without fear or shame. But Sri's act of veiling had brought a division.

The Muslim veil is many things: badge of modesty; shield of family honour; armour of purity; entry into purdah; act of piety; token of female subservience (or liberation); political (or fashion) statement; personal sacrifice; repression (or expression) of personality; conformism or personal choice (or both); action or reaction; retreat to the past; embrace of modernity. Its meaning varies among the young and educated, the rural peasantry and the newly radicalized, as it does between traditionally segregated societies, the multicultural West, and modernizing Asian cultures. Wearing a headscarf to the market in Egypt is not the same as putting on Islamic garb in a European school; nor is 'veiling' in school equivalent in France, England and Java.

In the West we are used to seeing Muslim women in headscarves, gowns, even the full face-veil. Images of Afghan women in blue tent-like garments still fill us with horror and pity, but lesser forms of veiling no longer surprise. Covering, like display, we now understand, is culturally relative. Naked or covered, what once shocked hardly merits notice. Besides, there are highly educated, articulate young Muslim women in the West to tell us that veiling is a form of freedom and liberation, a rejection of the commodification of the female body and enslavement to male lust. A woman does not need a body or even a face to participate in public life.

This logic is as alien to most of Indonesia as it is to the modern, secular West. In the world's largest Muslim nation, and especially in Java, a woman's physical presence, her appearance and comportment, are as much a part of her public character, her way of being in the world, as a man's. That presence is gendered, feminine, even sexual. But a woman is not therefore a sex object; nor is a man defined as a sexual predator. The village is not the jungle. A man's gallantry or respect towards a woman is not disguised lust. Whatever her age or status, he can respond to her as a woman without the implication of intrigue or insult. (This is different from the cultivated neutrality of much Western behaviour.) Men and women alike wish to appear polished and pleasant, fair representatives of their sex, even if they cannot be beautiful. But physical allure, if dangerous, is not shameful. Women are not perceived as the natural victims of men: they can attract or accept the man, sometimes they can pursue him; and they can say no.

To Javanese, all this seems – or once seemed – simple and obvious; and if it does not fit our picture of Muslim societies, then, clearly, our picture is wrong, or at any rate, partial. Meekly, uncomfortably, we recognize more and more extreme statements of Muslim ideology as authoritative. We accept that men – certain men, justified by their beliefs – cannot control their violent impulses, and that women are to blame if they are provoked. We accept that the price for women's safety is their seclusion. But Java shows that there are other ways of being Muslim; other ways that are threatened by the puritans and by our acceptance of the puritan view as legitimate and representative.

To understand the meaning of veiling in a Javanese village, it does not help to think of Middle Eastern Muslims or South Asians, with their traditions of segregation, their strict division of public and private worlds, their codes of honour and shame, and their greater sexual inequality; or of young European Muslims with their politicized sense of injury and pan-Islamic solidarity. Imagine, instead, the impression of your own mother or sister suddenly covered. Imagine, further, that you live in an intensely sociable community where doors are always open, where 'standing out' and 'being different' are deplored, where the essence of good manners is to make others feel 'at home', and where relations between men and women are relaxed and equable. In such cases, the veil is more than a breach, it is a social offence.

What compounded the offence in Sri's case was the apparent lack of meaning. Not being Pakistanis or Arabs, the people of Bayu reacted with incomprehension. To them, the veil did not signify modesty or obedience to the patriarch. It meant only fanaticism. Practically – for the veil is not just a symbol – it entailed loss: loss of community, of personality, of one's body. And to be present but absent – disembodied – was to be a ghost.

Sri would not talk about it. Perhaps she could not explain. Benny – away on his prawn farm, another absent presence – had approved, but had not ordered the change. The veil put his wife out of bounds; she could not stray. But perhaps that was her thinking too. Her hasty, disappointing marriage and sudden veiling had the effect of a fall from grace, as after a moral lapse or social embarrassment. We wondered whether she was punishing herself: she seemed chastened, lost. Her small face – made smaller and rounder by the scarf pinned tight under the chin – was grey and wistful. She still occasionally flicked through her magazines, glancing at the world of fashion, pop stars and bright young people to which she had once aspired. But she had lost more than that. She was no longer at home in the world. The act of veiling had made of the world something hostile.

In Bayu, the house is merely somewhere to sleep: you live outside, on the verandah, in the yard, between houses. You eat on a bench at the side of the house, calling out to others as they pass, *Drop in!* You wash at the spring; take a nap under the eaves. Children wander from yard to yard; women pound rice or pin out washing, talking across to each other, walking between kitchens. The village is home. Sri had taken to living indoors, the house shut up. She had made an island of her parents' house.

'What's this!' shouted Sae, arriving home from the fields and dropping his yoke of coconuts. 'Has everyone gone away? Has everyone died in this house?' And he flung the door open. His wife, Sutri, had taken to crying. 'I feel as bad as when Sri was taken from me as a baby.' But it was worse than that. Sae, for once, found the right words: 'She has been taken from herself.'

When the door was shut Sri would throw off the veil. But as soon as visitors arrived – there were not many now, the door a deterrent – she would scurry to the back and change. It was more than a covering. To see Sri before and after was to recognize how a garment can impose a bodily style. Spontaneity gave way to a slow deliberateness, a certain stiffness of the upper body, the head now frozen on the shoulders, the arms heavy and impeded. Even the face, framed tightly in white or black – one had a choice – lost expressiveness and personality. In the tropical heat the veil was a penance.

Wan, who had grown up with her, shrugged and tried to make a joke of it: 'Might as well live under a sheet,' he said. But Bu Mari could not bear to look at her. (It was the women who were most offended.) Only Sofía still brought a smile to her face. She would pick her up and whisk her away, petting her and nuzzling her cheek. 'Ah, come along with Aunt Sri!'

Drus was preparing for the pilgrimage. The other candidate haji that year, a middling farmer named Buwang, held a feast and hired an Islamic teacher to give a talk. Drus entertained on a bigger scale, inviting notables from other villages, paying for all-night recitations. He was staking a claim. In recent years his businesses had taken off. He had teamed up with a Chinese partner and was dealing in motorbikes and fertilizer. In five years he had doubled his land holdings. The event should reflect his success.

On the night of the feast I was away in Alas Purwo, but Mercedes helped out. Drus's wife, Siti, had been a friend, especially in the early days – a counterweight to the overbearing Mari. Mercedes often spent time with her as she minded the shop. She called her 'older sister Siti', and Siti, in turn, called her 'younger sister Mercedes'. In Javanese there was no age-neutral term of address; but the familiar usage showed complicity. Though never openly taking our part, Siti would explain Bu Mari's ruses and manipulations and her little schemes to divide and rule in the neighbourhood. Lacking the usual Javanese delicacy, she spoke frankly about her life and the lives of others. But when she had bruises to hide she would avoid Mercedes' company. Her small son was one of Sofía's most dedicated admirers, and Siti always called him 'Sofía's betrothed'.

The feast went ahead; the village came; but there were none of the usual obligatory donations. Uniquely, a pilgrim's send-off is unreciprocated, a pure material loss. Since equality in the village depends on reciprocity, on keeping even, the feast was a claim to class superiority. Mere riches counted for little – Hadi, the mill-owner, Drus's equal in wealth, was treated like any other villager – and poor hajis were unregarded. But a rich haji, one who gave without receiving in turn, had a slight moral advantage. His pretensions were flattered: people spoke to him in High Javanese (or its rustic version better known in Bayu); he was addressed by title as Pak Haji, Mr Pilgrim; he could take his place in the front row at Friday prayers. Drus coveted these honours.

The feast, as Mercedes reported it, was more than usually lavish: Siti dishing out ices and sweets, Drus playing the great man and patron. The talk was all of money. What a lot of meat, what extravagant sweets, what wealth! Nobody commented on Drus's personal piety. (He was making the trip alone, leaving Siti to mind the business.) But that was in the nature of village society: the pilgrimage brought no *religious* distinction. As the headman said, 'It's a matter of buying a name. And if you can't live up to it, your star falls. Look at old Nakib up the road. He ruined himself on the haj. Had to dump his second wife and sell off his fields. And now nobody even bothers to speak to him in High Javanese. They just say, Hello, Haji, as they would to anyone else. A headman is always Pak Lurah, even after he retires. That's something I won't let Drus forget!

To make a name for yourself, to gain ceremonial prestige, you have to exceed the usual festive requirements, and village custom allows only a haji to do this. There were two other recent hajis in the village. One, an upright but stingy man, had not made the most of his title. The other, Haji Sartono, was universally liked and admired. The biggest landowner, he was famously generous with his sharecroppers. He had helped out many debtors. He was charitable. And he was passionately fond of cockfighting – a vice which endeared him to the village. (Generosity was oddly apportioned: Haji Sartono's mother was married to Ran, the diviner, and lived in poverty. Nobody thought this unusual.)

Haji Sartono was genuinely pious, and a good man. There seemed little chance that Drus – even Haji Drus – could emulate him. 'He has fouled the village', said Pak Lurah after Drus had pressed himself on a woman labouring in his fields. And despite his newly discovered piety there were solid Muslims – men like Bu Lurah's father – who would not speak to him. Nevertheless, the haj and the feast marked a definite step up, an attempt to put things straight.

Before you go on the haj you have to pay your debts and settle your quarrels, ask people's forgiveness, or you won't come back, said Noto the carpenter. *The Bedouin will get you. If you're a cheat, you'll be cheated. If you've killed, you'll be killed. Haji N. in Glagah had been a soldier, a district commander. He was a violent man. People laid bets on his not returning – up to a hundred thousand rupiah, they were that confident. But before he went he wiped the slate clean, did the rounds. He came back a reformed man.*

Village Islam had its factions; but they were never as clear-cut as those of the city. Village life required compromise. The vanguard – the reformers and zealots like Aris – were mildly scornful of the hajis. For them, the pilgrimage was the least important pillar of the faith. It had something of idolatry in it, and was an obvious sop to personal vanity. Islam would advance through the efforts of poor, dedicated men like themselves, not through the self-serving piety of the rich. But perhaps Drus, with his money and connections, could be useful to the cause.

The problem was that the cause – a puritan, grass-roots Islam, hostile to local tradition and political compromise – lacked a suitable vehicle. The evangelical groups active in the big cities and university campuses were scarcely known in places like Bayu. And the extremist organizations dedicated to worldwide jihad were, as yet, mere rumours. Bayu's reformers had humbler ambitions, and they would work with whoever could help them. But the possibilities were unattractive. Muhammadiyah, the modernist organization, was puritan in outlook but city-bred and technocratic, unappealing to villagers hopelessly wedded to their spells and prayer-meals. With a dead face, Aris himself had told me as much. Nahdlatul Ulama (NU), the home of orthodox traditionalists, the rural pious, stood a better chance, though it was further from Aris's interests. NU stood for saints and chanting, obedience to Islamic leaders, the wisdom of tradition. Between them, these organizations commanded the allegiance of seventy million Muslims across the nation. For the new activists like Aris, they were too dependent on political elites, too tolerant of diversity. But you had to start somewhere. With Drus's patronage, NU might establish a foothold. Bayu's pious could then find their own way. Better that, better anything, than the headman's impious fudging.

One evening, after a notably feeble prayer-meal at the house of Sukib ('His first for many years,' said Jona. 'He's only doing it because his wife is sick and he can't afford a doctor'), a small group lingered over coffee to talk about the pilgrimage – with Drus present it was hard to talk of anything else. The host, whose high-decibel voice I knew well from the call to prayer, spoke little. He nodded and smiled, anxious to please: he was not a neighbourly man and had nothing to say. But he was championing Drus, and after each of Drus's pious declarations, he would say (already using the title), 'The haji's right, there.' Or, '*Insha'allah*, may you return safely!'

Not waiting for him to finish, Drus, with glistening eyes, turned to another of the guests. 'You know, Mustari, for the first time in my life I feel awake. That's what I told the wife. I said, "I have just woken up to my faith." And I feel my faith getting stronger by the day; almost like a force. I look around and I think something is beginning here. Did you notice how full the mosque was on Friday? After five hundred years, Islam is finally making progress.'

'Indeed, indeed,' said Mustari, twinkling at me. 'Even Andrew was there. Recorded the sermon, didn't you?'

Mustari was entitled to twinkle. A man of nearly sixty, he had joined the cause half a century before Drus. Islam was his life. But it was the born-again Muslims who now had the initiative.

'With me and Buwang, that'll make four recent hajis,' Drus went on. 'I won't be ashamed when I visit my teacher at Lebaran and he asks me how the village is doing. The people of Bayu will be able to hold up their heads proudly.'

'And it'll be thanks to you, Pak Haji,' said Sukib, darting a glance at me. Like Mustari, Sukib was a Muslim of the old school, a seminarian. I had never met him on home territory but – strange to say, in so domestic a civilization – the prayer-house was his true home. Away from it he was like the office worker who feels naked out of his suit. But there was also something damaged about him. He had the unnatural greyness of a man who has recovered from a long illness. His smile, a defensive grimace, did not connect, like the smile drawn by a child.

We talked about the death of Sugito, the tambourine man, and what had happened to his father-in-law. Mustari, a prayer-house stalwart, Sukib's rival for the microphone, said, 'One whose faith is strong cannot be possessed. In my view it wasn't Sugito's ghost that possessed the old man but an evil spirit. See, there are two types of creature: spirits and humans. Spirits can be good or bad, like people. You can't know until you question the possessed person.'

'Spirits are from fire,' said Sukib, and added quickly, 'According to the story.'

'One who doesn't pray is unprotected,' said Drus with a thin smile.

I thought of the widow keening over the corpse, her father unconscious in the back room, his arms stuck up in the air, and the undeviating column of worshippers bound for the mosque. And I remembered Untung's dismay as he looked around for helpers.

The worshippers could have stopped, that day, I said. A man had died. What good was piety without humanity?

Mustari said sternly, as if stating an unpleasant incontrovertible fact: 'Sugito was not a good Muslim. One can't judge others – that's for God alone – but his death was a punishment. One's fate is written.'

We broke up soon after this, and I regretted my words. But as I walked home, something occurred to me. In discussing the progress of Islam in the village, the quickening of the faith, they had not mentioned the first veiling. Had Aris been present, I was sure he would have noted it. But for these men, the traditionalists, it was not part of their understanding of piety. Sri had confounded them as well as her impious parents.

Drus's departure almost coincided with our own. We had been in Bayu almost a year and a half, and the more attached we became to the village the less justification there seemed to be for remaining. Mercedes wanted to see her family in Mexico. My investigations had run dry. And Sofía was becoming Javanese. We had to leave.

Now nearly two, Sofía had the Javanese of a two-year-old, the responses and gestures of her Javanese playmates, and, in a way we could only begin to understand long after we had returned to England, she *felt* with a Javanese sensibility. Feelings are the subtlest differences between cultures, the hardest to conceive, but in ways only partly accessible to conscious thought they register the flow of behaviour and shape the tone of our relations with others. Feelings of different kinds and quantities are what separate North from South, Latin from Anglo-Saxon, East from West, and all the tiny subregions and classes that lie between these great opposites. This is one reason why emotion vocabularies are only partially translatable and exiles never feel at home. Sofía had learned to be a Javanese child. More than this Bayu was her world. Home was exile.

'Leave her with us,' they said. 'She belongs to us now. You can have her back when you return.'

We promised to return.

People did not leave Bayu. They married in the village or close by. There were few migrants, no famous sons or daughters in Jakarta. Except for the pilgrimage – which is a kind of social death and rebirth – nobody goes away for very long. As visitors we had settled in, defied expectations that we would go. We had confirmed Pujil's boast to the plain-clothes intelligence man, that night on the town:

people who came to Bayu couldn't leave. Like the agricultural extension worker from Mojokerto who had come for two months and stayed ten years, they always felt too much 'at home'. Besides, the anthropologist always outstays his welcome. By the time he goes, people – he himself – have forgotten why he came: he has ceased to be a guest.

We had seen out four harvests, two Lebarans, numerous marriages and circumcisions, surprisingly few deaths (this was not Nias; in Java people grew old) and we were still there. Our stay had come to seem permanent. And because one day was much like another – fieldwork goes on and on until it does not go at all – there seemed no reason why things should ever be any different. But of course we had to leave.

Three years later, the second period, it was very different. We could never shake off a temporary feel: they knew we would go in the end.

With Bu Mari as chief cook, we organized a banquet for twenty-five men and their wives. It was more than a neighbourhood feast. Jona, Misti, Siti, and Bu Lurah were prominent helpers; but so were the Sangkan Paran matrons. And the guests were a balance of mystics, pious Muslims, and ordinary villagers. Warno's litany spoke to them all.

Late the following afternoon we took the ferry from the port of Ketapang, north of Banyuwangi, to Bali. On buses, pickups, and motorbikes, over a hundred villagers came to see us off. We hired two minibuses for the village children. Suhem brought a dozen of the mystics in his van. From Banyuwangi, Bayu's day-labourers drove in convoy, three to a motorbike. And Untung cycled the ten miles alongside our pickup, laughing as he overtook us, racing ahead.

The dockside was a scene of ragged emotion as Pak Lurah, Wan, and Untung carried our boxes over the gangplank. Bu Lurah held Mercedes in a tight, un-Javanese hug. Jona and Misti were weeping as they let go of Sofía; Sri, wiping her face on her veil; Warno, composed, smiling. And the dockers, standing back, oddly respectful, astonished at two white people in tears as they boarded the boat.

In hats and sarongs, big and small, mostly barefoot, they spread out in a line along the harbour wall, the silhouette of a Javanese village; and there they remained as the sun went down, unmoving until the boat was out of sight.

PART TWO

17
Katri

Katri was a quiet, prim, demure girl of seventeen, keener on school than on Javanese dancing. She was pretty, in a village way, but not at all flirtatious. 'She doesn't have an eye for boys yet. Won't even talk to them,' said Untung, her father. 'Some of her friends are already engaged. But Katri wants to finish her studies. Maybe go on to university, like Sri did.'

'You'd never believe it looking at me, but I used to have her figure,' said Nur, her mother. 'But I want to fatten her up a bit. She'll never get a husband otherwise.'

Four years earlier, during our first stay in Bayu, when it was Sofía's Descent to Earth and a child was needed to act as Sofía's horse, everyone said: *Katri*. 'The horse has to be someone of good character,' said Aunt Jona. 'Steady character, of a solid family.'

None solider than Untung's. And Katri played the part well, even smiling as she went down on all fours and let Sofía ride her around Jona's yard (specially cleared of peanut shells for the occasion). It was one of those quirky rites of passage that marked the life cycle in Java. As in the Empty Prayer-Meal and the Seven-months porridge-squirting, the humour was partly in the queerness of the actions, partly in the attitude: the sense that the ancestors were having a laugh at the expense of the living, making them do ridiculous things, and the best one could do was play along. Ritual and laughter went together in Java. But it was the spectators who laughed rather than the participants, for whom it was always half-serious.

Jona and Mercedes had cooked a tray of rice porridge, a dimpled sheet of white, speckled with brown drops of cane sugar. Jackfruit leaves were arranged round the border to serve as spoons; and at either end a rice pestle, 'to show the child that she will make a living from rice'. Around the mat sat the neighbours' children, and at the north end, under the eaves of Jona's house, the midwife, an ancient white-haired woman who had delivered half the village. She lit incense in the clay brazier and held Sofía in the fumes, murmuring blessings.

Mother Earth and Father Sky, here's a child from the heavens – don't be startled – descending to earth – the reward is star porridge, her mother and father owe no debt. Then she gently placed Sofía on Katri's back, fed rider and horse, dabbing the porridge in with her hand, and led them off on a circuit of the baked-earth yard.

'*Ao*! Bu, she's enjoying it! Trusts the horse,' said Misti, reassuring Mercedes. 'Ma Item won't let her fall off.'

After completing the circle, the midwife put Sofía down beside a chicken coop under which a mirror, a packet of face powder, a corn cob, an onion, a pencil and a fieldknife had been placed. They lifted the coop. Which object would she choose?

Sofía cooed and looked up at the smiling faces. Then she reached to grab the red onion. 'Ah! Onion. A farmer!' said Jona.

'Wait, she's going for the face powder: a lady, a dancer!'

Bu Mari stooped over and turned the tray. The pencil stood out. When Sofía picked it up everyone clapped. 'That's the right one! Fitting! Just like her parents.'

A few days after this event, people commented that Sofía was looking fatter, cried less, and babbled like a Javanese baby. If so, she owed it to Katri.

Katri's docility did not prevent a certain independence of mind. She prayed: her parents were both abstainers. She fasted: her parents had never done so. (But throughout Ramadan, her mother got up before dawn to cook her breakfast.) And, like many of the other girls, she attended Koranic classes.

'In principle, I don't object,' said Untung, in his patient and methodical manner. He was a primer in Javanese, his sentences as neat and composed as his appearance. 'The content hardly matters – they don't understand the Arabic. But the discipline is good for them. Teaches them endurance and self-control. These are important for Javanese people.'

I said: 'But you didn't do the classes, did you?' And he repeated the riddle about learning 'to recite in Ponorogo' (a town to the west), meaning, in Javanist word-play, 'recite one's body', know oneself. Sitting still, following a discipline, was part of that.

With his neat movements and his slow, deliberate speech, Untung conveyed a sense of self-control: more than that, an air of decency and acceptance. He was not well off, but he did not wish for anything more. Or what he wanted was within his compass. Nur – squat and sturdy, with a mirthful laugh – was less steady, easily affronted. She had lost several children. But they were matched: he handsome, handy, conscientious; she solid, capable, a touch envious. They were a couple.

Like Noto the carpenter, Untung and Nur were 'lay' Muslims. Their observance of the Islamic holidays – the celebration of the Prophet's birthday, Idul Fitri, the annual slaughter of an ox during the pilgrimage month – was a kind of community service. Nur would be grating coconuts or hefting rice pans in the communal kitchens while Untung, deferent and dapper, ushered the pious to their seats: services that were necessary but always taken for granted. To serve was to be forgiven one's laxity. The alternatives – Pak Lurah's indifference, the mystics' waiver (which could sound like casuistry) – were harder to carry off, riskier. But Untung and Nur served not out of fear: they helped because they were decent and dutiful and wanted to belong to a village where differences could be harmonized. Smiling, ever willing, they made the concessions.

Although Untung was the nephew of Warno he had never been drawn into mysticism. 'I'm not ready for it yet,' he said. 'It's too heavy.' But how did he know? His father, who had died at the end of our first period in Bayu, was a simple man. He had lived next door to Warno and was the only one of four siblings who had not joined Sangkan Paran. Untung had married at eighteen and moved to the central part of the village, away from most of the mystics. He lived near Mustari, one of the regular prayer-leaders. Their wives, who owned adjacent house plots, were sisters. Living among the pious and the indifferent (and the merely ignorant), rarely hearing full-blooded Javanist talk, he had made his accommodation; but it was an act of positioning rather than a considered choice.

Nur – unschooled, practical – was simply non-observant, a non-believer; but women were judged less harshly. Village Islam was led by men: a man needed an excuse.

Where did that leave Katri? The diversity of her parents' and grandparents' generations – the animists and pantheists; the Berkeleyan idealists; the devout, whether fierce or mild; the seminarists and magicians; the were-tigers and sorcerers – had given way to something much simpler. For Katri's generation, the delicate compromises of the past would no longer be necessary. The social minuet would become a march. But it was not just the steady pressure of institutional Islam – backed increasingly by the state – that had brought about this change; it was a collective failure to respond. And the failure had begun a generation earlier when Untung was a boy and Java was torn apart by religious and political strife.

Three doors down, at the headman's, it was the same story. Jan, Pak Lurah's son-in-law, was planning for the pilgrimage to Mecca. He was grooming his son, Hari, now five, as a model Muslim. Yet Jan's father, the mill-owner, was a dancer and musician, a member of the mystical association. And so it was all over the village. Of the many ways of being Javanese, only one was being transmitted, only one was taught in schools, endorsed on television, sanctioned by law: the Islamic way. Or rather a certain vision – puritan, rule-bound, conformist – of the Islamic way.

There was also, of course, modernity, the way of the West that came at you from all directions. (It was this word – *West*, *West*, *West* – that burst like an expletive from the sermons of visiting preachers and fell less violently but no less disdainfully from the lips of politicians and officials. A dirty word.) In the future there would be a simple choice: to a be a Muslim – of a certain kind – or to be corrupted and Westernized. That was how Aris, the lathe-operator, and Tompo, the religious teacher, saw it; and their opponents – the Notos, the Maris, the Jonas, three generations of headmen, even Jumhar with his ramshackle prayer-house – were letting it happen.

So Katri attended classes in Arabic recitation. At school she learned about Muslim history – a black and white tale of conquest, colonial defeat and resurgence – and 'proper' Islam. On Thursday and Sunday evenings she sat with other young women, gowned and scarfed, in the prayer-house (our neighbourhood prayer-house, not Jumhar's), to do the chanting. She did the five prayers; she fasted. But the shadow play, the Javanese-Indian epics, poetry and the dance held no attraction. The Javanese arts were old-fashioned and difficult; the dance was shameless.

Untung lived right up against the prayer-house. Built as an act of piety by a harvest broker who had since moved out of the village (he had left his wife for a mistress), it was a modern concrete structure of hard surfaces and echoes. Like all the prayer-houses in Bayu, its territorial claim was asserted by a megaphone. Five times a day, when the call rang out, in the evenings during chanting, and more or less non-stop throughout the Fast, Untung's house shook under the assault. Windows rattled; glasses jangled in their cupboards; the cat ran out. With the megaphone switched on it was impossible to sleep, speak or even shout. But nor, during active periods, could the family escape to their fieldhut, since Nur had to be at home to cook for Katri, and Katri had to be near the prayer-house.

There was something pitiless and defiant in the noise, an aggression that was un-Javanese. It meant, at the very least, a breach of neighbourly consideration, even of the respect due to kin. (But Katri, obedient to the call, was not judged disloyal.) Mustari, Untung's own brother-in-law, broadcast sermons to the neighbourhood berating the lax, promising hell to backsliders. And Sukib, his rival prayer-leader, knowing Untung was in bed, would twist the dial until the feedback screeched. Somehow Untung retained his composure. Tolerance could stretch no further.

'I went in this morning – it was still dark – and said, "Can't you turn it down a little, Man Sukib? We want to hear the words distinctly." But he just scowled and turned it higher. Once I corrected him on his pronunciation – you'd be surprised how much I know – and he blew his top. I told him it was sinful to mispronounce the Koran. He ran to Mustari – actually ran – and there was a big row. But a lot of people hate Sukib and nobody hates me; so you have to ask yourself who is the better person.'

'He doesn't join in neighbourhood feasts; he won't do village repairs or help at weddings,' said Nur, wrinkling her nose. 'And he tells us *we'll* go to hell because we don't pray.'

'When it comes to the Last Judgement, that's my affair, not Sukib's,' Untung concluded; then added, with a grin: 'Though if he was doing the judging I'd be on my knees five times a day.'

'Why is it always him with the microphone?' I said. 'Even during chanting. Don't the others mind?'

'He insists. Getting him to share it is harder than tearing a baby from its bottle. That's why some have defected to Jumhar's prayer-house.'

'That's why he switched *from* Jumhar's,' said Nur. 'Jumhar had said to him, *Take your turn*.'

We had been away for three years, and in the months after we returned to Bayu, in April 1996, there was a rash of weddings. Two, three or four of them at a time, they were suddenly in fashion. And if the groom's side hired a dancer with her band, so did the bride's, even choosing the same woman. (Wan said: 'If Bayu folk could die in batches they'd do that too.') After the weddings came a sudden crop of engagements, also explained as 'following the fashion'. And it was then we heard that Katri was informally betrothed, like several of her classmates. The youth in question, Surya, lived in the hamlet of Sumbersari near the village shrine. He was nineteen and worked in the ice factory in Banyuwangi. Whether speeding about the village on his motorbike or dancing all night at wedding receptions, he was the not-very-black sheep in a traditionally 'white' neighbourhood. (Sumbersari was devout but conservative, as keen on prayer-meals and diviners as the rest of the village.)

Katri's parents were not worried about the future. Engagement didn't mean much. Once the date for a wedding had been set, there was an exchange of tokens, and an annual visit to the prospective in-laws kept the promise alive. But most betrothals fell through.

One day, near the end of term – it was exam time – Surya took a corner too fast and came off his bike. News went round that 'Katri's fiancé' was dying in hospital. It was the first time the engagement had been referred to publicly, and the announcement caused more surprised comment than the boy's mishap (you don't die from concussion). Still, villagers packed the district hospital eager to see the injuries – a pickup truck went down every day – and Katri found herself thrust to the fore as sympathizer-in-chief, with her parents anxiously in tow. She missed her exams; and what had started as a rumour – perhaps only a whim on her part, a desire to be grown-up – suddenly became a fact.

'I'm worried about Katri's education,' said Untung. 'She'll have to repeat the year unless I pay a bribe of a hundred thousand rupiah to the headmaster. And then there's the school fees, transport to Banyuwangi, and then college . . . My *ekonomi* won't stretch to it.'

'Are you worried about her interrupting her education or carrying on with it?'

'I don't know. She's always followed the example of Sri. But things went badly for Sri.'

And then Surya came out of hospital and everything changed. Only a week later was Untung, in his slow and steady way (like his uncle Warno, without the philosophy), prepared to tell me what had happened.

'I came home from the fields and was bathing at the back. It was after dusk, no one at home; Nur next door. Katri had asked her mother for a hundred rupiah to buy sweets and she'd just gone off to the store. I came out in a towel, still wet, and was surprised to find two men from Sumbersari just sitting there in the front room, smoking, cool as you like. Not even a *May we come in?*

'"Don't mind us," said one. "We didn't know you were home yet. Thought we'd wait." The other said, "We've come here on an errand, sent by Man Karto [Surya's father]."

'"And what errand is that?" I said.

'"Katri has been taken home by Surya. She's now in the house of Man Karto."

'"Since when?" I asked. I was pretty stunned.

'"Not long ago. Just before dusk. But don't be alarmed: she is well. Man Karto has sent us as go-betweens."

'They were taking their time, see; spinning it out, so Surya and Katri would reach sanctuary before I could give chase. When they had gone I fetched Nur, who fainted with the shock. We got the old folks round and held a conference. Should I go to Sumbersari immediately or leave it till morning? We agreed that Nur and I should go there at 11 p.m. And so we did.'

When my daughter was abducted they took her to the river, said Elan, the irrigation official. *The boy splashed water all over her so she was soaked – that was the excuse to carry her away. Then he took her up to a safe house in Sumbersari. She changed clothes there and he sent out a message. There was no prior engagement, so when the go-betweens came to tell me, I was staggered. I ran up to Sumbersari to make sure nothing bad had happened, that there was nothing to gossip about. They were married two days later.*

'"Ah! Untung!" said Man Karto as we walked in. He made us sit down before we could say anything and his wife served us tea. I said: "Listen, Man Karto, we're paying you a visit this evening, late as it is, because there is a certain need."

'"And what need is that?" said Man Karto. "Speak your mind."

'"It's like this. Just after sunset I had visitors. They told me that Surya had stolen Katri and brought her here. We've come to verify the facts. Where are the children now?"

'"Asleep at the back."

'Katri was woken. She burst into tears as soon as she saw me and her mother. Surya wouldn't look at me. I took them by the hand and said: "Surya, did you bring Katri here of your own desire, or on your father's orders? Katri, did you want to be taken or were you forced?"

'They both said it was their own wish.

'I said, "I am sad that you can't control your desire and wait for the proper time when you can make a living and are ready to be parents. Why do you want to leave me and your mother?"

'Katri said: "Surya loves me, Pa, so I love him."

'I said to Katri: "You'll be the responsibility of Surya and his parents now. Mind you are not reluctant to please them. Don't be shy to ask how to cook the soup. *May you both prosper.*"'

'See, Katri can't make a living. She doesn't know how to do anything except study,' said Nur. 'A woman should be able, like me. If Untung is without work for a while it doesn't matter. We can always manage with what I earn in the fields. As for Surya –'

I could see their disappointment, their fears for Katri: an only child, taken from them on a whim and married to a tearaway. But they had misjudged Surya. Perhaps shaken by his recklessness, or his new responsibilities, he became pious. In the evenings he began to join the others for chanting. He stayed on for extra prayers during the Fast. And within a month Katri, ever the pupil of Sri, was wearing a veil. Not the full face-covering veil of Arabia – nobody in Java wore that – but the heavy garb of prayer, the burka-like gown and head covering.

For her parents this was a different kind of shock. Marriage by abduction was a local custom – romantic, forgivable. It could be put right. And if things went badly, well, she could always remarry. But the veil was new, inexplicable. It was not Javanese. Sri's veiling three years ago had been tolerated as something unique, perhaps a response to the haste of her marriage or the failure of her studies. But two in the same neighbourhood – the two leading girls – could not be excused. Others would follow.

Untung said: 'I won't permit her to wear it. It's wrong to stand out. It's offensive to others.' Nur said: 'She was always proud of her hair. She was so pretty.' Yet it had been her own wish, not Surya's.

Again there was no explanation, no attempt to justify. The circumstances were similar to Sri's: a sudden romance, the end of an imagined career (teacher? civil servant?), the prospect of living the life of a peasant with city aspirations. How to dignify this personal failure, this acceptance of little? Katri said, simply, to her mother that she was a Muslim and that was how Muslims now dressed. (*Only on TV*, replied Nur.) She may have married into the most backward part of the village but she could show them how to be modern; she could set the style.

For her parents there was some consolation. They provided the best and biggest wedding that year: two female dancers, hundreds of guests, four days of celebrations. And when discussion turned to who should be the bridesmaid, everyone said: *Sofía*. Katri had been her horse: it was fitting.

Our return to the village after three years had been easy, almost a homecoming. Daniel, aged two, had fought off the unfamiliar hands and pinches, but was intrigued and delighted by everything: the animals, the rivers, the constant laughter that greeted him. Java was an amusing and inexhaustible game: he grasped it with both hands. On arrival, Sofía, now five, had simply sat on Aunt Jona's lap and relaxed. She could not know how or why she felt so 'at home' (in their phrase): it was the gentle crowd, the excited smiles, the warm pressure of interest, the end of indifference: Java. We learned that her devoted friend Andi (some eight years older), had been speechless with shock at our departure. His father, Mustari, had had to take him to a healer for a cure. Now they were back together, and Andi resumed his role as official best friend. Others proclaimed their grief at our absence. Elan, the quiet man, one of Mari's regular callers – he had been a follower of her husband, a member of his death squad – looked at me with sad eyes and said, 'I cried after you left; I wept for three months, hardly ate or slept. You ask my wife here? Did I eat or didn't I?' ('No you didn't, dear; you wasted away.') It was untrue of course, though kindly meant. I heard other long-term visitors – Javanese visitors – assured of similar devotion and retrospective grief. Such statements made a claim on you of a rather complex kind. It would be offensive to express doubt, even though both you and they know it cannot be true; and because, in playing the game, you accept it, it obliges you; it holds you closer.

We moved straight into the empty house belonging to Pak Lurah – one he had built for his parents, who preferred their rustic hut at the back. Now there were four of us we could no longer be lodgers of Bu Mari; and we were glad to be free of her jealous supervision: we had grown up.

The house was plain concrete, with louvred windows, a verandah and the heavy wooden furniture preferred by headmen. The sofa and chairs were fixtures, since the headman had painted around them, economizing on paint and effort. The green walls were marked with their ghostly white template, like the shadows of a radiation attack. At the back, joined to his parents' house, was a big airy kitchen, bamboo-walled, with a well. On hot days, Ma Witri, the headman's mother, would sprinkle water from a bucket onto to the dirt floor to cool the air. The beams of the kitchen were rat-runs and the rats, big fearless creatures, would hop down and raid the larder-cupboard. We set traps, spread a proprietory glue called No-Rat, and put little piles of poisoned rice at intervals along the beams. In the mornings I would dispose of corpses and half-dead rats, picking the remaining hairs off the No-Rat square and replacing the bait in the middle. I never dared use the phosphate (a fertilizer of some kind) that the headman's father, Winoto, used in his own house, once massacring twenty-six rats in a night.

One morning we were awakened by a scream. The cook had let himself into the kitchen and found there – attracted by rats or the chickens next door – a cobra, arched and poised to spit. He stood on the bench whimpering, a dishcloth held to his face. (Javanese cobras spray their poison at the eyes.) The piercing scream dispelled my normal timorousness with animals and I was able to stun the snake with a broom handle. Winoto killed it with a machete and burned the remains to prevent the return of a vengeful mate. The story circulated for days.

In our new quarters, we became close to the headman's parents. At sixty-five Winoto was already an old man, reduced and stringy but still tough. In his loose black smock, his panama hat pushed back off his high forehead, he seemed to drift along, weightless. His face was hollowed by toil. But he had once been strong. In out-of-town cattle markets he was still remembered as a champion kick-fighter. (You struck at your opponent's shin then braced yourself in turn.) In another Osing custom, no longer practised, he would tweak a man's nose over his coffee, daring him to respond. Sometimes, hardly caring whether his wife was out of hearing, he would tell me about his scrapes. During the troubles in the sixties, after a villager – one of the death squad – had 'named him' for a communist, he had revenged himself by taking the man's wife to a hotel in Genteng for two days. 'Ha! That taught him!' he boasted, raising a bony fist and giving me a death's-head grin.

Ma Witri, small and thin, prematurely old like her husband, had a mock frown to match his open-mouthed smile and a sudden barking laugh that was her comment on the world. Always with her hands full, she had the brisk, bluff manner of a ward sister. 'I'm bold,' she said. 'I say what's what.' When her older sister had stirred a family quarrel, she had slapped her (lightly) on the face and the two old women had stopped talking for a month. When people said what she called 'foolish things' – usually over the megaphones – she humphed and briskly went her way. She had no arguments against them, only herself.

Ma Witri always wore a chiffon jacket of faded purple and a brown batik sarong, her thin hair coiled behind. A woman's hair told of her station in life. Young women were proud of a luxuriant black mane, smoothing it back, tossing it flirtatiously. For her last photograph with Mercedes, the one she wanted to be remembered by, Sri had taken off her veil and shaken her hair free. Matrons kept their hair shorter, bulking it out for feasts with a false bun. Old women like Witri had a thin depleted coil, greasy and streaked with grey. Sofía remembers being taken to bathe down at the river and messing with her thin oily locks.

The old couple were fond of the children. Winoto, spotting Daniel, would put down his yoke and cancel his trip to the fields. Daniel would climb on his back, shouting with joy, and they'd go to feed the cows. Ma Witri would get Sofía to pick up the chickens and bring them into her house to roost or help her to fetch the eggs in the morning. Every day she brought the children a bucket of warm water to wash.

It was Bu Lurah who had proposed Panji, her childhood friend, as cook. He had worked in Bali, running a stall for the Javanese construction workers, and he was the best festive cook; but now he was back in Bayu, scraping a living as a tailor. I called on him one afternoon as he was cleaning out his poor little house – a hovel opposite that of his parents at the end of Noto's block. He was nervous of me, embarrassed about his circumstances, but I helped him carry out some old broken furniture and empty boxes to a bonfire in the yard and soon we were talking. One of the boxes was swarming with cockroaches – not dozens, but hundreds – and as we tossed it onto the fire, they scattered in all directions. Our frantic stamping attracted children, who joined in, and soon there was a riot of stamping and shrieking. Watching me, Panji cried with laughter. After this it was easy to agree terms. We paid him a weekly wage ('whatever you like') and every morning at eight o'clock he came to our house with a basket of vegetables and stayed until noon.

Panji was big, soft, bear-like, with shoulder-length hair and a round, smooth face. He had a gentle, lilting voice and gossipy tone. He wore a sarong, and his loose T-shirt showed breasts. He was a wandu, a man-woman.

From the beginning I was struck by his intelligence and his knowledge of village affairs. I was interested in the classification of emotions, and he spent hours with me discriminating minute shades of meaning. He knew the complicated, overlapping genealogies of neighbours, their intrigues and secret avoidances; he could point out when people had married a forbidden category of relative and the disasters they had unwittingly caused.

But it was his kindness and humour that endeared him to us. He became another of Mercedes' closest friends. And after she had taught the children in the morning (Sofía missed her first year of English school), she would join him for a coffee or they would sit on the bench outside for a leisurely hour. Their laughter would draw Siti and Bu Lurah, and the hour became an afternoon.

The kitchen was rarely empty. Mosque permitting, we woke to the smell of coffee roasting – Ma Witri raking the beans over a wide, flat pan – and the shrieks and slaps of Panji and his friends: the dancer from the dragon show, a transvestite who ran a night stall, and a make-up artist from town. While he cooked, they preened and primped, comparing notes, telling of their flirtations and quarrels. It was through Panji and his visitors that we learned about the stormy, brittle world of wandus.

In Javanese thinking, male complements female; the world goes by in pairs. Yet couples split, husbands stray, divorcees get left on the shelf, and boys will be girls. Humans are not always neatly one thing or another; desire confounds reason; the world is not as it should be. The man-woman and the randy widow, ancient cultural inventions going back to pre-Islamic times, acknowledge the fact of human diversity and polymorphous perversity. They are part of the Javanese tolerance. And when people ask about life in the West, they say, 'Do you have widows and wandus in your village?' as if both are necessary to a well-functioning society.

Wandus are females in male bodies or the other way around, said Noto the carpenter. *A week after a child is born, the parents give the midwife a chick matched to the sex of the baby. If the chick's sex is crossed – and it's hard to tell: you look for a raised or reddish crest in the male – the child will grow up a wandu. A boy will like playing dolls and carrying things on his head; a girl will go in for climbing trees. There's nothing you can do about it. Panji's father made that mistake. Panji says it was deliberate – his Pa didn't have a male and took a chance.*

You are two, said Warno the mystic: *male and female. But which predominates determines whether you are a man or a woman. With wandus there's a balance – no, not a balance, a conflict. I don't believe it has anything to do with chicks: matters of sex are in the nature of things.*

One of these friends, a slight, effeminate creature with red-painted nails and a squeaky voice, said he'd been a wandu since he was a toddler. Did that mean he felt like a woman? I asked.

'Ooh! I couldn't say. What does a woman feel like? What does a man feel like?'

'The point of being a wandu,' said Panji, 'is that you don't know if you're male or female. Can *you* remember what it was like to be male?' he asked his friend.

Kus, the dancer in the dragon play, was different. He had been male until adolescence. He knew both sides.

'Do you think he's pretty?' Panji asked, when he had flounced out.

'No, he's too strong,' I said. 'Those arms.'

'It's because he works in the fields. Mind you, he only does planting, with the other women. He won't do men's tasks. He's very popular, you know.'

Kus lived with a young man in the west end of Bayu, cooking and keeping house, using love magic to keep his interest. The man's mother disapproved, saying her only son should have a proper wife. She wanted grandchildren. When, one day, he brought home a wife from another village, Kus fainted and 'cried loudly for a week'. But the three of them now lived together, Panji didn't know by what arrangement.

'The wife calls Kus *older sister*, but Kus doesn't answer. He's angry and jealous. Wouldn't you be?'

But the wandus were not faithful or monogamous. Nor were they the object of purely homosexual interest. Youths in need of company for the night, and lacking a widow, would knock at their doors. They lived a soap-opera life of infatuations, betrayals and snubs.

Panji told me about his childhood. He was one of five. His older brother was the mother's favourite. She had always resented Panji, complained he wasn't a proper boy. 'I feel awkward with her. If I run short of rice I won't ask her for any. My brother takes what he wants.'

His mother used to hit him, saying he wouldn't 'learn to be male'. He preferred playing with girls and wouldn't go to the fields with his father. But his father, a rough type, was kind to him and combed his hair every morning before school. When he was twelve, Panji said he couldn't bear to live with them any more and his father built him the shack opposite, where he cooked for himself and made a living selling snacks. For three years he lived fraternally with another wandu from Rogojampi. Ronny did the make-up for brides and grooms, hiring out the stage sets on which they were enthroned. 'He was beautiful in those days,' said Panji. 'Always chased by men. And he became rich.' When Ronny's sister got married, a troop of Bayu women – former customers – had gone to Rogojampi to pay their respects. Among the guests were 'five hundred' wandus from all over the district. Misti had brought back the report.

'Did they take money or rice?' Panji had asked, meaning: Did they go as men or women?

'They took a bowl of rice and an envelope of money,' said Misti.

'Ah, fitting! Half and half.'

Panji lived alone, but he had many friends among the village women; then there were the old flames who dropped by, and the children he had fostered.

'Lasio has always called me Ma: when I fostered him I had long hair like a woman; his daughter calls me Granny. And then I fostered Ilah's son. Ilah was one of my childhood pals, like Bu Lurah. We were a threesome. When the boy was little, everyone thought he looked too much like his Pa – that's bad – so they gave him to me. Who knows, his father could have died young otherwise. They held a prayer-meal with red and white porridge and market sweets. Same with Katri, she resembled her mother, so I acknowledged her as mine. That was only in name: she never moved in. Ilah's boy was more like my own son. He slept beside me, and when he cried I'd give him the breast. He called me Pa. Now he calls me Man [uncle]. But he's a big lad now and rather shy with me.'

Listening to Panji, I began to see that wandus were not just the beneficiaries of tolerance. The flux of village society – the merry-go-round of marriages, gender switches, child-borrowing and ritual inversions – made tolerance, perhaps even religious tolerance, possible. If you wanted a recipe for harmony, one that valued difference, mere ideology was not enough. Relativism made Java special; it kept the peace. But it grew from a common experience of change, of changing places.

How could you be a hard-liner when nothing was straight?

*

Weddings came in two parts, first the Islamic ceremony, which could be done at short notice and required only the presence of the principals and a Muslim official; second the social wedding, which was also the traditional ceremony. Marriages between divorcees required only a prayer-meal, but a first marriage was always a big affair involving most people in the village. Both parties to the wedding held separate receptions, a day or two apart. It was obligatory to attend, to donate, and – if you were a neighbour – to help. With so many donations – fixed now at Rp2,000 for male guests, two kilos of rice for female guests, plus quantities of coconuts, bananas, cigarettes and sugar from neighbours and kin – all ultimately repayable, there was a complicated balance of credit and debt.

A glimpse at Untung's ledger gives some idea.

COSTS (in thousands of rupiah; Rp1,000 = $1)

Cow (bought from a neighbour)	850
Extra meat, 40 kg	300
Rice, 400 kg	300
Payment to man who looked after and slaughtered cow	75
Dancers and orchestra	300
Stage and 150 chairs, tables, bunting	100
Stage sets, throne, costumes and make-up artist	160

Gamelan orchestra (from east Bayu)	100
Lighting for three days and nights	80
Loudspeakers and amplifier	75
Firewood, 16 m3	80
Roofing and scaffold	20
Bananas, 500 branches	225
Eggs, 30 kg	75
Coconut oil, 80 kg (homemade, from copra)	240
Raw cane sugar	85

INCOME (x Rp1,000)	
Cash donations by 938 male guests	2,300
Rice, 1.5 tonnes, later sold to a rice factory	1,116
Sugar, 450 kg	675
Cigarettes, 136 cases	1,156
Coconuts, 2,200	440
Eggs, 50 kg, all used in the cooking	125

The total outlay was 1.5 million rupiah (roughly £1,000, or four to five hundred days' wages for a man); the income about 5.6 million. All donations are repayable at guests' future weddings and circumcisions. Sri, for example, contributed 120 coconuts, paying back, with an increment (and thus indebting Untung), the hundred coconuts received at her wedding three years before.

Besides these utilitarian exchanges, women and girls bring gifts. But these too are standardized and repayable. Katri's ledger happened to be her last schoolbook. It began, in childish script, with notes on 'Statistics and their Function' – a school lesson; it ended with lists of crockery (*Ana: 6 bowls, plain; Sri: 8 plates, patterned, returned; Aseh: set of 6 glasses, small*). Her back room, stocked with goods to be recycled at others' weddings, was like a warehouse.

The wedding – the joining before the ancestors – was in Sumbersari, at the groom's reception. I remember flowers, bunting,

Freudian cakes on sticks; intense heat and noise; Daniel wriggling on my shoulders; a procession, a swelling crowd, a storm of drums and tambours; bride and groom approaching under an arch; their thumbs joined; she breaking an egg over his foot; the diviner's blessing; the couple enthroned like king and queen, he with pencilled moustache and a wavy-bladed dagger in his sash, she sylph-like in tight costume, bare-shouldered, yellow-faced, expressionless; and on either side, fanning the couple, a bridesmaid, one of them Sofía, unrecognizable as a heavenly nymph.

For the first time in Bayu's unrecorded history, the wedding attracted reporters and university students, jostling for pictures, noting down 'Osing custom'. They had heard I was there: proof of authenticity.

The entertainment on the first night was a dancer: the bridal couple still enthroned, motionless like figures on a cake. I danced, and one of the bridesmaids burst into laughter. On the second day there was a shadow-puppet play, telling the story of the demon Kala, a source of death and misfortune in the world. All morning, shadows flitted across the broad white screen: an empty stage on which words could conjure a palace, a forest or the heavens. The puppets – always in profile, like ancient Egyptians – loomed from nowhere, slapping suddenly against the screen, then greyly vanished into the ether: the heroes long-nosed, with lacy crowns and slender arms, gentle and purposeful; the villains and monsters bulbous and pop-eyed, with violent gestures and wicked throaty laughs. Between the extremes, bumbling servants, dim-witted peasants, lecherous warriors, timid maidens and nagging mothers: a gallery of human types.

The puppeteer, a small neat man in a shiny jacket and brown batik turban, sat behind the screen with his hands in the air, twirling the flat leather figures, voicing the characters. Seated the other side, the audience saw only the shadows, but the puppets themselves were beautiful, with their delicate outlines and symbolic colouring (red for anger, white for purity), the puppeteer's movements a marvel. The stories were from Hindu-Javanese mythology, adaptations of the Indian epics. Through them the puppeteer projected a certain vision of human nature, of cosmic balance (upset then restored) and the hidden powers of the universe. If the profundities passed you by – the speeches, unscripted, could be highly wrought – there was a good story with battles and lots of jokes. And to keep the audience going, a musical accompaniment: the pulse of a drum and a rippling orchestra, with gongs and ethereal female voices (the singers, kneeling in their tight sarongs, elegantly fanned themselves and flirted with the players).

The Kala tale, all chases and burping ogres, was comic but serious. Its telling was an exorcism. Surya and Katri, as only children, were the 'food of Kala', designated for death. Only the puppeteer could release them. So, too, those children belonging to inauspicious sets – twins, a boy and a girl, boy-girl-boy. Altogether some twenty villagers had joined in the exorcism. At the climax, wreathed in incense, the puppeteer incarnates Vishnu and defangs Kala. (Vishnu, in Muslim Java!) Then the 'puppeteer's children' line up with bride and groom to be doused with holy water. Deliverance.

Two days later, a corresponding event at Katri's house. Before an audience of village elders she recited from the Koran. During the prayer-meal that followed – a long and solemn affair – a motorbike skidded in the road outside and the crowd gasped as one, several women leaping up and shouting, 'My child!' But no one was hurt and the prayer-meal continued. In the evening, the couple sat enthroned while a dancer performed. There were three changes of costume and scene: Hindu-Javanese, Mataram (the classical Muslim kingdom), and Egyptian pharoah-Angkor style. Katri resplendent. For such glory one cast aside the veil.

Within a week another neighbourhood wedding: the festivities a little dimmer than Katri's; the ushers and cooks weary after a sleepless week. The bride was marrying into a pious family in another village and she, too, after sitting in state – a bare-shouldered Cleopatra sheathed in silk – adopted the veil. Her parents, nominal Muslims like Untung and Nur, could do nothing to stop her. But it was a sudden change, another jolt. When Sri had first gone veiled, she was one of the girls who had whispered 'ghost'.

18
A Speech in the Mosque

On the Prophet's birthday Jumhar held a celebration – a Muludan – in his rickety prayer-house, the Light of Paradise. Children danced about with eggs on sticks; sacred books – lives of the prophets – were smoked in incense; there was joyful singing; and in the evening a hired preacher came, his sermon broadcast by megaphone.

Preachers were usually arranged by our old housemate Wan – nominally a Christian – who would tell the speaker roughly what was required: something on birth control, women's activities or the importance of parents, with a few prayers and a mention of Pancasila, the state ideology in which the five recognized faiths were proclaimed equal. Nothing controversial: it was a 'mixed neighbourhood'. This time, however, the paramedic had intervened. Yusuf was of Aris's party, a reformer and zealot, a scourge of the headman. He was one of the teachers Jumhar had 'let go' from afternoon Koranic lessons, the man who, in Jumhar's metaphor, had wanted telegraph poles instead of trees with branches. Jumhar had reason to fear his influence. Soon after arriving in Bayu, Yusuf had married a pious girl and had since then confined her to the house. Pale and thin, veiled now, she crept between her parents' home, where she and Yusuf lived, the mosque and the prayer-house.

I had first met Yusuf when I called on his father-in-law, Ali, who lived in a lane near the Light of Paradise. Yusuf might be the face of the future: he had to be reckoned with; but it was the father-in-law whom I found the more interesting. Why had he given his daughter to such a man? Why make the concession? The question could not be asked, but it was another light on the problem of how Java had passed from one generation to another, from the indifferent parents to the veiled daughters and chanting sons. Unlike the parents of Sri and Katri, Ali was an observant Muslim, one of Bayu's traditionally pious. His perspective on the new Islamic fervour would not be the same.

A fattish, middle-aged man, Ali was seminary-educated and conservative, generous in manner. His home was a comfortable nest for the cuckoo. Built only two years ago, much visited by government officials and promoters of tourism, the house was not exactly traditional but, as Ali said – and he might have been talking about himself – 'inspired by tradition'. A visitor had once told him it was 'better than the real thing', and this was the phrase he repeated to strangers, laughing at its oddness.

Ali's house was high-roofed and ceilingless, the corner posts made of a dark hardwood, ornamented at the joints. The wall panels were of bamboo strips crossed in contrasting patterns, the weave looser towards the top, allowing light to enter in thin yellow beams. The airy interior was striped with shadow, motes of dust rising through the banded light. It was like living in a huge upside-down basket or a giant birdcage. Contributing to this aviary effect, under the eaves hung four ornamental cages containing songbirds and extravagantly plumed parrots. The golden light, the moving bands of shadow, the polly-phonic hoots and tweets: it was enchanting.

Ali was rich enough to indulge his traditionalism. Unusually, he still kept a field of native rice, the kind that did not require pesticide or fertilizer. The hard stalks had to be harvested with a handknife instead of a sickle, and the first sprigs were brought home in a ritual bundle called *Dewi Sri*, the rice goddess. Ali had inherited a large plot of land from his grandmother. But like Drus, another traditionalist with outside connexions, he had ties with a Chinese dealer in town. He was a peasant-entrepreneur. Together, Ali and the Chinese had built a bungalow in the hills and there they would go on their motorbikes to 'relax', sometimes taking a prostitute from town, sometimes hunting in the woods. (Ten years ago, Ali had shot his brother dead, mistaking him for a deer.) When Ali talked about the bungalow in the hills he praised the 'panoramas' and 'the healthy experience of nature', again with his uncertain little laugh. It was a foreign perspective, perhaps that of the Chinese partner. No one who worked in the fields ever expressed any pleasure in the landscape. *Landscape* implied distance, not engagement.

Ali had a small boy's pleasure in dirty talk, and he would giggle as he told me about his exploits, while his wife scoffed sarcastically as she moved about the house. I assume that this talk had finished once the paramedic moved in. Perhaps it helped to account for his daughter's willingness to put on the veil.

That day when I had first met Yusuf, we were seated around the table in the big front room, our voices echoey among the peeps and squawks from the birdcages. Yusuf had taken his place at the table with quiet assurance. He was tall and thin, with a military bearing; he wore a black cap and had the beginning of a goatee – a consciously Islamic look. His wife – veiled, pallid from a life indoors – sat silently at the back.

In the presence of the paramedic, his imposing son-in-law, Ali seemed nervous, deprived of conversation. It was a reversal of the proper hierarchy, the older man deferring to the younger.

We had talked about the forthcoming Birthday and Ali had reminisced about previous occasions, the amusing and eccentric preachers of the past. Yusuf had listened in what I took to be silent contempt. When he began to speak down to me, using the familiar 'you' form reserved for juniors and children, Ali had not reacted. Perhaps he thought I hadn't noticed; but there was no polite way to respond to the rudeness of a clever man. I had tried doing it back – getting an infantile 'you' into every other sentence – but Yusuf, his black eyes glittering, seemed not to mind. He smiled thinly and continued the lesson, if anything more pointedly. Out of regard for my host I could not get angry (and to be angry in Java is to lose). After a few minutes I left, humiliated.

Yusuf's chosen speaker was a rising cleric, a firebrand from one of the more radical seminaries to the north of Banyuwangi. To Jumhar's constituency, gathered under the eaves that night, he was a new face, an exotic. He had a young man's fluffy beard, a full-length gown and a white turban: the fancy dress of fanaticism. His voice was harsh and he gripped the microphone like a weapon. Jumhar and his father, the old Koranic teacher, sat at the front, wringing their hands. As the rant proceeded, they shook their heads and stared at their feet. (So Wan told me: I listened at home with burning ears.) There was a big change in the world, said the preacher, and things were different now for Muslims. Indonesia had joined a free global market. Western influence was flooding in. Three hundred and fifty years of white rule had not infected the Indonesians with Dutch ways; nor had three years of yellow rule infected them with Japanese ways. But two years of satellite dishes (he was a city man) meant that people *were* now infected – they were rotten, like a carcass with maggots. They watched American soaps like *Baywatch*, they saw white flesh, they listened to Jewish propaganda. What were the signs of rottenness? Girls in trousers, consorting freely with boys, Muslims ignoring their Islamic duties, sending their children to state schools where they were taught lies. All that a child needed to know could be found in the Koran and the sayings of the Prophet.

The 'tourist village' planned for Banyuwangi would bring new horrors: Western people behaving like animals; and villagers could be infected by this animal behaviour and become animals themselves. It was the job of Bayu's pious to be vigilant and punish offenders, to impose the Fast, to encourage Islamic dress. Satan was clever. He worked through the Americans and the Jews. The Jews were like the Chinese: parasites on the hard-working Indonesians, infidels. It was the job of Muslims to declare war on them, to recognize them as the enemies of Allah. All over the world, Muslims were at war with the infidel – in Palestine, in Bosnia, in Sudan, in Chechnya. But even in Muslim countries – Algeria, Egypt – there was a battle for the faith, a war against the pharoah. In Java too, the time had come to choose your friends and enemies, to show others where you stood.

The villagers enjoyed a good talk; they appreciated a story with a moral, and they expected to be mildly chaffed. But the preacher either misjudged his audience or didn't care. He scolded the young for imitating the West and the old for indulging them; he chided girls for 'behaving like whores'; he cursed the headman for 'following Satan' (this must have been Yusuf's information). Nobody present would escape hell if they continued in their wickedness.

Blank-faced, unruffled, Noto, Jona and the others drifted out, the lax and the faithful equally damned. Nobody replied; only the diehards stayed till the end. Next day, Jumhar and his father toured the neighbourhood, shuffling from house to house in their white shirts and black caps. They even called on us, 'in case you heard'. It was a rare sight: a father and son, cap in hand, making apologies. They struggled for the words: they hadn't known: it was a different type of Islam: Yusuf had forced their hand, cheated them. Next year they would let Wan run things.

The villagers heard them out politely, and with the same blank faces, the same air of listening to a problem that did not concern them. Privately they were angry, and as the indignation mounted I had the impression that some of the preacher's targets were pleased: they had the advantage of the insulted; and if they felt sorry for Jumhar, for once they were in the right. 'We hate people like that,' said one old man with sudden passion, imitating the preacher's gestures, his staring eyes. 'What we wanted was a bit about the life of Muhammad, a few stories, not insults and reproaches. You can't wound people's feelings. That's not religion.'

Noto said, '*Barat-baratan* [aping the West]. That was his charge. But what about *Arab-araban*?'

This had been Jumhar's plea. The gown, the beard, the ranting: it had all been a big mistake, a horror show, and Yusuf 'the needle man' was to blame. Everyone agreed. But the damage was done and during the remainder of our stay Jumhar suffered a decline. So, despite appearances, the preacher had his victory. And what had seemed at first a modest recovery, a reassertion of Javanese values in the neighbourhood, was actually a setback for the most moderate prayer-house. Officially, the preacher had flopped, Yusuf was exposed, and the neighbourhood had balked, strengthening the position of men like the carpenter. But these small reverses for a militant Islam counted for little. Yusuf was now enrolled on the mosque committee, joining forces with Aris and Tompo, the village school's religious teacher. They could hope to dominate the moderate voices, the mosque official and his followers. And Jumhar's loss was his rivals' gain, as the prayer-house where Sukib presided became the focus of piety, with louder chanting, bigger classes, and a new spirit of activism. (Untung's house fairly roared under the megaphones.) Haji Drus recruited Aris to give informal instruction to the neighbourhood children. Attendance was now solid. There was a momentum, a quickening of the faith. And the ratchet effect of Koranic classes, school and television meant that the young could move only one way.

The gentle backlash provoked by the preacher's visit had not been enough to quench youthful enthusiasm, merely to redirect it. And the change was quantifiable: purer (less of that), stricter (more of this) and, of course, louder. Most social scientists would call it Islamization, but that would be to accept the ranter's charge that the newly pious – Aris's flock – had not been proper Muslims, when what they were becoming was a different kind of Muslim: conformist, obedient, stricter in ritual observance, less open to other kinds of spiritual experience. The quieter Muslims had shown that they would not be browbeaten. But they could be left behind.

The main Birthday celebrations were in the mosque. Like the prayer-house events, they drew the lax as well as the pious. A few stayed away. Sae said, waving a labourer's hand, 'You know, I don't hold with all this fuss.' *Fuss* was what he called Sri's veiling; so was chanting. 'When I think about it, I'm ninety-five per cent Christian – like my brother-in-law, Pak Arjo. Now *there* was a man who hated fuss: a man of principle.'

Some of the mystics decried any public worship. 'They are like children,' said the old headman above the clamour. 'Children go where the noise is. They follow the crowd: they *see* only the crowd, the loudspeakers, the propaganda. They can't see that the Prophet's birthday is symbolic. It means the birth of humanity; just as *Koran* means *ukuran*, measure: the measure of man.'

But a good number of the mystics did turn up, even if they sat in the wings where they would not have to join in the communal prayers. Like Untung and Noto, who ushered the mosque elders to their places at the front, they had come to show solidarity. Muludan was part of village life; and the mystics, by their own definition, were Muslims too. They could take part without committing themselves to more.

It was my third Muludan in five years, and it was different. In the run-up to a general election – always a staged event with a predictable outcome – there was national concern about social unrest, 'conflict between groups'. The local resurgence of Islam had fed into party politics in a way unseen since the 1960s. Following Suharto's coup in 1965, Bayu had switched from Sukarno's Nationalist Party to Golkar, the new dictator's party machine. Arjo, as leader of the Nationalists in Bayu, had overseen the defection: a painful and self-denying decision: a move, in effect, to accept the inevitable and stay out of politics. For three decades, Bayu's pious minority had accepted the policy and voted, like the rest, for Golkar instead of the official Muslim party, guaranteeing the village subsidy and allowing access to government patronage. Villages with votes against the government could be punished; they were left behind in the race for development: so, at least, it was understood. For three decades, locally and nationally, Islam had been politically weak. Yet although Suharto had neutralized the religious parties, through education and government funding he had permitted, even encouraged, a more orthodox society to develop. And a society that held orthodox Muslim values and social goals would, eventually, want leaders who represented its interests. During our three-year absence Haji Drus had set up Bayu's first branch of NU, the conservative Muslim organization. In front of his store, with its bags of fertilizer and tin buckets, he had put up the green NU board. This was hardly a radical act: despite its millions of supporters, NU was politically docile. Regionally, one more branch counted for nothing. But to raise the flag in Bayu was a provocation, a rejection of the cultural compromise. To declare oneself for Islam – when everyone was

Muslim – was to break the truce, to say you were one type of person and that alone. So it was seen.

There had been riots in Jakarta and sporadically across Java. Suharto had engineered a split in the opposition Democratic Party and set his thugs on its supporters. Islamic clerics close to the government were alarmed by a new outspokenness among secularists and had organized demonstrations. Nationally there was a security alert. And a week before the Birthday celebrations the district army chief called a meeting in the village hall.

We were told it was a 'training' session, to 'build social harmony' and to warn of 'certain dangers' – the spectre of communal strife raised at every election. But the meeting had a further motive which I only heard about later. Drus had complained to the Office of Religious Affairs about the mystical association Sangkan Paran. As an NU branch leader he felt 'bound to oppose unbelief'. ('Unbelief' was a hate-word, a political slur the NU leadership avoided; but Drus was still learning.) How could the authorities allow this godless organization to prosper? The treasurer was even threatening to put up a Sangkan Paran board in front of his house. If nothing were done about it Drus 'wouldn't be responsible for any disorder that might follow'.

In the village hall – an open-sided pavilion joined to the headman's office – sat three grim-faced men in uniform. Facing them across the table, in two blocks either side of an aisle, were Bayu's orthodox – all men – and the Javanists – men and women. It was the first time in thirty years that they had divided: village life did not normally permit such clarity. But sensing controversy and the awkwardness of disagreeing with one's neighbour, they had separated. The public forum, the unspoken motive, the larger dimension – of town and nation – had made it seem natural. Had it been a prayer-meal, they would have sat down together, just as naturally, to bury their differences, finding in its symbolism their common humanity. For thirty years they had known no other way.

It was the man in green, the army chief, who spoke. In Indonesia green trumped grey: the police chief, sleek in his grey shirt and epaulettes, was just for show. Beside them, in sweat-patched khaki, the headman looked defensive, resentful at the intrusion. Their presence implied he had lost control of events. They would say things that shouldn't be said.

The soldier stood under the lamp, a bull-necked, balding man in his fifties, his creased forehead shining with sweat. Before his martial prowess the audience was respectful, attentive. His face was dark from long days in the sun. He had served in East Timor.

Like a preacher at the start of a sermon, he announced his theme: SARA – the acronym for racial, religious and political conflict. He spoke of wreckers and saboteurs, criminals who wanted to impose their ways on society. People might have heard about the riots in Jakarta and Surabaya, he said. But they shouldn't worry their heads about why such things happened: it wouldn't do them any good. The wild bull (symbol of the Democrats) had two horns – two factions – and they were fighting each other. (His hands locked horns.) Perhaps it was a fight to the death. But why should *we* care? Let's stay out of it. As long as our crops are sold and our bellies are full, what concern is it of ours? Young people might be flocking to the bull, but older folk know where their interests lie. And when it comes to the election, one has to think carefully before voting. Think of the consequences: think where progress lies. It's like someone catching a bus. If you want to go somewhere soon you get on the bus that's almost full. You don't get in the empty one behind.

The audience nodded, impressed by the analogy. The army chief was a decent speaker, even a bit of an orator. Sarko, head of village security, listening in the front row, would remember the empty bus in his future speeches. People in Bayu hated to be left behind.

The soldier moved to the gap between the two blocks of villagers and stood with his hands behind his back, chest puffed, on parade. He had heard about tensions in the village of a delicate nature. He wouldn't name names: all he wanted to say was that Indonesia required all citizens to acknowledge a religion, but it didn't ask more of them than that. Mystical groups were recognized in the law and could worship in their own way. It wasn't for others to dictate to them. They were the responsibility of the Ministry of Education and Culture: the Office of Religious Affairs couldn't interfere. Mysticism wasn't religion. And it was against the law to pressure others to pray or fast or to slander others who wanted to sleep. Unrest and factionalism played into the hands of 'certain groups' who would bring down the nation. He didn't need to remind them of what happened in 1965, the Time of Madness. He himself had had to line people up and shoot them, three hundred at a time. He didn't want to do that again.

After his mild rebuke of Muslim proselytizing (received with faint smiles by the Javanists), he spoke respectfully of local Islam. He mentioned the hajis. How much did the pilgrimage now cost? Nine million rupiah? Such financial sacrifice showed how 'thick' was their faith. They had 'graduated' in their religion. But they shouldn't rest on their laurels. There was a national association of hajis to make sure that they kept up their standards. Islam was winning converts worldwide: Muhammad Ali and Mike Tyson had converted. Why? Because they saw that Islam was the best religion. But not everyone thought like that. He himself knew what it was like to live among the faithless. He had been stationed in Flores, in East Indonesia, among Christians and animists, people with no religion. He wasn't always welcome but he learned to adapt. In Flores there were two categories of food: ordinary and special. Ordinary food was rice and maize. Special food was rat, pig and dog. As a guest he was always presented with special food. But he didn't complain, not wishing to hurt the feelings of his hosts. He would simply have a drink and pretend to eat. At night he prayed to Allah to be transferred back to Java. He prayed non-stop for three months, and then – *Alhamdulillah* – after many requests had been turned down, he got the letter sending him home. This was proof of the grace of God and the power of prayer. He himself had proved it.

At this there was much nodding among the pious, as if the soldier's recall from Flores really counted as theological proof, a point in their favour. Throughout the hour's discourse (a whole hour: he could have gone on for two), the police chief had not moved, but he too affirmed the power of prayer with a slow, considered nod. Pak Lurah shifted uncomfortably in his seat. The soldier's piety was a reproach; at least, the pious would see it as such. He had cackled appreciatively at the anecdotes – the 'special food' – but now he looked away.

The soldier ended with a brief recruitment speech. Any young people out there should think of signing up for their country: his door was always open. He recited the code of conduct pronounced by a soldier every day; he spoke of the importance of discipline, the obligation of every citizen to defend the country.

At the end – like everyone else, I think – I rather admired him. Perhaps he was corrupt, a bully, even a killer. But he had principles, and they were spoken with such conviction that you could not simply cry hypocrite. That note of piety and self-sacrifice, the jokey self-deprecation and paternalism, the hint of necessary violence, was struck by every Indonesian leader from the president down. It was what the headman couldn't do. To bang heads together, to remind people of the greater good, to warn of collapse and the dangers of difference: short of force (and the uniforms were a reminder of force), these were the skills of leadership. This was not a democracy.

But if the headman lacked these skills he had others, better suited to village life. And the village had evolved other means of dealing with difference: the prayer-meal, the neighbourhood routines, the exchange of children, the ties of kinship and marriage. A headman required only knowledge and impartiality, the virtues of a chairman. If things turned nasty he could call on Sarko.

The Muludan in the mosque followed two days later, the soldier's warnings and the public division still in the air. There had been more riots: rumoured, officially denied, hardly reported in the television news. Like Lebaran, but with less of the obligatory good will, Muludan put faith on show, and the solid turnout of activists and the ordinary pious was triumphalist, a rebuke to the slackers.

The mosque was in the western part of the village on a flood plain down by the river. To reach it, you walked up the hill, past the village office, and then turned left off the road and down a broad stepped path a hundred yards long. It was a big airy building in gleaming white concrete, with a shining dome topped by a pair of huge megaphones: a statement of modernity as well as of faith. Today the mosque was packed. I sat at the back with the hajis and Pak Lurah on sofas set aside for the notables; in front of us, our perks, tea and cakes. While a girls' group sang praise songs, young men moved through the seated congregation handing out clove cigarettes. Muludan was a social affair, not just a religious celebration, and every man attending had brought a tray of food, taking home the tray of another man in an indirect exchange. There was always more food than needed. A madman from Tamansari took away the surplus trays on a bicycle.

It was a political affair as well as a social and religious affair. The two main speakers, inevitably uniformed, were the district secretary and, once again, the army chief. Each spoke for an hour without notes, mixing warnings with jokes, prayers and songs. A leader was a moralist and entertainer, an agile propagandist who could switch from sermon to karaoke. There was no officialese, no tapping of the microphone: that was for the amateurs, the youngsters who did the introductions and read out the 'protocol' (whose first line was always 'Item One: Reading Out of the Protocol'). Burly, loudmouthed, astonishingly fluent, the district secretary praised the village for its harmony and devotion to steady profits; he teased the villagers about their addiction to prayer-meals and their parsimony – so few cars and such big harvests! He chided them for not paying their taxes. And he warned them of dark forces, seeds of division. The soldier, less jovial, repeated his strictures on SARA – sectarianism – and the necessity of tolerance. But he was less even-handed than at the village meeting. Now, when he spoke of Islam's advance, of Mike Tyson's recruitment and Saddam Hussein's defiance of the West, he did not mention the mystics or the predicament of the quiet, harried majority. 'One need not be surprised that more people are coming to Islam, that Java's Hindus and Christians – the false converts of 1965 – are returning to the fold: they recognize that Islam is the most perfect and complete religion. But one *should* be surprised that those who call themselves Muslims can't be bothered to pray and won't fulfil their obligations. One should be *very surprised* that they have "Muslim" stamped on their identity card but don't behave like proper Muslims.'

This brought spontaneous applause, shouts and bursts of laughter. Heads turned. Some heads stayed very still. At least half the congregation was compromised. Pak Lurah, seated next to me, clenched his fists. He wanted to reply. But he was a poor speaker and the timing was bad. The activists, on home ground, would resist. I whispered to him, 'Is it the place to rebuke them?' He showed me a little paper in his hand with three points scrawled on it. He had written: *rise of fanatics*; *NU their shelter*; and *radical preachers*. 'It's my right as headman,' he said hoarsely. 'I have jurisdiction in the village. They can't come here and insult us.'

But the cheering and mocking shouts – not heard for a generation – had made the event a triumph for his enemies. He would be shouted down. I said: 'You can't speak now. They are celebrating their victory.' And when the secretary bounded up to the microphone for an encore, he turned to me, blinking, and with an expression not of fear but confusion, said: 'I won't do it now, then, since the secretary will say the right thing. He's like me, *nasional*.'

The secretary said his piece and warbled a song, flashing his white grin. Then, when the Muludan praise songs broke out again, the congregation stood up. At the back, the notables – the hajis and visitors – were deep in their sofas. None got up. But then Drus stood, and, following him, the other hajis. They were all standing now; everyone except me and Pak Lurah. I would have risen automatically like the rest; but I could not leave him isolated. The moment was long: yet I had to stand or else risk giving offence. I tugged his sleeve and stood. He passed his hand over his face, sweating, and said, 'Dizzy!' Then he rose unsteadily to his feet amid the chanting. He looked about to faint.

After the Muludan broke up (the madman from Tamansari peddling away unsteadily under his baskets of food), I was pressed to eat with the speakers and hajis. We sat on the floor in Haji Sartono's house around a banquet prepared by his large household, the secretary sprawling like a Levantine prince, one knee in the air, eating enormously. The soldier had gone – SARA calling – but the secretary, with his wide mouth and big laugh, entertained us with songs. Pak Lurah had excused himself. He went home and vomited, defeat and humiliation translated into illness. He was not mentioned during the meal.

Java had been Islamizing for five hundred years; Banyuwangi, at its furthest shore, for rather less. In so long a story there were few turning points: what Islam claimed, Java claimed back. The ebb and flow of orthodoxy had blurred any clear lines. But in the few years I had known the village that third Muludan stood out. A personal defeat for the headman, the event was a rebuke to the lax, the lay Muslims and the principled abstainers, but it was also a defeat for the middle ground – the decent, faithful, tolerant types like the mosque official, Jumhar and Pak Lurah's father-in-law who deplored controversy and whose instincts were always to include, to celebrate and to compromise. Some of them, misled, had joined in the jeering. It was how the village could crack apart.

19
Monkey Business

The headman's illness baffled me. Sometimes it was an old man's cough, a chesty nicotine attack that shook him like a convulsion. Sometimes it was a fever that he gave in to, blanketed pitifully against the world. Sometimes it was more of a fog, a deep gloom that would lift as he put on his uniform and strode slowly up the road to the village office where the orderly world of pie charts and government registers awaited him. In the afternoons he lay inert on the little bamboo bench outside his mother's hut or sat there spooning the soup she had prepared for him. Like a man retired from active life – the village would go on without him – he watched his father tending the cows or laughed at the children playing in the yard. 'Our children don't play like that,' he said, a touch disapprovingly, as Sofía and Daniel drew Hari into their game of prayer-meals. 'Hopscotch or buying and selling. But prayer-meals, no. You can't play at prayer-meals.' With the flowery offerings, the mud-rice cones and incense sticks (but those they had seen in Bali), it was preposterous.

He obtained a monkey for Hari, an orphaned animal from the forest bordering a village up the mountain. It was a macaque, I think, silvery-grey with a black, alert face and mobile brows eager to communicate a language we did not understand. They kept it on a chain outside and fed it papaya and scraps. When Hari lost interest and the monkey became morose and snappy I took over the feeding and negotiated a longer lead, sometimes untying it altogether. 'Not too long: it'll hang itself in despair,' said Pak Lurah with a sudden empathy. 'All the more reason to let it go,' I said. ('It' was really 'him', but the language ignored gender.) Bu Lurah protested. 'We can't let it go. Hari will be upset. When it's too big we'll take it back to the forest.'

There was no concept of a pet. People laughed when I told them that English people combed their dogs and took them for walks: the man serving the dog: the world turned upside down. Animals were for food, or – like songbirds – for amusement. 'Hari's chickens', bantams kept by his great-grandmother at the back, were both. They amused, then they were eaten.

Sometimes the monkey came into the house and sat on the table or climbed on my shoulders, its slender, leathery hands light on my neck, like a woman's gloves. Finding nothing, it would hop down and steal into the kitchen, making eyes at the cook. Panji was half scared, but his gentleness appealed to the monkey. 'No mother! No mother!' And after fending it off, he lifted his shirt to give it the breast. ('See, it just goes there naturally!') Could anything be more flexible than Javanese kinship?

I took it for walks on a long leash around the neighbourhood. It would dash ahead, hurdling over washing lines, upsetting trays of peanuts and baring its gums at the laughing faces. I loped after it while the women and children ran for cover. Pak Lurah found this hugely amusing and soon he was doing the same, sweeping through backyards with the monkey springing ahead. I can see him now like the Pied Piper, trailing children, laughing hoarsely as he scattered chickens and screaming women. Then he would go back to his bench shaking his head and coughing gigantically. Alternately gloomy and high-spirited, he had lost the easy, stolid indifference that was his armour against the critics.

One day we were sitting watching the boxing on television when two men pulled up in a tinted-window jeep. They were journalists working for the Golkar party newspaper. They looked at me with distaste and said they had something private to talk to him about; but Pak Lurah said quietly to me, 'Stay here,' and took them a little to one side, only half out of earshot. There was no tea, no pretence at hospitality. Glancing back at me now and then, they sat in a huddle, and finally, after a surge of voices they walked straight out, not looking back, and drove off. 'They were threatening me,' said Pak Lurah. 'They couldn't do much with you here, but they wanted money or they would make up some story about me and publish it in their rag, try to get me fired. Pran [the headman of Mandaluko] told me they did it with him.'

'What did you say?'

'I told them they could write what they liked.'

He shrugged, but I could see he was bothered. Blackmail was an occupational hazard, like the taunts of the fanatics and the anonymous complaints sent to the authorities. There was a PO box for these 'canned letters', as they were called. In Suharto's state of narks and creeps they were encouraged. One of the district officer's regular correspondents – Pak Lurah thought it was Rapi'i or Pujil, longtime rivals, men with uniforms – had complained that he had mismanaged funds. Again, he shrugged off the threat: he had nothing to hide: everyone knew he did not solicit bribes. If it was Rapi'i – a man who had crossed him in village meetings – he would expose him: *his* hands were not clean; he drove one of only three cars in the village, something unattainable on a headmaster's salary. 'Rapi'i is richer than me and I've got four hectares of salary land as well as my own fields. How is it possible?' I remembered how Rapi'i had left a newspaper article on my table after calling one day. The article had been about the immorality of the West and the need for Indonesia to be vigilant. He had said nothing to my face.

Hari was not one of the children's regular companions. Son of a would-be haji, grandson of a headman, he was groomed for solitary distinction. He didn't run about with the other children. Nor had he acquired the sharing ethic, the disposition to give way and appease younger playmates. The selfishness which parents indulged had an effective cure: the laughter of the yard; but this Hari had yet to suffer. Like Western children trained in the rights of possession he would struggle over objects, claim the biggest portion. Life, as yet, presented no resistance. His mouth was a smear of brown sugar, his tiny teeth already rotten, his hands sticky and outstretched for more.

We took a party of children and mothers to the coast, packing them in a Colt pickup hired for the day. (Jan – like father, like son – would not loan his vehicle and wanted too high a price.) The seaside, as recreation, was a novelty. To most of them the sea was as foreign as snow, though the Straits of Bali were only seven or eight miles away. Southwards lay the bay of Pampang, the largest fishery in Indonesia. At Muncar the brightly-painted outriggers lined the bay in their hundreds. In the deeper, wreck-haunted waters pirates still operated. Northwards, where the straits narrowed to a fast-flowing channel, the coast was bleak and poor: ochre cliffs and a hinterland of deciduous, rust-coloured forest, monkeys high in the trees.

It was here, along the straggling shore, that we parked. We left the pickup among the fishermen's sheds and approached the unfamiliar water, the sea a greenish grey, almost black where it slapped and frothed against the sand. The day was windy and overcast and the black beach – the volcanic sand like dried, granular mud – was striped with twigs and stones. Fishing boats with painted eyes and pronged prows like marlins pointed outwards across the straits to the mauve bare hills of western Bali.

While the children floated past in the warm, strong current, their mothers, seated on the beach, hair blowing in eyes, shouted instructions. Untung and I stood in the waves as human anchors. Drownings seemed likely. But Hari did not swim. His mother said he was afraid of the water and would get dirty. While the other children lay in the shallow surf or bobbed and gasped on the brink of happy deaths she went to a stall among the sheds and bought him a fluorescent ice. By the time she had returned, holding out the toxic bait, he was dangling between aunts Nur and Jona, uncertain whether to laugh or cry. Coaxed by Mercedes, the women had hiked their sarongs up to their knees and waded in. '*Don't photograph us!*' they pleaded. (How white their legs! How winning their embarrassed laughter.) 'Hari's loving it,' they shouted back to the anxious mother. And he began to float, joining the rest who were gliding by at walking speed along the shore. Perhaps he would turn out like the others after all.

*

How you became a Javanese person was a complicated business, but it had a lot to do with the world of children: close yet loosely structured, intimate yet unattached. Unlike the intense, indifferent, aggressive world of North European and American children, with their games of dominance and exclusion, their pride in possession, here boys and girls played together, the older looking after the younger. Without toys and prized objects there could be no envious struggles; without competition, no appeals to 'fairness', of who had the right or who was first. Being older by a year meant conceding, showing the younger ones how to yield, laughing at their selfishness. And giving way meant acknowledging the superior needs of the group, not submission to the strongest. It helped that every child was 'older sister', 'older brother' or 'younger sibling'. (Unadorned names were used only to infants.) So the loose egalitarian groups had a structure of regard, and if you couldn't accept this you stayed clinging to your mother's skirts, an overgrown brat.

It was this careless yet orderly world of the yard, the river and the playground – always on the fringes of adult activity (the washerwomen and harvesters, the festive preparations) – that turned savage infants into civilized Javanese. If childcare were left to adults, babies would never grow up; they would never 'become people'. Knowingly spoiled by adults, small children were monsters of selfishness and whimsicality. When they cried they were sweetened, their mouths plugged with sugar; when they complained, they got their way. A visitor once brought a sprig of mountain berries, and after Daniel had pulled them all off, crying at his handiwork, the headman's mother patiently sewed them back on. When Hari was offered Daniel's toy – a plastic ball with geometrical holes and shaped inserts – his mother simply pushed in the shapes for him. To learn was to risk frustration. In games of chance, they encouraged him to cheat.

Not all parents were equally indulgent, but if a mother tried to assert discipline, a neighbour would intervene, reward in hand. A child's will was sovereign. Only other children could break it.

One day Sri's son, now aged three, climbed the roof pole of our house and refused to come down. Sri, hampered by the veil, awkward in her difference, had left him in the charge of a neighbour, a particularly silly woman, who stood beneath him for half an hour, her hand as his seat, begging him to descend. Irritated past endurance, Bu Mari, who had been watching, slapped the neighbour on the arm and stalked off. Sri herself would have known better than to interfere.

Children under three or four were 'not yet people'. It took the bigger children to socialize them, forcing them to share, laughing at their sulks and whims. They too had their rivalries and quarrels but they managed them in a peculiarly Javanese way. When we printed photographs of the outing – the drowned and the saved – and passed them around, Andi confessed that he was not on speaking terms with Taupik, another boy his age. Hadn't I noticed? Taupik had snubbed him in class one day, and they hadn't spoken for a month. One could play in the same group and maintain a distance: together but apart. Other children understood, but they did not take sides. It was a way not to fight. In the end, after weeks or months, something would happen to restore relations. But grown-ups could go on for years, long after the offence had faded. There were famous cases: husbands and wives who still slept together but did not speak; in-laws who communicated through third parties. Panji, our cook, had not spoken for ten years to a neighbour who had thrown a bucket at him after he had told her she was too fat. She would buy food from his stall by pointing and leaving the money. Why not make up? 'We can't. We're ashamed.'

Childhood had its own laws, its own ways, and these were not like those of the West which we take to be universal. Children knew best how to manage their affairs. What they learned in the yard – to tolerate difference and avoid conflict; to belong without excluding others; to feel mutuality; to restrain, rather than assert, oneself – enabled them to live together as adults. And adults for the most part let them alone. Once they were out of danger – of falling into fires or being abducted by spirits – they were free to roam. Only rarely did a parent intervene.

School was different. School took the high moral tone of the New Order, the authoritarian, paternalist state that Suharto had built. It was school that turned children, though hardly yet Javanese, into Indonesians.

I spent a few days in the primary school: Mercedes took Sofía along to 'kindergarten'. Kindergarten was more like a school than a nursery. Six days a week from 7.30 to 9.30 the children sat at desks and chanted back to the teacher. They drew and sang. They played games and ran races. Above all, they learned to be Indonesian citizens. Under the benevolent gaze of the president (his portrait unchanging, or merely ageing, while that of the vice-president was swapped every couple of years) a child took its first tottering steps into the bureaucratic state. And all over Indonesia, with its hundreds of languages and cultures, they were doing the same. It should have been depressing: you wanted to be outraged at the drills and flagpole parades. But it was riotous, impure fun. When they chanted the constitution or roared the national anthem they did so with such zest – such pleasure in the simple joy of shouting – that you smiled. Of course you had smiled, too, at the jokes of the military commander. Inside the uniform there was always a charm.

The children arrive early, shining and eager, to greet the teacher and kiss her hand. 'Morning, Bu!' 'Good morning, Master Hari!' Then they sit three or four to a bench, the boys mostly with the boys, the girls with the girls, filling the benches even if there are spaces at other desks. Among the pupils sit the mothers of new children, expansive on the tiny chairs. With as much enthusiasm as the rest, they join in the tuneless songs and do the actions. At the front stands Bu Sus with her three-year-old son in a sling on her hip. If the children are noisy, she sings louder, keeping her smile. She never speaks crossly; never tells them to shut up or sit still. The class is a constant ripple of shifting and chatter that suddenly finds focus in a loud patriotic song or a chanted reply. 'Altogether: WE WASH OUR FACE AND HANDS!'

The emphasis is on learning a skill: copying a drawing or reciting a sequence of letters. Hari knew the alphabet and could count up to sixty but could not read or use numbers; at Koran school in the afternoons he was already memorizing Arabic prayers, again without comprehension. Learning is imitation, repetition. Rather than drawing a flower from the imagination, the children copy one from the blackboard. There is a certain way of doing it, of picturing the Platonic flower, and having mastered this skill they can go on to more difficult tasks: an umbrella or a motorbike. Andi once drew for me, from memory, a complicated picture of a helicopter, like a technical drawing, complete with drooping blades and tail propeller.

These imitative practical tasks (origami a favourite) are completed without evaluation. The teacher ticks the work but expresses no approval or criticism; there is no sense that one child did it well, another badly. One cannot fail. In loud sing-song voices, the children repeat the days of the week, the parts of the body, the names of president and vice-president, the colours of the national flag: facts on an equal footing. And then Bu Sus walks towards Master Hari or Sister Titi and points to her stomach, asking the Indonesian word. They show no fear of getting it wrong, no awkwardness or confusion. And if they falter Bu Sus gives them a clue. Pointing to her head: *kepa— . . . kepala!*

Since the kindergarten lacks teaching materials she goes from desk to desk drawing an outline of a camel in each child's notebook ('The Prophet Muhammad rode one'), repeating the operation thirty times. The children fill in the hump with coloured pencils. The school possesses no funds for materials, nor can families afford them, yet the expenditure on sweets would fund a small library and every child requires no fewer than three uniforms – different colours for different days – and two pairs of shoes. To make them last, they walk home barefoot, shoes in hand.

Saturdays are for sport, usually races. In one race there are pairs. Each child runs against an opponent for a stone on the other side. One wins, the other loses. But there is no further knockout, no competition. Most of the time is spent watching.

The building, like most rural schools, is a hut with a corrugated roof and mesh-covered gaps for windows. The playground – an expanse of bare earth, tufted here and there with grass – has a swing and a broken slide, but there is little play, for breaktime is devoted to eating. All morning a man stands in the yard selling candyfloss and bowls of bean porridge. Most of the children bring sweets. Sofía, having none, was the object of adult pity.

During lessons the yard is crowded with mothers and grandmothers, some of whom stay the whole two hours watching through the window-gaps and shouting instructions. *Sit properly! Don't take off your shirt!* Huddled among the matrons, Mercedes was able to shout Spanish translations to Sofía, her words taken up excitedly by the others: *Sientate! Responde a la maestra!* (These parrotings were strangely accurate, giving an illusion of comprehension: Javanese are good mimics.) But maternal love is alert to any disturbance. Should a child cry or fall over, its mother runs in and comforts it or whisks it outside for more sweets. A scuffed knee ends the day. It is not the graze that matters but the emotional response: a startled child is prey to the spirits.

Primary school is hardly tougher. You attend with your classmates from kindergarten, children you have always known. To the customary brightness and confidence is now added the status of being a pupil: a status which gives schoolchildren a slight air of superiority among their peasant families, a sense of entry into a better world.

My first class was with the older children. Class 6, Civics. The lesson followed a book – so closely that the first time a pupil asked a question it was, 'What page are we on, Bu?' The teacher stood at the front, book in hand. She wore a smart frock and had short hair, in the town style. She began to talk about 'poor beggars', a semi-technical term in Islam that includes orphans and people without permanent jobs. 'Are there any in your area?' Leaning forward on their benches, responding as one, they all answered, 'Yes.'

'What do you feel towards them?'

'Pity,' they answered in unison.

'That's right. And what should you do for them?'

'Help them.'

'How should you help? You should do it *fr—*'

'Freely.'

'And that means without *expec—*'

'Expectation of return.'

'What programme has the government introduced to help backward villages with poor beggars?'

'Presidential Instruction.' They were sitting in a school funded by Presidential Instruction.

'And what decree?'

They quoted the number and year of the regulation.

The teacher gave some examples of people needing our help and pity: the victims of floods and fire, sick neighbours, people in road accidents. It was important to take gifts of food to such people, but it was more important to pray for them. Why? Because health is God's grace. So is sickness and death. Death is God's blessing. How do we know this? Because we can't decide for ourselves when to die: only God decides. She acknowledged, however, that people could hang themselves if they wanted to.

A girl at the front put up her hand and asked: 'Should you visit sick people if they are wicked?'

'A very good question. Yes, you should. Even if they are wicked we can pity them. And they'll feel grateful and may even behave better. Also, remember that because illness is God's grace, you shouldn't cry if you are ill. If you cry that's something to be ashamed of.'

After this the teacher wandered out and left the children alone. It was evident that the girls ran the class. One of them, a tall striking girl of about thirteen, came up to a boy sitting near me and pasted chalk on his face with the blackboard eraser. He didn't react.

The next lesson, with Class 5, was about tax. The teacher was a young man from Pacitan on the south coast. He wore a grey safari suit and had thick back-combed hair, like the headman. He spoke in the central Javanese dialect and in Indonesian. (If nothing else, children leave school accomplished multilinguists.) His style was confident and affable, a mixture of gentle scolding and jokes: the jokes inserted to relieve the tedium of the explanation. There was a difference, he explained, between obligatory taxes, fixed levies for specific projects like irrigation improvements, and voluntary contributions. With the latter, what mattered was not the amount but the open-hearted spirit of the gift: that was what won religious merit.

'Nobody likes paying taxes. But without them there'd be no development. Take road-building. Our road has been resurfaced: proof of the use of tax. What do I mean by proof? If you cycle along the new road you'll find yourself falling asleep because it's so smooth. Try!' (They laughed.) 'Remember what it was like five years ago. You could hardly walk along it. And now we have electricity. In the old days wick lamps. Then pressure lamps: they were hard work.' He mimed the pumping. 'Now we've all got proper lights. Ah! Clever Pak Harto [the President]. Now schools are everywhere, even in the hills, so that peasant children don't have to be stupid and tricked by clever people. Give me some other proofs?'

Someone called out, 'Mosques.'

'Mosques and churches and temples. That's right. So that each can worship in his own place. We couldn't have Muslims going into churches or Christians into mosques, could we? That would spell trouble. Separate buildings: tolerance. We all have our different religions, but we're equal before God. We're all born naked. Or perhaps you were born wearing a jacket . . .'

They laughed again in an easy way, happy with the teacher. And so the lessons went on, mixing facts with gentle moralizing, emphasizing feelings and proper behaviour, the wisdom of government. The materials were formulaic, memorable. But the propaganda points, made by teachers grateful to the system (their salary scales were pinned to a board in the head's office), were often unscripted.

School was undemanding: not a means to an end but a life-stage, like the Seven Ages, a step up from infancy. It asked only your presence. I saw children doze or talk quietly to one another, then pick up again, repeating the points aloud, like the words of familiar songs. Yet though classes were dull, in four days I heard few groans or sighs of boredom, no protests or misbehaviour. The teachers, relaxed but not over-familiar, were respected and liked; the children only sporadically engaged but never rude or troublesome. It wasn't much of an education, but it was enough.

Outside in the yard the carpenter's wife, Las, had a stall selling snacks at breaktime. She stood behind piles of cheap homemade sweets and drinks, beaming stoutly, joining in the banter. Everything was the same price, fifty rupiah, the smallest coin, and the children simply helped themselves. On a bald, dusty field boys were playing football. Girls and boys took turns swinging from a branch. The smaller children chased a sheep – exotic as a zoo animal – that had escaped from a neighbouring yard. This was the scene that Tompo, the religious teacher, confronted one day in Ramadan when he marched up to Las's stall and swept her wares furiously onto the ground. He had threatened to punish any child caught eating during the Fast. 'You are dragging the children to hell with you! Get out, temptress! Out with your sweets!' And she ran, wailing and terrified, back home to Noto.

20
A Village Coup

Mustari rises before dawn, makes his way through the yard to the creaking pump for his prescribed ablutions – the rinsing of mouth and ears, the sluicing of forearms and feet – and walks in darkness to the glowing prayer-house three doors down. The noise has already started: Sukib at his post, hand on microphone, rocking back and forth. As Mustari enters, wincing at the roar, Sukib half-glances at him through narrowed eyes in a semi-smile that suggests either solidarity or triumph. The tussle for the microphone is only part of their rivalry. If Sukib gets there first, he not only does the call to prayer but leads the prostrations. Only when Sukib is ill can Mustari be certain of this honour – one not much coveted in Bayu. For the rest, they have an unspoken compromise. Mustari gives the sermon, Sukib does the Arabic chanting and the devotional songs called, in Javanese, 'balm for the heart'. It is Sukib who controls the cassette player wired to the megaphone.

I think of Mustari, even in this loud company, as a lonely man. Sometimes his eldest son joins him, but usually he goes to the prayer-house alone. His wife, like most of the neighbourhood women, has never prayed; his young son, Andi, shows no inclination. Mustari prays alone as he works alone. His life is one of modest, solitary application: the struggle for cash, self-denial, the firm hand of family discipline. As a man of principle, he knows he is not much liked (though not actively detested like the stiff and singular Sukib), but it is usually he who presides over neighbourhood feasts. He knows the sequences of prayers, memorized in his boyhood seminary, the nineteen kinds of offerings and the incense-borne dedications to angels and spirits. One of the poorer Muslims, he regards the new-found piety of Drus and Jan (the haj, the seal on their wealth) with a touch of irony. Godliness takes a lifetime! But he expresses no criticisms – one must be tolerant – and shows no envy. The prayer-house regulars – Sukib, Drus, Jan, Aris – would not be his first choice as friends: but then he has no friends. Piety makes strange bedfellows.

In Bayu, Mustari possesses neither land nor relatives; like many others he has married into the village, but among the ungodly he has never felt quite at home. (The sentiments, like the pieties, come ready-made, but that too is part of tradition.) Untung, next door, whom he calls 'younger brother' – their wives are sisters – is hardly a Muslim, though his daughter has turned out well; the headman, further down, is a hard case; eastwards live the thick-skinned, insolent Jakis, then Wan, half Christian, running to fat, and the ignorant Ramelan, a man who dares to say (varying the slacker's formula), 'My plough is my religion.' Jan, though promising, is a mere boy; and Drus comes at a cost: his mistresses, his violent temper, his swaggering pride. In a godless neighbourhood it is his, Mustari's, duty to set an example.

*

For more than a month Andi had not come to see us. Mustari had banned him from playing with Sofía and Daniel in protest against something I had said. At least, that was how we interpreted it. One evening, after a prayer-meal, talk had turned to a lynching in another village somewhere in the hills. Mustari, who travelled the area on his bicycle doing carpentry jobs, had been there the day after it had happened. The victim had been dragged out of his house and cut down, the house burned. When the police came next day nobody knew anything about it. Nobody had seen.

Mustari – round-eyed, with a thin moustache and a lined forehead under his rimless hat – related the story with satisfaction. He used the word 'cleansing', and said that the area, like a stable, needed a periodic clearing-out. Had the village not acted, the sorcerer might have struck again: half a dozen people had already died that year.

'They took the law into their own hands,' said Pak Lurah. '*They* are the ones who should be punished.'

'Some things can't be handled by the law. When religious matters are at stake, you have to act on what you believe. That's how Java was saved in 1965. Believers knew what was right –'

'People die there because it's a backward village,' said Pak Lurah. 'If they dug proper latrines and didn't foul the stream they wouldn't get sick and die. It's nothing to do with sorcery.'

'Such things may not be denied,' Mustari persisted.

We sat quietly for a few uncomfortable moments; then another man spoke.

'I don't believe in sorcery,' said Elan, who had been one of the killers in 1965 and understood the difference between communists and sorcerers. Elan believed in karma. He wasn't proud of his past: he now saw the slaughter as wrong. A hard life – a year in the army, seven marriages, only one child – had not expiated his guilt. He turned to me, laughing, and said, 'I bet they don't have sorcerers in England, do they?'

The three of them waited; then the headman said, 'Well, were they right to kill a sorcerer?'

I thought of the carpenter's father – the magician – and the other lynchings I had heard about in Bayu. I thought of the peanut broker's husband and the dragon families, victims whose names were never cleared, children with tainted pasts.

'No. They murdered an innocent man.'

'Ah!' It was what the headman wanted me to say. 'Fanatics.'

That was a month ago. Since then Mustari's son had avoided us, not even coming to play with the monkey. 'Mustari's a difficult man,' said Nur, his sister-in-law, in a whisper. 'Untung and I have a hard time putting up with him: all those reproaches. Pak Lurah says the sermons are always aimed at him; we say they're aimed at us!'

I imagined them lying awake at night, the voice itemizing their faults, promising them hell. They were neighbourhood stalwarts: the first to join in house-building and the unpaid chores of feast and funeral (the days off work a double sacrifice). But without prayers and mosque duty their good deeds 'stank like sins', their services were 'no better than crimes'. So the sermons told them.

'Let him think what he likes, but keep it to himself,' said Nur. It was hard to remain a good neighbour when religion gave license to offend.

Cacophony is next to devilry, pandemonium. But loudness can also be sacred: the Arabic for religion, by coincidence, is *dīn*. During the holy month of Ramadan, *dīn* prevailed and people conceded to the noisemakers, weathering the harangues and the whistling feedback. 'It's their turn,' said Noto magnanimously: he was honing a windmill blade, speaking between the strokes. 'Let them do their worst! We'll show our forbearance. We are Javanese!'

'But so are they,' I said.

His son came out to listen, smiling, wanting to admire. Noto rested his plane and blew off the shavings, then sighted along the blade. 'You have to look at it this way,' he said. 'It's a kind of trial – makes us better people, more patient. Actually, the Islamic hardships – fasting, staying awake – are really Javanese: ways of training yourself. Only the noise isn't ours.'

Purwadi the mystic, owner of the windmill blade, said simply, 'Empty vessels.' The proverb was the same in Javanese.

They did their worst, exceeding expectation, and then, emboldened, they carried on. Weeks passed and still the noise persisted, clangorous, defiant, inescapable, invading your dreams and thoughts so that even moments of silence were tense with anticipation, like the gap between flash and thunder. Eventually, you heard the chants and calls in your head, a holy tinnitus.

Under fire, distance matters. Untung and the headman, either side of Sukib's prayer-house, were the front line. Thirty yards back, we too reverberated; the children moaned; Winoto's chickens flapped and regrouped. Across the road, a mango tree gave Bu Mari a little shelter, but Wan, destroyed by prayer, had taken to sleeping in the day. Only those in the far west, the mystics – dreaming of caves in forests, practising extinction – could sleep undisturbed.

The noise went on, but soon there was a different note, lighter, but unmistakable – the sound of stones dropping onto prayer-house roofs; not every night, but often enough to cause comment. First you heard the blare, then, in answer, the scuttling stones.

The message of the stones was heeded. To put it into words would be to risk 'misunderstanding' (*misunderstanding* meant *understanding*, saying what could not be said). Yet the protest could not be ignored: behind the artillery were respectable men, or so it was rumoured. The mosque official appealed for moderation. The megaphones were turned down a shade. And the scattered prayer-houses were repaired, new tiles prodded into place by men grumpily silent. Nobody risked a smile. Only Sukib in his castle was defiant. And when the headman stood blinking in the brightly lit archway at three in the morning and told him to 'tone it down', he slid a cassette into the machine, turned a knob, and ran home to his house near the fields.

It was on another such night, shaken by his trumpetings, that I walked – half crazed, half asleep – into the howling electric glow. (How strange and remote Jumhar's tranquil and shady prayer-house – built for another age – now seemed.) It was futile, I knew, but I had to see for myself, to confront my nightmare: a madman rocking with a microphone, a voice that never ended.

Prayers had not yet begun; Sukib was alone in his ecstasy, eyes closed, a finger in one ear, the microphone at his mouth. I pressed my face to an ornamental gap in the headman's wall and began to shout – 'It's very loud, Man Sukib! Could you . . . ?' – when something hit me, a puff of dust or sand that shot through the hole and felt like a sharp slap in the face. I blinked and peered again. An angry eye appeared the other side of the hole and with it Drus's indignant rasp: '*Lurah?*' Like impatient duellists, we marched in parallel to the end of the wall, then Drus closed on me, his fists raised, his black mouth open. 'You! What are you doing? How dare you!' I saw his teeth, his billowing robes, smelt his breath; yet no blows followed. As soon as I had grasped his collar he relaxed in my grip and I felt the fight go out of him like a drowning puppy, his voice rising from prophetic outrage to stammering whine. I remember little of what he said, except for that oddly neutral *sampeyan*, the polite form of 'you': a word for outsiders. To someone you intended to insult, the correct form was the dialect word *sira*. That was how Yusuf the paramedic had addressed me, repeatedly needling me with it until I responded in kind. '*Sampeyan*' was already backtracking.

Drus had been expecting someone else; or he had not expected me to stand my ground. But I too was puzzled. Had he been crouching behind the wall with a handful of dust (thus annulling his prayer-ablutions)? Or had he happened by and attacked on a reflex, instinct prevailing over sacred intention? Either way, I had received another's insult. And now the real target – lit from behind, hair sticking up wildly – appeared on cue in his doorway.

'What happened?' The headman was choking. 'Why this infernal noise? Sukib! QUIET!'

Though the sound died suddenly, we could not answer. Strictly, nothing had happened. I had hardly uttered my complaint; Drus had slapped the wall, not my face; we had not come to blows. Nobody had even said anything rude. Yet it felt serious, as if we were caught on the brink of something much worse. I had sleepwalked into someone else's fight. And if it was the headman's fight, not mine, it was also much more than that. Untung and Nur, the carpenter and the peanut women, Sri's many parents (perhaps even Sri), the neighbourhood, a good half of Java could have stood in my place. In the battle of the megaphone was Java's modern history.

As Mustari came round the corner into the light, Sukib ran off, his tail between his legs. Mustari looked from one to another.

'He was forbidding Sukib,' complained Drus, like child to father.

'No, I was about to ask –'

The headman raised a checking hand. 'Enough! Nothing happened. That man is driving us mad!' He passed his hand through his startled hair and said weakly, 'I haven't slept for three weeks. Now go back to bed or get on with your prayers!'

He closed the door and we obeyed.

*

Later that morning I went round to Mustari's to explain. He was sitting in the shade, on his verandah, in a sarong and singlet. He wore his customary black hat. He was guarded but courteous, a little weary. I felt like a fool. I *was* a fool.

'Yes, I know you meant no harm. But Sukib is not an easy man. *Turn it down, Brother Sukib!* He won't listen: that's his way. He won't give me the microphone. But you should understand, Andrew, that he has the right. It is his duty to proclaim the message.'

'Yes, but so loud?'

'As loud as it takes.'

'What if the neighbourhood refuses?'

Mustari explained in a patient Sunday-school voice. 'Then they are sinners and will pay in the afterlife. God counts up all the unpaid prayers and exacts a punishment. But at least the lax will get some benefit. They hear my sermon.'

'You can't force people to pray.'

'That's right. It was the Prophet Muhammad himself who said, *There is no compulsion in religion*. But you *can* force people to listen.'

I did not want to argue. I would never argue again about anything, ever. But there had been the moment with Drus that he had not seen. How to repair that? What had Drus told him?

'I won't talk about Drus. But he's a man it doesn't do to cross. If he sees you are too close to the headman he will take you for his enemy. Drus has friends you don't want to get mixed up with. A different kind of people.'

I said I regretted the incident – it was not my affair – and he seemed pleased, so pleased that I feared he had mistaken regret for apology. And if it wasn't my business to protest about noise, nor was it mine – over the heads of Untung and the rest – to concede to bullying.

As I was leaving, Mustari called me back. 'Listen, Andrew. Keep this to yourself. We don't want the story getting round the village or beyond. Think of the headman: it will damage his reputation. I feel sorry for him, I really do.'

This was untrue. But I promised I would not take it any further. Later that afternoon he sent Andi round to play with the children.

For a week nothing happened and I felt I could risk paying Drus a call. But I wanted a witness, somebody neutral, so I got Johan to accompany me: it was the Javanese way, to choose someone with links to both sides. Johan and his wife were childless; his wife did our washing. He was a regular at the prayer-house, a timid man who swept up after the evening chanting and turned out the lights: *piano* to Sukib's *fortissimo*. With his self-effacing bearing – sloping shoulders, complaisant smile – he was a favourite choice for usher at neighbourhood events. As the older brother to Aris, whom he resembled in everything but expression, his whole manner conveyed apology, as if by standing affably at his brother's side and shaking his head he could soften the harsh words. He was the quotation marks around his brother's diatribes.

'The haji will be relieved,' he said encouragingly. 'He knows it wasn't your fault.'

'What wasn't my fault?'

'I don't know. Whatever it is he's accusing you of.'

Drus was at home with Mustari and another activist, a man from a different prayer-house. We could hear them talking in low voices as we squeezed past sacks of pesticide into his parlour, with its showroom upholstery and Koranic mottoes pinned to the walls. It was a scene of peculiar dullness: Drus's tiring, pedantic voice ('According to my teacher . . .'); the room flat and shadowless in the dim fluorescent light, like a cardboard theatrical set. The men looked uncomfortable. Other hajis were content to be local notables, patrons of the poor, sponsors of cockfights and Islamic events. They did not take themselves for sheiks. They had no designs on the village. To visit them was to gratify their self-esteem but also to submit to an easy hospitality: the scattered cushions and trays of sweets, the poor relations serving glasses of tea, the sharecroppers and harvest contractors coming and going. But here the unfamiliar furniture made positioning difficult, the graded presence of a Javanese gathering impossible. Without the usual bench and coffee table there was no way of sitting on the sidelines, no way of dropping in. Enthroned in his armchair, Drus wanted to hold court. He wore the baggy robes of a cleric, with big Henry VIII sleeves that exaggerated his girth; on his small head, the haji's white skull cap. Forced to sit below him, the other men – his senior in years and knowledge – had to lean forward in their seats to mitigate the effect.

We stood on the edge of his circle.

'Pak Andrew's come round to pay his respects and put things right,' said Johan obligingly. Mustari and the other man twisted towards me with strained smiles. 'He wants to say a few words, smooth things over.'

Siti, who had rushed in, wiping her hands on a cloth, squinted at me with sympathy. She had a bruise over her eye. Nobody told us to sit down.

'Say your piece then,' said Mustari.

I tried to be conciliatory but not apologetic: I should not have got involved: it was stupid to quarrel: we should not blow things out of proportion: it was important to remain on good terms. The headman, I said, was with me in this.

While I was speaking Drus seemed to be composing himself as if about to make a declaration, puffing and making little irritable shifts of posture. Once again, I felt, I had taken him by surprise and he did not know what to say. But at my last sentence he groaned.

'Ah, of course he would! You are being used as a tool by others. And let me tell you this –' now wagging his finger – 'it is not your place either to stand by the headman or shelter him. If he is blocking progress in this village, your job is to stand out of the way and let us get at him. Otherwise, it'll be the worse for you. You have no business to question how we conduct ourselves, you a Christian –' He turned to the others and said in an undertone, 'An infidel!'

'Don't come here trying to make up,' he went on, his voice rising to a shout. 'We have nothing to say to you. *Each to his own religion*, said the Prophet Muhammad, peace be upon him. Our interest is in the others, the backsliders. I would be betraying my rank as a haji – and all the sacrifices I have made on the pilgrimage – if I didn't put people right. That true, Mustari?'

'Quite true, Haji.'

'So we shall turn up the megaphones as loud as we like, twenty-four hours a day if necessary!'

I said, 'That seems a poor justification. Some of the people you want to correct are very decent folk who don't need to be told by Sukib what is good for them.'

'They are ignorant and it is our duty to correct them. There's an end of it!'

Mustari, seeing my point, said, 'It's not enough to do right by others to be saved. Good works on their own aren't enough.'

But was piety on its own enough? Could you behave badly while preaching salvation to others? I dared not ask. The charge of hypocrisy was never made, perhaps because it was assumed. At every level of society from the president down, people in power said one thing and did another. In an odd way, this somehow confirmed what was said. Because no one could be held to account, measured against their words, the message itself remained uncorrupted. The fact that the Five Principles of the constitution – posted on every office wall, chanted by schoolchildren – were routinely violated, did not detract from their worth. You could lie to affirm a truth, kill in the name of peace. Politics in Indonesia was a double game, but so too was religion. Immune from criticism, remote from practical morality, religious authority was doubly sacred.

I nodded and withdrew, Johan wringing his hands in dismay.

The headman said so little that he could never be accused of hypocrisy. But in the weeks following the prayer-house incident his critics renewed their attacks. I was visited one day by the mosque official warning me about a letter in circulation that put a different construction on the incident. Drus, Aris and the others were accusing the headman of trying to ban the microphone; I was his spokesman. It seemed a trivial charge, but recent events made it serious. In Situbondo, a heavily Muslim town to the north, opposition to mosque amplification had led to riots.

Next day the headman and I were summoned to answer the charge. A clerk came on a bicycle and waited for a signature, but Pak Lurah was in no hurry and we sat drinking coffee until mid-morning. As we left the house, he said, 'Best not let them see where we're going. Drus has got his spies out. They'll think they've beaten us.' So we took a back road to the district office, through the rice terraces and coconut plantations, the motorbike winding round potholes and bumping along at walking speed. When we arrived at the little complex of white government buildings – neat yards, flag-poles, stencilled boards – the headman said, 'Just back me up. I'll do the talking.'

Our first district officer, five years ago, had been a mild, urbane man, with practised jokes about his servants – his light-fingered chauffeur, the maids with their superstitions and pregnancies. At Lebaran we had sent him a durian – the prickly, foul-smelling fruit prized by connoisseurs, the only fruit eaten by tigers – and he had promptly ordered a car round to collect us for tea. But I knew nothing of his successor. I had been lazy.

The new district officer – a cautious, slight man in a mauve safari suit – sat between two uniforms: the local military commander and a man from the Orwellian Sospol (Sosial Politik) department. Before them on the table, in an opened folder, was the letter of complaint which had been referred upwards from the Office of Religious Affairs and had bounced between state agencies, no one sure whether it was a matter of public order, sectarianism or local politicking. The letter – by turns abrupt and rambling – the district officer now read out to us. When he had finished, he laid it down carefully and looked at us without irony. Pak Lurah, who had permitted himself to snort at the contradictions, said. 'So how many of them were supposed to be witnesses? One, two or eight?'

'You tell me.'

'Only Drus, Andrew and Sukib were there – and me. Sukib was busy chanting. Mustari arrived later. Nobody else.'

'What about their accusation – that you want to stop them broadcasting?'

'We want them to turn down the volume and limit the early broadcasts to the call to prayer. Cut out the sermons and the cassettes. That's what everyone wants. Nothing more.'

'Is that what you told them?'

'We have never told them anything else. In fact, we have only ever *asked*. They won't be able to deny it.'

The district officer sighed and said, 'What is your relation to those who have signed?'

'Drus is my cousin's son; the others are semi-family. This is a family quarrel that should never have come to you.'

'Aris has complained about you more than once, as you know.'

'He's a young man. Too much enthusiasm.'

At this the military commander said: 'He's a religious teacher, I suppose?'

'He's a factory worker. He never even went to a seminary. Nor did Drus. They come over all pious, in the new style. They want to take over and do everything their way.'

The Sospol agent said, 'So they vote against the government?'

Again the headman remained loyal. 'No, Pak, we're all Golkar.'

'That's not what I've heard.'

The headman shrugged.

The Sospol agent asked me about anthropology, and then said: 'Do you know the phrase *kambing hitam* [black goat]?'

Yes, I said; we had the same concept: scapegoat.

'You are the scapegoat of the scapegoat. They want to bring down the headman – he's in their way – and they'll use you as an excuse. They'll drive you out to get rid of him.'

The headman laughed bitterly. 'Aris calls me Abu Jahal!' It was an odd accusation at the end of the twentieth century, but insults came no stronger. Abu Jahal was the Prophet's arch-enemy. Drus and Aris were fighting Islam's oldest war, the war against the infidel.

Like most Javanese, Pak Lurah could not think in absolutes. *Abu Jahal* was a playground taunt, part of a ridiculous game, like the robes and the screams. The game was dangerous, like any politics, but the fancy dress – the religious aspect – was absurd. The newness of the new style – the nature of its challenge – was not yet understood.

'How do you propose to deal with them?' said the district officer.

'Anyone who disagrees with them they call *kafir*, unbeliever,' replied Pak Lurah. 'What can you say? With such people you can't find a middle way. They'll eat you, given the chance.' Having made of the quarrel a family affair – therefore nobody else's business – he was free to criticize.

The district officer closed the folder and said that he hoped the remainder of my stay would be peaceful. He hoped – perhaps that meant *expected* – the headman would be able to put his house in order. Then he pushed back his chair and stood up. 'Gentlemen!' he said, and indicated the door.

We climbed on the motorbike and Pak Lurah set off with a grin. I felt reassured, impressed by the officials' common sense and their reluctance to interfere in village affairs. Correctly, they had scented a village coup, a miniature Islamic revolution. They had grasped the play of personalities. Yet despite their files and networks of informers they knew little of Bayu's practical politics. Or, like most townspeople, they assumed – the mistake of 1965 – that peasant politics was a simpler, rustic version of the real thing, with sharply defined power blocs, distinct religious constituencies split along party lines. That would be to reckon without kinship and community; without, especially, the collective symbolism of the feast. If you didn't know how children were borrowed, how religious distinctions were blurred through marriage and how adversaries were held close through gift-exchange, the village must appear more fractured than it really was. (I once told a group of Banyuwangi experts about a Hindu-Muslim prayer-meal I had attended in the south: they were frankly incredulous.) Without knowing how differences were managed, talking about difference was about the worst thing you could do. Just as the army chief in his mosque sermon had misjudged the villagers, creating divisions by talking about them, the Sospol agent had asked, incredibly, whether Bayu's activists were 'in the majority'. In Bayu, the very concept of a majority was alien. The one thing you never did was take sides.

The riots in the northern town of Situbondo had begun after a court case. The man on trial was a Koran instructor named Saleh. In a town of white-walled seminaries and famous Islamic teachers, Saleh was a very minor figure. But he had approached one such teacher and asked him to restrict the use of loudspeakers in his mosque. On this same occasion, Saleh had been accused of expressing heretical views (for example, that the Koran was humanly authored). He had then slandered the recently deceased head of another seminary, saying that he had died an unholy death in hospital.

The Islamic teacher, an important man, had carried his account to the police, protesting blasphemy. His campaign succeeded and Saleh was duly brought to trial. To all appearances, it was a manufactured scandal, started for obscure reasons. But passions were high and, in the ensuing court case, sessions were repeatedly adjourned as demonstrators, chanting death, overcame the police. At the final session, held under siege, Saleh was sentenced to five years for insulting a religion, the teacher's word counting as proof. But the demonstrators, numbering several thousand, were not satisfied. They burned down the courthouse (Saleh was saved) and then rampaged through the town, burning Christian schools, Chinese businesses, and twenty-five churches. The churches – why so many in a Muslim stronghold? people asked – were a separate issue. But grievances combined. And the result was that a Protestant minister and his family died in the flames. When arrests were made, the rioters turned out to be mostly religious people, pupils of the town's many seminaries. But there were also reports of men on street corners with cans of petrol, giving directions while armed policemen stood idly by. As with other such incidents, it was difficult to pin the blame. And the language of uncertainty – 'provocateurs', 'masterminds', 'hidden forces', like the spooks and were-tigers of an earlier age – served only to name the fear. Some people claimed to have spotted army boots on the 'agents of chaos'. But this too was uncertain.

At first, in any case, it was all rumour: the riots went unmentioned on television and radio; the newspapers were contradictory. But disturbance itself was contagious and the authorities feared the disease would spread south to Banyuwangi, the next big town. They cut the road and put troops on the streets at night.

Banyuwangi was not Situbondo. Its ethnic mix was different, its religious schools scattered and obscure, its hinterland partly Muslim in the Bayu fashion: inclusive, mystical, determinedly tolerant and – since 1965 – unpolitical. Why would anyone riot? But the effort to contain the violence failed. Rumours, anonymous phone calls late at night, slanderous leaflets dumped in mosques and prayer-houses suggested a counter-effort. The sources – and, curiously, the targets – were said to be Muslim leaders, accused now of sorcery and conspiracy. Islam was not the problem: Islam was being made the problem.

Pak Lurah, who had recently installed a phone – Bayu's first – received police warnings that lynchings could be expected. And then, not long after the first such killing in the hill village, a man living less than a mile from Bayu was murdered as a witch. This time – so it was said (everything was hearsay: to demand proof was to expose oneself to suspicion) – a truck had pulled up outside his house in the darkness and masked men had got down and performed the deed. The village head had conveniently been away on business. This was more frightening than an angry mob. The word now used – a new word in the lexicon of fear – was *ninjas*, like the masked raiders in Chinese horror films.

Suddenly, the dawn broadcasts had a different context. The tired denunciations now connected to a different story, but one begun elsewhere by people with different, unfathomable intentions. The stray connection made life unpredictable in a way that villagers found queasily reminiscent. As in the 1960s, the time of political massacres, they felt out of their depth, disoriented. If townspeople, men in uniform, did not know how things worked in the village, villagers knew even less what was driving events outside.

Perhaps because the neighbourhood was finally listening, resentment over the prayer-house revived. Drus's brother-in-law, who lived next door to Bu Mari in a big shady compound, refused to help him carry timber from his fieldhut. ('He hung his head in shame,' boasted Jakis. 'He wouldn't dare call *me* an infidel.') People stayed away from the evening chanting. One or two pious types dared to call Drus a fanatic. But collective disapproval – outright ostracism was unthinkable – only inflamed the activists. They now began to make trips outside the village to rally support. We watched the motorbikes come and go, heard rumours of violence planned and carried out. And caught up in the fear, we wondered how long it was safe to remain.

There was a sharpening of internal boundaries, a scrutiny of outsiders. In Banyuwangi, for the first time, we faced whistles and catcalls – shouts of *Whitey*, *Shit*, and the oddly colonial *Boy*. In the covered market, among the crowded stalls, Mercedes felt the hard stares of youths. But town was orderly and well-lit. With its barracks and patrols – the military a slumbering Leviathan – Banyuwangi was still safe. It was the hinterland, the night, that was dangerous. Over the next year, more than 250 people died in the Banyuwangi countryside, killed by mobs and 'ninjas' in a witch-craze. Outside Africa – and the witch-hunts of seventeenth century Europe – there had been nothing like it. The victims in villages near Bayu had been the first.

For a few terrifying months the spooks and demons – were they *out there* or *in here*? – loomed and flashed in the darkness. Misfortune found an explanation. Fantasy lodged in a neighbour, a kinsman, a rival: the familiar suddenly grotesque. It seemed that the terror of the 1960s had returned. But the battles of that era had been ideological, an argument over what kind of society to create. Now the terms of conflict were cultural – or hazily existential. What kind of Muslim am I? Do I want to be modern? Who *am* I? Who are *they*? Questions that could not be turned into slogans or parties; indeed, they barely surfaced in consciousness. In place of ideology there was fear, confusion and anxiety. Only the machinery of death was familiar: the poisonous rumours, the semi-official lists of names, the black-clad death squads.

Our enemies are in ourselves, said Warno. *We must struggle to overcome them. In the shadow play they are the monsters.*

Who was behind the violence? The dying regime? Dissident generals? Islamists? In the Javanese view there was always a puppeteer. But some said the witch-craze was home-grown. In the face of Islamization, or Westernization – the one a reflection of the other – the killings seemed like a fit of local hysteria, a last spasm of local ways. Or perhaps a reaction to the fading of state power (most of the killings took place after Suharto's fall in 1998). These were some of the theories. Briefly, the reporters came to Banyuwangi and, following them, the social scientists. By then the stories had been worked up, the explanations rehearsed. In Java it was useless to arrive when the fires had burned out.

The few certainties were violence and fear – and, with them, opportunity.

One day Pak Lurah had a visit from his old friend Pran, the headman of Mandaluko. Seeing the antique motorbike parked across the road, with its gleaming chrome tank and Pran's aviator goggles dangling from the handlebars, I went straight over. The door was open. In the afternoon heat the parlour was dim and cool; a fan whirred in the corner. The two men, of a similar age, were examining a sheet of paper. Pran – mild, bespectacled, droll – had obtained a copy of a letter of complaint that Bayu's rebels had drafted in his village. His brother, a devout Muslim, was a friend of Aris; they had used his house. But the brother had shown Pran. The two friends turned the letter over, pointing out the errors, commenting, half amused, on the authors, people they had grown up with.

'That bit was surely Aris,' said Pak Lurah.

'No. Only a schoolteacher could say that,' said Pran.

Pak Lurah looked at me with a sour grin. The coup was on again.

In the bureaucratic state there is a protocol for mutiny: secret meetings, petitions to the district office, a signed accusation in triplicate. Even a coup requires permission. These were the visible signs.

We did not know where the conspirators went on their motorbikes or what encouragement they received from outside, what larger frame the village coup was being fitted into.

There were stranger aspects that suggested a potential for violence, even a link to the squalid murders in the hills. One night, Sarko, head of village security, saw a light burning in a fieldhut north of the mosque. He walked there in darkness and peeped through a slit in the bamboo wall. Inside, lit by a pressure lamp, Drus, Aris and the other malcontents were gambolling and tumbling about in the straw. They chanted prayers and uttered spells and oaths. A man Sarko didn't recognize was instructing them in martial arts and 'invulnerability magic'. Sarko called it 'ninja training'. One of those present – an observer, not a participant – was Mustari. Standing in the dark, his face pressed to the slit, Sarko had also been shocked to see his son-in-law: a friend of Wan's, an idler, a tambourine man who had recently 'got religion'. The conspiracy had spread beyond the acknowledged zealots.

These days Drus was hardly ever at home. He had cast aside his business for Islamic politics. The headman joked about it. Drus had switched brands, he said, and now smoked Jarum and Super, two popular brands of clove cigarettes. *Ja-rum* was a contraction of 'rarely at home'; *Su-per* meant 'likes women'. But it wasn't women – or not for the moment – that Drus was chasing.

Know your enemy. I came outside one morning hearing squealing. Across the road, in front of his store, Drus was crouched down with his back to me. Three or four children watched from behind a fence, their hands held to their mouths. He was castrating a cat. When the operation was over – from a distance, it seemed complicated work, a struggle – he dipped a rag in a kerosene barrel and rubbed it over the wound, then stood up and faced the children with a glare. Later I asked Mustari's son about it. The cat might die, said Andi, because Drus didn't know how to do it properly. He had made a mess. People normally got an expert to do the job. But Drus did his own dirty work. At Lebaran, when an ox was killed, Drus wielded the knife.

The rumours continued. The private meetings went on. Several nights in a row the headman was awakened by threatening phone calls. He did not report them, not knowing who to trust. And he succumbed again to the bouts of coughing and fever that had afflicted him after his humiliation in the mosque. I wondered about my fieldnotes: the books and tapes that could be seized or burned in a moment. Any trouble and I would have to account for myself: my findings would be examined by the authorities, perhaps for evidence against others. I went through my notes and blacked out names and incriminating gossip, heretical depositions, mentions of the communists and the killings of the sixties. As the headman's guests – then friends, now allies – we were no longer safe. His protection was a liability. But the risk was impossible to gauge. Violence in Java was random; that was part of the fear.

The danger – incalculable, perhaps imaginary (that toll of 250 dead had hardly begun) – made for a double life. Day was sunshine, clarity, openness, moderation, reason. Night was rumour, noises off, waiting. At night we made plans to leave, we listened to motorbikes draw near, throb or stall outside the house, then fade away. We checked on the children. In the morning we laughed at our fears.

After a week, the headman and I were summoned again to the district office. I expected bad news: I had seen too much to be allowed to continue, and my fate was tied up with Pak Lurah's. But the district officer had decided to back him. By the time we arrived at the office – late of course: the headman stolid even in decline – he had lined up fifteen conspirators for a showdown, or rather a *show* showdown, since the two sides would not be allowed a proper confrontation. What was it about? The right of a village to choose – or keep – its leader (a right denied to the nation); the possibility of pluralism; the limits of militant Islam.

How to live plurally, how to manage intolerance, how to defend ordinary liberties: on a bigger stage, these had become the dominant questions of the day, not only in Indonesia but across the Muslim world and beyond. It was odd that the district officer, appointee of an authoritarian state, should be their arbiter today; but civil servants –

even under the dictator – could be decent men. They worked within the system. They had other values. They were still Javanese.

In the small hot room, like a classroom with rows of wooden chairs and a blackboard, a signed petition – now a little crumpled – lay on the table at the front, a collective demand for change. The leaders – the paramedic and religious teacher in their government uniforms, Aris, thin and intense in his black hat – occupied the front row. They wore an air of expectation, even triumph. The others, awkward in their village clothes, shrank into their seats. Village life depended on a pact not to raise differences, not to stand out. But this was what the district officer, brisk and schoolmasterly, now demanded. He made the fifteen signatories stand up, one by one, to state their complaints and whether they were willing to settle the matter. Yusuf, the paramedic, quickly got to his feet. 'Not you. You'll get your turn. Now sit down,' said the district officer.

The charges – impiety, corruption, autocracy – could not stick. The headman, seated with me near the district officer, away from the fifteen but not quite facing them, winced as he listened. But his injured pride counted for little. The district officer wanted peace, and peace was about compromise not facts. Aside, he told Pak Lurah, 'You must let them have their say, take it on the chin.' Aroused Islam could not be confronted.

Sullen, separated, the rebels had lost their collective voice and with it the confidence to strike. Mustari, a little wearily, his hands resting on the back of a chair, said, 'I came here to settle. I never expected anything more. We just want to be allowed to pray.'

'Who is stopping you?'

'Well, no one.'

Jumhar, who ran the moderate prayer-house, the Light of Paradise, said, 'I never actually saw the letter. I didn't know what it was about. Aris dragged me along.' His face showed agony.

Unable to grandstand, small in his black woolly cap, Drus found himself denying the contents of the letter.

'But you signed it. Did you read it?'

'Yes, but –'

'Well?'

'If I climb down, where does that leave us? *He's* still there and we've lost prestige. What rankles is that nobody comes to the prayer-house any more.'

'Carry on as usual. Things will return to normal.'

It was the right thing to say: nobody should be pronounced in the wrong, nobody humiliated. And after pledges of peace and awkward handshakes we were permitted to leave. Outside in the hard sun, Sukib wheeled his bicycle towards me and put out a dry stiff hand. 'It wasn't me. I never wanted –' He squinted at me with his half smile then, with surprising grace, swung a long leg over the saddle and pedalled away. Only Yusuf held out. He stayed inside, arguing the case. Through the window I saw him standing over the district officer, a sharp thin figure prodding the air. And when the district officer rebuked him for his aggressive stance – 'like a tiger about to devour its prey' – he broke into a violent rant. The door swung shut and we could not hear the reply, but when he came out Yusuf was, in Jumhar's words, 'pale with stress'.

Gently, cautiously, the state had done its work.

The megaphones blared, the prayer-house regulars returned. For Drus and Aris, the headman's survival notwithstanding, it was a modest triumph. Peace was possible, even enforceable, but the cost was mainly on one side. And just as the district officer had been unwilling to confront the militants, so ordinary villagers preferred peace to anything else. The headman and Bu Lurah blanked Drus and Siti, boycotting their store; but this was nothing unusual, and others dared not fall in with them. Misti, who had brought us fruit on the day following the prayer-house incident – her gesture of sympathy – meekly made her purchases. Her husband, Jakis, had an older quarrel: Drus had married his sister. But in principle – Javanese principle – quarrels did not ramify. When they did, disaster was sure to follow. Only Jan's behaviour surprised. Far from backing his father-in-law, the man who had given him house and daughter, Jan remained close to Drus, even accompanying him on a tour of the saints' graves. 'I've already paid,' he said weakly. Besides, it was recommended for one about to do the pilgrimage.

I never again spoke to Drus. But one day we found ourselves at opposite ends of a long straight path that ran through the western part of the village. I saw his cloaked, strutting figure, ragged and menacing, two hundred yards away and saw that he saw me. He had a long minute to consider his action. Yet neither of us could concede victory by turning off the path. And so, like the estranged lovers at the end of *The Third Man*, we walked straight towards each other, almost brushing, and then straight past, gazes fixed ahead.

21
Ancestors

Bayu in 1992 had seemed settled, almost static; the orthodox, mystical and animistic elements finely balanced; the social arrangements that supported them guaranteed by traditions so old they were barely questionable. Bayu in 1997 was much the same – daily life carried on as before – but the balance had been upset, and the inertia of habit was no longer enough to set things right. As elsewhere in the Muslim world, it was the accumulation of incident, the failure to recognize and respond, and the general desire for a quiet life that had allowed a certain form of Islam to advance. The megaphones (the voice of aggressive orthodoxy), the attacks on a secular leadership, the politicizing of piety, the revived prestige of the pilgrimage (what was old, and old-fashioned at that, suddenly new and modern), the pressure on schoolchildren to conform and – most puzzling of all – the vogue for the veil had changed the rules of engagement. There was no hiding place: every family felt the changes and faced difficult choices. And if Indonesia, and in particular Java, lagged behind the rest of the Muslim world in the march to purity and internal division (to be followed, depending on who had the upper hand, by external confrontation), that was not because it was furthest from the Islamic heartlands, but because it had most to lose. Malaysia – as distant from Mecca, as lately converted – had long ago become as scrubbed and stiffly puritan as seventeenth-century New England.

In the month before we left, two weddings showed how much the changes hurt, and how difficult they were to resist.

Our neighbours Misti and Jakis were ordinary village farmers: plain, hard-working, resilient and thrifty. To these peasant virtues they added the Javanese even temper and empathy. It had been Jakis who first came over to offer his support after my clash with Drus, his sister's husband. A man who thought nothing of climbing a sixty-foot palm tree in a gale to fasten a windmill was not likely to be swayed by a megaphone. Misti, in contrast, was all mildness; as mild as her husband was tough.

They were comfortably off because Misti's mother owned a block of Grade A land west of the village and let them farm it, though, cannily, she had not yet handed over the deeds. At Lebaran Misti wore gold in her hair and celebrated lavishly. Jakis hardly ever changed out of his rough working clothes. Nobody regarded them as anything other than ordinary, and yet their ordinariness showed a lot about Javanese civilization. They were its product, admirable in a way, but what they had to pass on – apart from the virtues of plainness and poise – was quite limited. They had no formal Javanese culture: the world of the shadow play, the performing arts and the mystical philosophy passed them by. Nor were they practising Muslims. Like everyone, they hosted neighbourhood feasts, with their appended prayers, and submitted to the usual rites of passage; they attended the mosque at Lebaran; but they believed none of the dogmas. 'Of course the Koran was written by men!' said Jakis. 'Do you think it dropped from the sky?' And this open disavowal – safe, because no one was listening – meant that they had no desire for the supporting roles in village Islam that Untung and Noto, more substantial figures, had perfected. Strictly, then, there was little they could do to shape or mould their children; indeed they had little desire to do so.

It was different with the older generation. Misti's mother, Tari, apart from being a solid landowner, was a true Javanist, even an arch-Javanist. She belonged to a cult centred on the shrine of a holy man, a semi-legendary figure from the Hindu period. Every week she went there to meditate and sprinkle flowers. She had never prayed to the Muslim God, and said, in the Javanist way, 'There is nothing outside.' Her husband, whom she dominated, was devoted to his ricefields. But he was also a follower of the shadow play, and knew the stories and characters. They had no other sons or daughters to follow the tradition. Misti, who attended the holy man's shrine at festivals, like many of the villagers, had married a man without Javanese learning. And the grandchildren knew still less. So when the boy Urip, now a young man of twenty-two, proposed to marry a pious orthodox girl from another village, only the grandmother was seriously upset. She had wanted him to marry the cousin of Jan who, like the candidate haji himself, had a claim on the family rice mill. She liked Jan's family, who were Sangkan Paran veterans – though that was another case where Javanism had skipped a generation.

Tari had given Urip a motorbike for his birthday and now, in protest, she took it back. It was the girl's veil that provoked her. 'How can a woman do that?' she said, smoothing back her silver hair and smiling at me. 'How can she lose herself in that way?' When the return of the motorbike had no effect, she took back the gold jewellery that she had passed on to Misti and her daughter Ana. For this she was criticized.

The middle generation was caught. Misti was a conscientious daughter but also an indulgent mother, Jakis an instinctive atheist. Neither had wanted a connection with a pious family, but they 'wouldn't dare' tell Urip what to do (as Wan informed me). Besides, marriages were fragile; it might not last. And there were plenty of mixed couples in Bayu: in the long run, things evened out. 'The girl will grow out of it,' said Jakis. 'Tari is bothered because she wanted a landed family, that's all.'

It might have been true. Tari had said, 'How can she work in the fields if she's wearing a veil? She'll bring them to poverty.' But she had not objected to Ana's fiancé, a poor boy from a Javanist family in east Bayu.

There was no possibility of discussion. Tari and Jakis had not been on speaking terms for years. The old grandfather was not a talker. And Misti hated controversy. Jakis said: 'Your mother can't dispossess us and she can't take her land beyond the grave.' Besides, he was resolved to have a proper Javanese wedding, with a gandrung. When Drus had asked whether an Islamic preacher would be giving a sermon, Jakis had replied, 'Yes, Preacher Wulan.' Wulan was a famous gandrung, a professional flirt who, in her time, had captivated half the village males. Let the pious family fret in the background, Jakis didn't care. His son would get exactly what he wanted.

The wedding went ahead. The grandmother stayed away, weeping – she told us – in her fieldhut. Misti wept for her mother's absence. The bride's family – a small, defensive crew from Delik – sat grimly inside with Haji Drus, ignoring the dancing. After it was over, Urip and his bride went to live with her parents and we saw little of him again.

The other wedding was similar, but the effects were less predictable, messier. Again, it was a mixed match, the girl – veiled – from a pious family in Krajan, the boy from a household that was only loosely Muslim. But the boy's father was Noto the carpenter, and that made a difference. Where Jakis and Misti were detached from village Islam and irrelevant to its progress or decline, Noto was one of those who helped maintain the cultural balance as, so to speak, a lay Muslim. His father had been the magician, learned in Arabic prayers, whose death at the hands of a lynch mob had excused Noto from active service. To know the prayers was to expose himself to allegations of sorcery, misuse of the scriptures. That was what had happened to his father in an era when mastery of Islamic liturgy qualified one to deal with other supernatural affairs. After his father's death, Noto had told me, his brother had been visited by an apparition: *Don't come looking for me in Alas Purwo*, it had said. *I am a tiger.*

Better not pray, then, or associate with the pious: it was enough to usher and stand occasional guard of honour. And Noto had a different compass. The arts were his passion. With his own gamelan orchestra and dance troupe, unlike Jakis and Misti, Noto had something to pass on.

The boy Marko, knowing his parents would object to a veiled bride, had eloped with her. He was nineteen. The elopement, like

Katri's, was staged as an abduction: in Bayu even the exception had to follow custom. They lived a week at the girl's house and then came back to Noto. In the big rambling house, smelling of raw timber and half-finished furniture, there was still plenty of room. Las and the daughter Rita (whose husband was away in Bali), coarse women with loud voices, would hardly mind a young girl. Marko returned to helping his father.

The new couple settled in, but the veil caused friction. The other women, physically exuberant, carelessly clad, could not bear it. To them it seemed a reproach, a constant reminder of what they were not and did not want to be. They had the simple view that all religion was hypocrisy and that the veil hid illicit lusts. 'Huh! Veils! As if *they're* more honest than others and wouldn't do it given half a chance,' said Las, aiming a jet of red betel juice to her side. 'She even wears *socks*!'

Rita curled her hands and twitched her hips, adding mischievously: 'Like a gandrung.'

But Noto would make the best of it. Marko was still his son; he deserved a proper wedding celebration. And a child's first wedding is one of the great obligations in a parent's life. A mixed marriage? Very well, let it be a mixed reception, with a gandrung one night and a preacher the next. He would invite the whole village and would put on a show to impress the bride's contingent, veils and all.

It certainly wasn't done in my day, said Ma Witri. *To hire a preacher for entertainment at a wedding! I can't think what's come over Noto.*

Again it was gandrung Wulan – overbooked that year in Bayu, but she was, they all said, the best. I couldn't judge. To me, a gandrung's voice quickly wearied: the high pitch, the elongated vowels and swooping changes would always be alien. I preferred a gandrung when she danced and let the band take up the tune. A two-handed drum, a violin (held against the chest like a gun), kettle gongs, a triangle and a big hanging gong: a slow-burning musical combustion. In the lead-up there was a groove: the violin playing low, holding a chord while the drummer wove dashing rhythms around the rocking gongs. Speed against slowness, movement against stasis: it was the sound of anticipation, an unbearable holding-back before climax. I had been with people who, hearing the sound float over the fields from another village, felt drawn there and immediately leapt on their motorbikes. But the gandrung is all about irresistible attraction. *Gandrung* means 'madly in love', 'infatuated'.

As the music rose above the noise of guests – the women grouped around the stage where bride and groom were enthroned, the men relaxing at tables, smoking or finishing their meals, the whole arena strung with bunting and lights – gandrung Wulan, with mincing steps, shuffled into the dance space, a patch of hardened earth that was Noto's front yard.

A gandrung's 'beauty' is different from that of other women: enticing and immodest but stylized, controlled, something offered and withheld. There is an element of caricature. Wulan was over thirty, a 'widow' (no gandrung is married), and no longer a beauty, but the costume, the voice and the music made her, in local estimation, not simply beautiful but the very image of desire.

The costume was singular: a gold-and-black bodice pinched at the waist, a batik sarong drawn tight to emphasize curves, white socks (no shoes), and a crown of gold leather displaying two figurines of Gatotkaca, a romantic hero from the shadow play. Over her bare arms and shoulders hung a red silk scarf. With bangles, rings, long fingernails, red lipstick and a pale, powdered face, she was equipped to seduce.

The MC was Hadi, father of Jan and owner of the rice mill. Like Noto, Hadi was an arts impresario, with his own gong orchestra. (How painful that neither of their sons had ever danced!) He had taken groups on tours of Java and knew all the local gandrungs. At fifty he was already a grandfather with a paunch, but he still danced with conviction. As he approached the gandrung – hands cocked, face raised greedily in a grin – I noticed his wife smiling.

Hadi did a turn with Wulan and then presented a scarf to Noto, the host, the only older man who could outdance him. The gongs and violins began to swing again and the new pair moved around the arena, the gandrung retreating with tiny steps and shimmering smile. At the end of a musical line they were face to face and they rocked their hips in synchrony before Noto swerved away, a faint smile on his lips. Then it was the turn of the guests.

There were two principal styles: a courtly duet – the man poised and erect, the woman with arms outstretched and knees slightly bent – and a faster pursuit which could suggest a suitor chasing his coquettish prey or being led by the nose. Younger men tended to overdo the aloof, masterful style, catching the gandrung's scarf when she flicked them with it or turning away scornfully, then bearing down on her in retreat. But Joko, the mystic's son, had perfected the softer, 'infatuated' style. While the three other dancers – on the corners of a square – preened and twirled, awaiting their turn, Joko put on a sweet smile and with fluttering arms approached the gandrung as if to steal a kiss.

During the intervals she sang at tables, taking requests and tips that she passed back to the band. Sometimes the notes that were passed to her contained lyrics alluding to mistresses and lost loves. For those in the know, the allusion was clear.

In Tamansuruh there's a house
With writing on the walls.
I know you're someone else's wife,
Both skilled in deceit.

Which brought, anonymously, the following riposte:

Better chanting than the pilgrimage;
Chanting wins the greater merit.
Better a mistress than a wife;
A mistress gathers more rewards.

There was even a song for Marko:

Black shirt, black trousers
Won't fade in the wash.

Mother and father don't like it
But, forbidden, you can't withdraw.

Songs of the prodigal son, the girl spied in the fields, the forsaken wife and jilted lover. The show was a celebration of erotic love, of pursuit, rivalry, coquetry and conquest. And that, as I now saw, was the source of Wulan's attraction, her special skill: to evoke love's unruly power in the respectable setting of a wedding. While the bridal pair, around whom the whole thing revolved, sat enthroned and motionless in their finery, guests and gandrung explored the forms of human passion – longing, disappointment, jealousy, rapture, lust and fascination. For better or worse.

The final night of the five-day affair – there had also been a shadow play, *Gatotkaca Marries* – was given over to an Islamic preacher. Dharsono wasn't a cleric, the head of a seminary, but an evangelist. Tall, bareheaded, urbane in his safari suit, he was one of the best speakers in the district. I had heard him twice before and had even recorded his hour-long sermon one Lebaran. Noto had chosen well. Dharsono's gift was for judging the character of an audience. He managed without hellfire, without the insults that had driven villagers from the Light of Paradise. Not for him the bearded ranting of the new men. Dharsono's Islam was a tolerant religion in which there was room for everyone. Nor did he have the cleric's self-congratulatory piety (their standard exhortation was to 'love and respect the Islamic scholars'). The jokes were against himself or his household (I thought of the old district officer with his light-fingered servants and pregnant maids); the prompts to piety were teases, not reproaches. And there were sudden flights of song. Dharsono was sure of a grateful audience.

No, Andrew, I will not listen to a preacher, even if he's doing it next door, said Ma Witri. *I don't care who he is!*

A reception committee had organized microphones, a podium and Koranic readings by young people, the visit dignified by the tokens of modernity. Noto's niece, cloaked in Islamic garb, was the link person in charge of *protokol*. In her heavy black gown and white headgear only her face was visible. But the covering – like the uniform of a surgeon or a nun – deprived even the face of personality. In the pale neon light it seemed to float above the upturned heads of the audience. Her voice, untrained, was a monotone.

Asih lived at the back of Bu Mari's in a house overlooking the fields. We knew her through the children, who played with the baby goats in her yard. Sometimes she would sit with Jona's peanut women, but she didn't join in the banter and seemed embarrassed by the jokes. She shared a house with her widowed mother (Noto's sister) and her husband, who was an ape-man in the dragon play.

Asih had a special fortitude. Mercedes once met her staggering along the path to her uncle's, on the point of giving birth. Because her mother was not at home and she did not want to bother Mari, she was walking there alone to get help. Serious and pious, she might be, but like others in the family she had disapproved of Marko's bride. To robe up for a preacher was one thing; to veil in daily life was a step too far.

Asih finished her prayer at the microphone and turned to get down from the podium. But something had caught her eye. She halted and stared intently into the darkness to one side of the arena, past the bunting and lights to the trees at the back. Then she lost balance and tottered forward, as if about to faint, before someone rushed to her aid. A fussing with papers at the microphone covered her exit while the next reader took her place. The preacher hadn't noticed.

They carried her into Noto's house and laid her on a bench, rigid and mumbling, surrounded by anxious, weeping relatives. While the preacher began his melodious sermon, unaware what was happening in the dingy kitchen nearby (unaware, too, of the extraordinary opportunity for evangelism it presented), the young woman went into trance and began to convey messages from the spirit world to her assembled family – her first request being to remove the veil. As she later explained, she had finished her recitation and looked up to see a huge tiger – her grandfather! – standing in the dark beside the house. He had taken her to sit with him under the big starfruit tree at the back. It was her grandfather who now spoke through her. He called upon his son, Noto, and reminded him of his responsibilities to his widowed sister who had no income and had to fend for herself. Had he taken her a sack of rice after the harvest? Had he included her in the preparations for the reception? Why had Marko failed to visit the family graves before the wedding? Was it because his new wife forbade it?

The tiger spirit had closed with the familiar warning not to seek him in the forest and had ordered roasted bananas and seven glasses of tea to be placed at the foot of the starfruit tree where Asih imagined she was sitting. (This was immediately done.) The seven glasses were for the seven dead souls who now spoke through her.

It was a family reunion in which the living spoke directly to the dead. The interviews were conducted by Noto's cousin, the mosque official (who gave me the best account: at the time I was enjoying the sermon under the stars). Solid, reassuring, he sat beside the murmuring girl, crumbling incense on the brazier and patiently questioning each spirit in turn, satisfying their worries and then, one by one, dismissing them. When Asih went cold and stiff, he had massaged her limbs and back ('I was bold enough: she's my niece') and forced the possessing spirit to speak, then he threatened to 'burn down its house if it took her away'.

Ancestors were hard to please. They wanted their customs honoured; they wanted to be acknowledged. With a hint of humour, the mosque official acted out the seance for me, doing the voices, now gruff, now wheedling. Noto's mother – wife to a were-tiger – had been a strong woman. She had reproached the young couple: *Why didn't you leave offerings for me? How could you forget to tell me about the wedding!* Another spirit – he wagged his finger and arched his eyebrows – complained of the bride, *She walked out of the cemetery and didn't leave flowers. Said it was unnecessary to ask our blessing*. It was the reformist heresy.

Marko, the groom, had wavered but followed her that day, said his uncle with a sigh. 'Led by a scarf.' It was clear his sympathies lay with the dead. 'See, the old folk were angry. They can't be ignored.'

In the kitchen Marko had knelt beside his stricken cousin and was chastised for marrying a 'foolish girl'. Other spirits arrived, voicing other grievances. Finally, Noto's nephew, graduate of a reformist university – a doubter by definition – had been summoned by his dead mother and made to introduce his baby son to the spirits. Shaken, wilting under family pressure, he too had knelt and submitted.

By now an hour had passed. Asih was sitting up, smacking her lips. She shook hands with the graduate and blindly touched the baby (the mosque official shook my hand, apologetically touched my face), then called for the bride. *Where is she, stubborn girl? She won't work. And she threw away my flowers. But Marko, you must be good to her. Stay here with her. Now say a prayer for me and let me go home.*

The dramatic illusion. Under the blind hands I shuddered lightly and the mosque official laughed, pleased with his performance. A man impersonating a girl impersonating a spirit. Echoes of echoes. But that was how the supernatural world was created.

His work done, he had held the brazier under Asih's bench, recited a prayer and sent the spirits away.

Noto's bid to exorcise the past had failed. But the ancestral protest – a return of the repressed: for once, the cliché seemed justified – had come from a surprising quarter. In picking Asih – a sensible, phlegmatic woman of impeccable piety – the ancestors had made their point with maximum force. Tradition would not be denied; nor, on an Islamic occasion, would it be sidelined. However strong the claim of Islam, it could not be allowed to exclude other claims: the need for social harmony, the demands of the ancestors, and older traditions which a modernizing Islam would throw out. And it was because village Islam was not yet fractured, polarized into parties and factions, that change could still be resisted in this powerful, unanswerable way. If the spirits were, as the mystics maintained, 'in ourselves or nowhere', then to deny them was an act of self-denial, a kind of madness. That was Asih's message.

The point had been made. And next day, Noto – red-eyed, ashen – said to me: 'Now even Marko will have to believe.' Yet only a week later bride and groom again absconded, going back to her parents in Krajan.

'Don't they worry about what will happen?' I asked the mosque official.

He stared at me for a moment, round-eyed, perhaps remembering, and stroked his goatee.

'Well, yes, for a while. But that's young people for you. That's love.'

22
Separation

Why do we equate life with our separate lives? 'Life is indivisible,' said Warno. 'If I tell you to fetch a bucket of water, I don't say *this water* or *that water*. It's all one.' In the village, daily life was shared. You grew up with people, attended their weddings and prayer-meals, shared their misfortunes, helped dig their graves. And at every waking moment they were around: tending the next field, sweeping the yard, sitting on your doorstep in the evenings. As you fell asleep you could hear their coughs and murmurs through the wall. Their presence was the inescapable condition of your existence. *I* was always *we*. (Yet there was no Osing word for 'we': you said *isun kabeh*, 'I-all'.) In death or life, nobody was ever really alone. If you moved to a different part of the village, your old ties fell away but there would be others just as strong. It wasn't depth or continuity that counted but the sustaining presence of others, like Frost's silken tent. One could drift between families and neighbourhoods, marry and remarry, but the gentle embrace of the community was constant.

In the West – or perhaps simply out of the village – you pursued your 'own life'. Of course, you had friends and relatives and at regular moments your lives overlapped with theirs; but your path was separate. An individual destiny, with goals and obstacles, life was 'what you made of it'.

We knew what it would be like to return to the isolation and boundedness of the nuclear family: an adjustment of shape; a shock for the children; separate lives. The villagers could not know, but they knew it was hard – indeed, for them, almost unimaginable – to leave the village behind. Hajis left too, but only to return in glory. They were the Javanese exception: men and women who sought distinction, spiritual merit; they wanted to stand out. But their path was well trodden, a collective march. In Mecca they joined two million others in the ultimate experience of sameness: a sameness that was oneness. Then, duty fulfilled, they returned to what they had always been, farmers and merchants, villagers, plus title and white cap. They still belonged.

Our farewell prayer-meal was similar to that of five years before, though this time we were proper hosts, no longer dependent on Bu Mari. At dawn Mercedes and I went with Panji to the market in Banyuwangi. The headman's mother, who had kept our chickens, now blessed and slaughtered them. Misti and Bu Lurah supervised the kitchen.

We combined the banquet with an all-night reading of the story of Joseph, honouring in turn the neighbours and the village elders. Warno spoke the litany, his words, even his unspoken interpretations, now familiar. Signposts to the infinite. I looked along the rows of seated men – the black caps, the serious, patient, good-humoured faces, the batik sarongs. I noted the red and white porridge (Ma and Pa), the five-coloured porridge (for my spirit siblings), and the rice-cone of misfortune steaming gently through its banana-leaf covering. As the Joseph book passed from reader to reader, pausing halfway to be smoked in the incense, the old headman Harsono turned to me and said (knowing what I was thinking): 'I am old. I've done everything a man can do: marriage, children, great-grandchildren, war, revolution, hunger, plenty. I've only got one thing left to experience. But I tell you, I'm not worried by these new folks, the riots and the noise. It's been happening for five hundred years, ever since Demak.' Demak was Java's first important, but short-lived, orthodox Muslim kingdom. The challenge had never gone away, but white-haired Harsono and the others would see it off. 'As long as there's the Joseph story, the dragon and the prayer-meal the village will be safe.'

A week later, in the midst of Jan's preparations for the pilgrimage, we left. We had nothing to go back to, no jobs or settled life, nothing planned: it was too soon. And the children were now village children, at home among the chickens and goats, followers of the dragon. Too soon.

But Jan's pilgrimage had brought our neighbourhood to a pitch of piety, and it was hard to remain. With nightly Koranic readings, amplified chanting and a procession of pious visitors – Haji Drus and the conspirators to the fore – Pak Lurah spent as much time out of the house as he could. His ageing parents, happier in their hut at the back discussing cattle prices and footrot, carried the wood and water to Jan's kitchen or wordlessly served coffee at the front. Even Hadi, Jan's father, was obliged to sit with the hajis and chat politely with visiting VIPs. 'Now where is *your* Mecca?' he quoted to me, but it was under his breath.

Despite the old headman's assurances, the village had changed. And we wanted to leave with a different Bayu in mind: the Bayu of Jona and her peanut women; of Noto honing his windmills, stalking the gandrungs; Jumhar in his creaking prayer-house; Wan crouching to the guardian spirit in the dead of night; the mosque official giggling through a wedding. The Bayu of Joko in his sarong and blouse; of Untung's stories told in slow and perfect sentences; of Purwadi stiffly meditating while the mystics watched with bated breath; of Panji and the men-women screaming with laughter; of Misti's smile and Pak Lurah's deflating cackle.

We refused most gifts, but Jona came secretly at night with a jar of coffee she had roasted and ground. (Back home its taste vanished: magic could not travel.) And on the last day, Pak Lurah came round with a mask he had commissioned from the dragon troupe, 'so Daniel will think of us'. It hangs now as a charm on his bedroom wall: a glaring, grinning, red-faced lion-dragon, with inflated nostrils, popping eyeballs, and little brass discs on springs either side of its fangs that quiver nervously at the slightest touch. The headman could not imagine a boy growing up without a dragon. He made the sounds: *Ding-dang ding-dang, gong ding-dang*, and then said: 'You'll come back, won't you? No you won't.'

Throughout our years in Bayu, Mercedes had remained close to

Sri. And when Sri married, and kept more to her house, she became her most regular visitor. With the front door shut, they would sit with the children or talk under the trees behind the house. Sri had never lost her love of Sofía: she combed her hair and nuzzled her, made a fuss of her. But now she had a son, she wanted him to be different from the others, independent, not one of the crowd. He was a mild, quiet child, disengaged from his playmates, though he became a good friend of Daniel. Sri feared for his future. 'Perhaps we'll go away and live in Jember,' she said, 'away from all his mothers.' She caught him up in her arms. 'He's *my* son!' It was a Mexican sentiment. Before we left, she brought Mercedes a gift, perhaps the only thing that was really her own. It was a scarf her brother had brought from Timor, a homecoming from the war. It bore Sri's name embroidered in gold lettering.

On the harbour they spread out again – not so many as before ('I'm not saying goodbye again,' said Warno, 'but I'll be waiting for you'), but enough to stop the traffic and clog the quayside.

In the morning we had gone up to the hamlet of Sumbersari to take leave, crossing the stream for the last time, up the slope through the tall trees to the cluster of houses on the hill. A breeze swept across the ricefields and a windmill, big as a cartwheel, whirred and throbbed on the tallest palm. On the way back we passed through the old cemetery, stopping briefly in its dappled light, and Mercedes had said, 'You know, I'd be happy to be buried here among the ancestors.'

As the ferry moved away – the ropes cast off – a motorbike detached itself from the crowd and drove to a vantage point on the far end of the quay. It was Pak Lurah in batik shirt and Bu Lurah, side-saddle, her arm round his waist, in her festive finery. And as the boat swung north and headed out into the straits, it was the two of them we could see, waving and waving.

Index